The
Devil

To K the bad angel

The
Devil

IN TUDOR AND
STUART ENGLAND

Darren Oldridge

First published in hardback entitled 'The Devil in Early Modern
England', 2000
This fully revised edition first published in 2010

The History Press
The Mill, Brimscombe Port
Stroud, Gloucestershire, GL5 2QG
www.thehistorypress.co.uk

British Library Cataloguing in Publication Data.
A catalogue record for this book is available from the British Library.

ISBN 978 0 7524 5739 0

Typesetting and origination by The History Press
Printed in Great Britain
Manufacturing managed by Jellyfish Print Solutions Ltd

CONTENTS

LIST OF PLATES 6

PREFACE 7

1 INTRODUCTION 9

2 THE DEVIL AND THE ENGLISH
REFORMATION 30

3 *LIVING WITH THE ENEMY*: PROTESTANT
EXPERIENCES OF THE DEVIL 57

4 THE DEVIL IN POPULAR CULTURE 78

5 WOMEN AND THE DEVIL 114

6 POSSESSION AND EXORCISM 136

7 WITCHCRAFT 162

8 THE CHANGING FACE OF SATAN 193

APPENDIX: SELECTED SOURCES 202

NOTES AND REFERENCES 220

SELECT BIBLIOGRAPHY 238

INDEX 247

LIST OF PLATES

1. The Roman Antichrist (Thomason Collection, British Library)

2. The scene of judgment, from the dying room of St Wulfstan's monastic hospital in Worcester. (Courtesy of Worcester Museum Service)

3. The triumph of faith over Satan (Bodleian Library: Douce B.Subt.266 Sig. M4r)

4. The persecution of 'all that professes the worde of God' (Bodleian Library: Douce B.Subt.266 Sig. H2r)

5. A 'monstrous serpent' (Bodleian Library: 4°R. 21 Art Seld(5) T/Page)

6. The devil as a headless bear (Bodleian Library: 4°C 16 Art Bs(4) T/Page)

7. *The Witch of Edmonton* (Bodleian Library: Mal. 238(9) T/Page)

8. The demon with a gun firing popish trinkets (Bodleian Library: Douce B.Subt.266 Sig. J1r)

9. The fool confronts the devil (Bodleian Library: Douce B.Subt.266 Sig. B1r)

10. The devil leads the way to sin (Bodleian Library: Douce B.Subt.266 Sig. D2v)

11a. The pope's reward in hell (Bodleian Library: Soc.2806 d. 16/6-14=A(vol.1) page 396)

11b. The fiend encourages murder (Bodleian Library: Soc.2806 d. 16/6-14=A(vol.3) page 29)

12. The devil claims a blasphemer (Bodleian Library: 4°C 16 Art Bs(48) T/Page)

13. Satan attacks a church (Bodleian Library: 4°C 16 Art Bs(34) T/Page)

14a. The pope as Antichrist (Thomason Collection, British Library)

14b. Archbishop William Laud as Antichrist (British Library)

15. Satan exploits the female sin of pride (Bodleian Library: Douce B.Subt.266 Sig. H3r)

16. Matthew Hopkins, *The Discovery of Witches* (British Library)

17. The dangers of Satan (British Library)

PREFACE

In a comic ballad published in 1736, a lovelorn young man made a pact with a demon. In return for his heart's desire, the man was obliged to find a never-ending task for the wicked spirit to perform. The task of writing a history of the Devil in Tudor and Stuart England would have probably sufficed. The Devil infiltrated so many aspects of religion and culture in this period that a comprehensive study of the subject is impossible in a single volume: indeed, ideas about Satan were almost as rich and complex as ideas about God, with the consequence that each chapter (and possibly each section) of this text could be expanded to a book-length study. The present volume attempts to survey the broad contours of English thought about the Devil from the Reformation to the civil war, and suggests some of the implications of this thought. It is hoped that future researchers will flesh out, and challenge, the picture that is briefly sketched here.

This book is a revised and updated edition of *The Devil in Early Modern England*, which was originally published in 2000. Readers familiar with the earlier text will notice several changes. The new version is more sensitive to the continuities between late medieval demonism and the understanding of Satan that emerged during the Reformation, while maintaining that a distinctively 'Protestant Devil' can be identified. For this and other insights, I am indebted to numerous studies that have been published since the first edition of the book, and notably Nathan Johnstone's excellent *The Devil and Demonism in Early Modern England* (Cambridge University Press, 2006). The areas in which my interpretation departs from Johnstone's are identified in the text.

Like the original edition, this book is written for general readers as well as scholars in the field. For this reason, as well as the desire to provide an overview of the subject, I have assumed a broad continuity of assumptions about the Devil among English Protestants.

(The extent to which these assumptions varied between different elements within the church is one topic that awaits further investigation.) I have used the word 'godly' to indicate those men and women who placed the practice of the new faith near to the centre of their lives: those whom contemporaries described as the 'hotter sort' of believers, and some historians have identified as 'experiential' Protestants. I have used the word 'puritan' in a similar sense, but more sparingly to avoid the impression that such people constituted a discrete block of opinion within the church.

On a point of demonic terminology, I have given the Devil a capital D to distinguish him from the multitude of infernal spirits that was recognised in Tudor and Stuart England. Contemporary writers often conflated wicked angels with their master, so that individual demons frequently morphed into Satan himself. I have adopted a more consistent approach that is, I hope, more useful to modern readers. I have also retained the lower case 'devil' in those instances where the sources appear to refer to an individual spirit.

The intellectual debts I have accumulated in writing this book are huge, and I have tried to acknowledge them fully in the pages that follow. I am especially grateful to those critics who identified lacunae and shortcomings in the previous edition. Many of these have now been addressed; but I have no doubt that many remain. As the master of 'crafty persuasions, deceitful and false illusions', the Devil is an elusive but tantalizing quarry. I hope this book will encourage others to take up the chase.

INTRODUCTION

THE DYING ROOM

In the late Middle Ages the monastic hospital of St Wulfstan in Worcester kept a room for the dying. Attended by carers and spiritual advisors, the men and women who were taken to this room were encouraged to make peace with their world and preparations for the one to follow. As they contemplated their final surroundings, they viewed painted images designed to help them with this task: a depiction of the Trinity on the ceiling, and on the walls frescos of Christian martyrs, offering models of patient resolve in the face of pain. Perhaps the most potent image was a scene of judgment (see plate section). This painting, which remains on the wall, portrays the archangel Michael holding a set of scales, with a human soul suspended in one of its pans. Standing at his side and facing the viewer, St Mary drapes a set of rosary beads on the balance to tip the judgment in favour of mercy. Clinging to the other pan, a demon seeks to drag the balance towards damnation. As they reflected on this spectacle, its original viewers may have gained some reassurance concerning their own impending fate. Mary stands shoulder to shoulder with the angel and is clearly his equal. The demon, in contrast, is a verminous 'imp': it has to stretch itself upright to keep hold of the pan, and already its exertions seem futile.[1]

The quiet drama of the dying room conveys themes that are fundamental to our understanding of the Devil in Tudor and Stuart England. Most simply, it provides a reminder that individuals engaged personally with demonic powers: Satan and his minions were not abstract ideas cut off from the world of lived experience. Nor, for the great majority of people, were they metaphors for other things, such as human wickedness or worldly injustice. While the Devil was intimately involved in the myriad sufferings of earthly life, he remained a living presence with a real character: a personality with whom men and women were obliged to contend. The image of judgment in the hospital also illustrates the highly integrated nature of pre-modern religion: the Devil belonged to a much larger scheme of belief, which comprehended the origins and destiny of humankind, the purposes of God, and – as the dying viewers of the painting were reminded – the weighing of individual souls. Satan occupied a central role in the scheme of salvation and damnation in sixteenth-century England, but his part made sense only in the context of this greater story.

Anyone viewing the paintings in St Wulfstan's hospital today will notice another quality that documents the religious conflicts of the Tudor age. The faces of the figures that populate the walls have been removed, leaving only spectral impressions of their personalities. St Michael and the Virgin are featureless ghosts. The defacing of the images was an act of censorship initiated by Protestant reformers determined to erase the Catholic past. The Reformation abolished the power of saints and denounced religious art in strict compliance with the commandment not to make 'graven images'; more deeply, it repudiated the whole system of belief that once sustained the men and women in the dying room. The Devil retained his central position in the new vision that replaced it. Indeed, he acquired a new status – in many ways more dreadful and intimate than the image on the hospital wall – in the religious life of sixteenth- and seventeenth-century England. The idea of Satan that emerged influenced many aspects of culture and politics, with effects that were sometimes profound and often contradictory. This book charts the rise of the Protestant Devil, and attempts to recover the experiences of those individuals who, stripped of the protection of the saints, were obliged to take up a lonely struggle against the personification of evil.

THE CHANGING DEVIL

'A belief in a supernatural source of evil is not necessary', wrote Joseph Conrad in 1911, as 'men alone are quite capable of every wickedness'. Few would deny the second part of Conrad's assertion, not least because of the industrialized violence that characterized the decades that followed his statement; but the concept of a personal Devil remains remarkably strong. For many millions of twenty-first-century westerners, the idea that a personal force lies behind the suffering and cruelty in the world seems a viable possibility; many others accept it as a matter of fact. To those who believe in the Devil, his presence is a constant and unchanging reality, and the historical approach of this book may seem challenging. After all, historians examine the construction and development of ideas over time, with the implicit assumption that these ideas are mutable and respond to the political and social circumstances in which they appear. Indeed, this book will argue that a distinctive – and distinctively modern – understanding of Satan emerged in the Tudor age. Such a historical approach is necessary, however, as it offers both believers and skeptics the best way to understand the Devil. This is because direct knowledge of Satan is unobtainable: even the most devout Christian (or talented necromancer) cannot possess it. As Jeffrey Burton Russell has argued, it is only through studying the idea of the Devil in human culture that we can understand him at all. 'The Devil is what the history of his concept is. Nothing else about him can be known.'[2]

The idea of the Devil has been strikingly variegated. Indeed, few figures in history have possessed so many diverse and overlapping identities. The various names for the Devil illustrate this tendency. The Old Testament character of Satan – originally an angel loyal to God who was permitted to test the faith of His servants – was transformed into God's enemy in Jewish apocalyptic literature in the centuries before Christianity. The Greek word for 'adversary' – the original Hebrew meaning of Satan – was rendered in Greek as 'slanderer' or 'accuser', and subsequently Latinized as *diabolus*, giving rise to the English 'devil'. The fallen angel whose starry descent from Heaven inspired the name Lucifer, or 'giver of light', derived from apocryphal books of the Old Testament familiar to early Christian writers. This figure was conflated with Satan in the New Testament: in Luke's gospel, for instance, Jesus 'beheld Satan as lightning fall from Heaven'. By the sixteenth century, the names Lucifer, Satan and the Devil were used interchangeably. More broadly, these names could also be used to describe a host of lesser demons, whose identities frequently merged with that of their infernal master.[3]

The many names of the Devil were matched by his multiple and sometimes contradictory attributes. Satan was both the enemy of goodness and the punisher of sinners – and in this latter role he appeared to enforce the will of God. Only the Devil's wickedness was relatively constant, though even this was sometimes challenged in 'merry tales'

that portrayed him as a comic or likeable figure. As the ancient opponent of goodness, the Devil was defined more often by what he was
not than by what he was, and his representation was correspondingly
pliant: in the phrase of the art historian Luther Link, he was a 'mask
without a face'. Link observes that no stable iconography of the Devil
emerged in medieval culture: he could be represented as a dragon-like
monster, a rebel angel, a corrupted version of Pan, a man, or an 'evil
microbe'. Rather than a fixed identity, the Devil was a loose assembly
of images united by their negative relationship to God; he was more
an abstraction than a real character. Such diversity was probably useful.
The sheer range of the images and qualities attributed to Satan made
him an exceptionally adaptable figure: in his various guises, he could
be pressed into the service of storytellers, artists, politicians and theologians of very different stripe.[4]

Tudor and Stuart representations of the Devil illustrate these variations. Satan was often depicted in grossly physical terms, not least in
printed ballads describing the fate of evildoers. In this spirit, some of
the earliest English versions of the legend of Johann Faust, a magician who traded his soul with the Devil, ended in a riot of carnage:
the Devil ripped Faust's 'arms and legs in pieces' and smashed his
head 'against the wall'. At the other extreme, some Protestant writers
such as the Kentish gentleman Reginald Scot portrayed the Devil as
a wholly immaterial presence: a 'secret force or power' that impelled
individuals to wickedness. In the vision of many preachers and devotional writers, Satan was a mighty spirit whose power extended over
all but those redeemed by Christ, and who continued to torment
even these fortunate individuals. A parallel tradition in cheap literature depicted him as a crafty but fallible trickster, frequently gulled
by resourceful peasants or beaten by fierce housewives.[5]

This array of images suggests that no single understanding of the
Devil achieved complete dominance in Tudor and Stuart England.
Nonetheless, it is possible to discern a consistent picture of the ancient
enemy that emerged in the work of English theologians during the
Reformation, and which can be described as the 'Protestant Devil'.
To create this distinctive image, Protestant thinkers drew selectively
from the well of ideas about Satan that existed in the late Middle Ages,
emphasizing some and neglecting others. Most notably, they stressed
the spiritual nature of Satan. The Protestant Devil was preeminently
a creature of the mind: an interior presence encouraging falsehood
and sin. This internalised idea of the Devil – a dark counterpoint

to the personal experience of God – diminished the importance of Satan's physical manifestations. As Nathan Johnstone has observed, English Protestants elevated the Devil's role as a tempter to the 'single most important aspect of his agency', and in this process they relegated his more fleshly attributes to secondary and largely theoretical phenomena. 'Whilst they did not deny the Devil's power to manifest physically', Johnstone writes, 'it is striking that they virtually ignored the possibility in their theological and devotional works'.[6]

The internalised view of Satan associated him with all forms of falsehood and temptation. As a consequence, he expressed himself most powerfully in his mastery of individuals, and his influence in the world appeared to rise or recede with the tide of false belief and irreligion. In 1652 Thomas Morton, the former Bishop of Durham, observed that Satan's title of 'prince of this world' (John 12:31) described his lordship 'of the generation of the wicked in this world'. As such, the extent of his kingdom was measured by the number of enemies of the gospel, whom the Devil possessed 'in the heart'. Such an outlook did not necessarily magnify Satan's power; but it meant that his influence seemed pronounced whenever sin and falsehood abounded. The early reformers struck a blow against the Devil by rescuing the gospel from Roman 'superstition'; but later generations discovered that his empire of deceit was resilient. Conflict over the true form of Christianity tended to amplify Satan's influence by focusing attention on his deluded adherents. At the same time, the reform of the church itself stripped away many of the rites and holy objects that had once shielded the faithful from his spite, as well as the saints that interceded on their behalf. Men and women had to face the Devil's temptations alone, often in the belief that they held sway over the greater part of humankind.[7]

English reformers, then, crafted from the traditions of medieval Christianity a concept of Satan that was both intimate and powerful. This concept was presented to a wide audience in sermons, devotional literature, chapbooks and ballads, including cheap broadsheets such as *Stand up to Your Beliefe* (1640), which presented the 'combat between Satan tempting and a Christian triumphing' as a lively dialogue between a humble believer and the enemy. The appeal of this message depended on the disposition of individual listeners and readers, and was not confined to any one section of the population. Devout Protestants were a minority in Tudor and Stuart society, however. In part, this reflected the fact that religious devotion in any culture tends to be a minority pursuit. Reformed Christianity was also more demanding than late medieval Catholicism, as the latter was based as much on the performance of ritual as the understanding of theological precepts. With its intense emphasis on scripture, Protestantism certainly required a fairly high degree of literacy in a predominantly oral culture. This helps to explain the relatively rapid spread of the new faith in urban areas, and especially London, where both education and print were most widely available. These factors ensured that committed Protestants remained a self-conscious minority in the sixteenth and seventeenth centuries, though they were well represented among the political elite. The rest of the population, characterized by the Essex preacher George Gifford as 'the common sort of Christians', retained many conservative religious assumptions and correspondingly 'unreformed' ideas about the Devil.[8]

This book examines the rise of the Protestant Devil in Tudor and Stuart England. Chapter two argues that the godly minority diminished the more physical and often comic representations of Satan that belonged to the common inheritance of the Middle Ages, and abandoned the belief that men and women could overcome the ancient enemy by their own efforts. The reformed image of Satan imposed considerable psychological demands on those who took it seriously, and these are considered in chapter three. The rest of the book is concerned largely with the effect of these ideas on English society as a whole. It suggests that Protestant theologians largely failed to convince ordinary people of their case, and much broader attitudes towards the Devil continued to flourish. Their efforts were not, however, entirely in vain. Some Protestant assumptions did achieve widespread acceptance, resulting in a partially reformed view of the Devil in popular culture. These developments were shaped by a coalition of theological, social and psychological factors, the effects of which are surveyed below.

SATAN, PROVIDENCE AND THE PROBLEM OF EVIL

If God did not exist, according to Voltaire's maxim, it would be necessary to invent him. The same is probably true of the Devil, since his existence helps to resolve an enduring and profound difficulty in Christian theology: the so-called 'problem of evil'. If God is perfectly loving, why does He allow the innocent to suffer? If He has infinite power, why does He do nothing to prevent it? These questions are raised by any instance of underserved pain. Theologians distinguish between 'natural evils' – such as famine and disease – and man-made atrocities like the gulags and extermination camps of the twentieth century, but both lead to the same basic dilemma: why does a good and all powerful God allow such things to happen?

The problem of evil dissolves if all earthly events – including famines and atrocities – are attributed directly to the will of God. This position was adopted in some books of the Old Testament, which present an unflinching vision of Jehovah as the fount of both goodness and suffering. The message is unusually clear in the authorized translation of Isaiah 45:7: 'I form the light and create darkness: I make peace and create evil: I the Lord do all these things.' This position entailed a humble acceptance of divine sovereignty in all its aspects. Less palatably, it also implied that God was not unambiguously good. The construction of a perfectly benign (and perhaps more psychologically satisfying) vision of God required an alternative explanation for the obvious evils in the world – and the Devil emerged in this role. Indeed, some Old Testament scholars have argued that the idea of an entirely benevolent God encouraged the transformation of Satan from His servant into His evil opponent in the centuries before Christianity. This process was completed in the New Testament, in which a wholly loving God confronts a wholly malevolent Devil. On this interpretation, it appears that belief in the Devil arises from the assertion of God's goodness.[9]

Viewed more narrowly, the Devil helped to resolve the apparent inconsistency between a perfectly loving and all powerful God and the presence of evil in the world. A good God would wish to prevent the innocent from suffering, and an omnipotent God could do so; yet human experience shows that this is not the case. One solution to this logical problem was to place an effective limit on God's power by arguing that he acted within constraints imposed by the disobedience of his own creatures. Such disobedience could not be avoided without the abolition of free will, which a loving creator would not impose. The first rebellion against the deity was led by the angel Lucifer, who devoted himself to the corruption of humankind once he was cast down from Heaven. Through his intervention in the Garden of Eden, the first man and woman were deceived into betraying their maker, and this act brought sin and death into the world. A similar argument could explain specific instances of innocent suffering caused by famine

Satan and demons, from the pamphlet *Newes from Avernus* (1642)

and disease: as a powerful spirit in rebellion against God, Satan could be held responsible for such 'natural evils'.[10]

The relationship between the Devil and God remained ambiguous, however. A tension existed between divine sovereignty and demonic agency: if the Devil was a free creature who disobeyed the Lord, did his freedom extend to complete autonomy? Such an assertion came close to acknowledging a spiritual power independent of God, and undermining His government. This problem arose whenever Christians emphasized divine authority, and came sharply into focus during the Protestant Reformation. For the German reformer Martin Luther, God was the ultimate cause of everything in the world, including events that appeared to be evil. The Devil, accordingly, always acted according to God's will. Equally, John Calvin cited biblical precedents to affirm that the Lord supervised the Devil's actions, as when 'he turned Pharaoh over to Satan to be confirmed in the obstinacy of his breast'. By taking this view, Protestant theologians risked the suggestion that God desired evil. Luther avoided this conclusion by making some careful distinctions. First, he proposed that occurrences that seemed wicked to us were, in truth, part of God's loving plan for the world. With our flawed minds and limited sense of perspective, we were incapable of seeing the goodness that underpinned all the creator's works. Second, Luther distinguished between the will of God, which was always good, and the will of Satan, which was utterly malign. While the Devil took a cruel pleasure in what he did, God allowed him to act for reasons that were loving and just. Thus 'God incites the Devil to evil, but he does not do evil himself'. [11]

In Protestant England these ideas were contained within the doctrine of 'providence'. This was the belief that God's hand guided every event towards His ultimate purpose. Providential thinking was applied to all manner of earthly affairs, and also reached into the world of spirits. 'Devils do much mischief', wrote the West Country minister Richard Bernard in 1627, 'but even by these also doth God work His will, and these do nothing without the hand of His providence'. Francis Raworth observed in 1655 that 'providence extends toward all rational and intellectual creatures, men and angels, good and bad'. Since God's intentions were benign and just, even demons were unwilling agents of the higher good. Their acts were performed with malice, but the divine hand ensured that their outcome was benevolent. As Edward Leigh noted in 1646, 'God well useth evil instruments besides and beyond their own intention'. In *A Sermon of Gods Providence* (1609), Arthur Dent adapted the words of St Paul to describe this strange marvel: 'so mighty and wonderful is God, that he is able to make the light to shine out of darkness'. John Milton dramatized this idea in *Paradise Lost*, in which Satan was tormented by the knowledge that 'all his malice served but to bring forth / Infinite goodness'. [12]

The doctrine of providence was illustrated in the more mundane context of an English murder case in 1603. Elizabeth Caldwell conspired with her lover and two accomplices to poison her husband with rats-bane; but their plot resulted in the accidental death of a serving girl instead. A contemporary account of the crime noted that Caldwell had been inspired by the Devil, but his aims were frustrated by the higher intentions of God. The failure of the plot proved to be the improbable route by which Caldwell discovered true religion, while her associates remained unrepentant slaves of the 'ugly fiend'. In this way 'the deceitful Devil, who hath sometimes permission from God to attempt the very righteous, was now an instrument to her sorrow, but her feeling faith the more increased'. Caldwell went on to exhort the crowd at her execution to resist demonic temptation, forswear adultery, and keep the Sabbath. Thus God used Satan as his tool, and the outcome of his actions was good rather than evil. [13]

The supreme power of God was further emphasized by the doctrine of predestination. Drawn from the works of St Paul and St Augustine, this concept was embraced by Martin Luther and the followers of the second-generation French reformer, John Calvin. In its Calvinist form, the doctrine asserted that God had chosen to save a portion of humankind – the 'elect' – from the beginning of time, and condemned the rest to damnation. This divine edict was immutable and could not be affected by the behaviour or 'merit' of individuals. In 1563 the idea was enshrined in the Thirty-Nine Articles which set out the official doctrine of the Church of England. According to the seventeenth article, 'predestination to life is the everlasting purpose of God, whereby (before the foundations of the world were laid) he has constantly decreed by his counsel secret to us, to deliver from curse and damnation those whom he has chosen in Christ out of mankind, and to bring them by Christ to everlasting salvation'. While the correct interpretation of these words was the subject of scholarly debate, the most influential Protestant theologians of the Elizabethan period were firmly committed to the doctrine. William Perkins placed it at the heart of his sermons and catechisms in the 1590s, and the doctrine was publicized by other devotional writers such as George Gifford and Arthur Dent. [14]

By underlining the power of God, the doctrine of predestination appeared to diminish further the Devil's role in human affairs. Not only did the Lord employ Satan as his instrument, but he retained control over the salvation and damnation of particular men and women. Although the ancient enemy wished to draw people into Hell for his own malicious pleasure, he had no final power over their fate. To human eyes, the decision of God to damn one person and save another might appear to be arbitrary and unjust, but – just like the existence of other apparent evils in the world – it reflected the deity's eternal wisdom and ultimate purpose for humankind. The faithful were encouraged to submit themselves to the divine will, and examine their consciences for 'signs' that they were numbered among the elect.

Protestant theology, therefore, offered a radical solution to the problem of evil. As Jeffrey Burton Russell has observed, the leaders of the movement were 'unflinchingly consistent in affirming the total omnipotence of God', with the result that Satan was reduced to little more than 'God's tool, like a pruning hook or a hoe that he uses to cultivate his garden'. The implications of this theology were not fixed, however. While the doctrines of providence and predestination set absolute limits on Satan's power, they proved to be extremely subtle (and supple) in their application. God's providential wisdom could confound human expectations. The divine plan was 'marvellous and unspeakable', as Edward Cradocke pointed out in 1572. Indeed, the Lord's methods could appear inscrutably harsh. As Arthur Dent explained in *The Plain Mans Path-way to Heaven* (1601), God did not spare his children from earthly afflictions; rather, he allowed them to suffer in ways that were ultimately beneficial, either in this world or the next. 'He loveth them when he smiteth them. He favoureth them when He seemeth to be most against them . . . He presseth them that He may ease them. He maketh them cry, that afterward they may laugh.' Thus God could employ Satan as an instrument to purify and chastise His people, both directly through temptation and indirectly by inspiring others to persecute the church. At the same time, the doctrine of predestination meant that He abandoned the unsaved to the Devil's wrath. These possibilities meant that the doctrines of providence and predestination were compatible with diverse interpretations of Satan's earthly power; and these interpretations reflected the world that reformed Christians perceived around them. [15]

In practice, many Protestant reformers came to emphasize the Devil's might, and placed the struggle against him at the centre of religious life. In this respect, the teaching of John Calvin was entirely typical:

> The fact that the Devil is everywhere called God's adversary and ours also ought to fire us to an unceasing struggle against him. For if we have God's glory at heart, as we should have, we ought with all our strength to contend against him who is trying to extinguish it. If we are minded to affirm Christ's kingdom as we ought, we must wage irreconcilable war with him who is plotting its ruin. Again, if we care about our salvation at all, we ought to have neither peace nor truce with him who continually lays traps to destroy it.

Many English Protestants joined Calvin's 'irreconcilable war' with Satan. This attitude was captured in the titles of numerous books devoted to the subject: particularly martial examples include John Downame's *The Christian Warfare, Wherein is First Generally Shewed the Malice, Power and Politike Stratagems of the Spirituall Ennemies of our Salvation, Satan and his Assistants the World and the Flesh* (1604), Henry Hoddesdon's *An Armory against Satan* (1616), William Gouge's *The Whole Armor of God: or A Christians Spiritual Furniture to Keepe him Safe from all the Assaults of Satan* (1619), and the anonymous *Seven Weapons to Conquer the Devill* (1628). Thus the potential of Protestant doctrines to allay anxieties about the Devil was not realized. In fact, the Reformation had the opposite effect. To explain why this happened, it is necessary to reach beyond theology to the lived experience of English Protestants. Here the most important factors were religious conflict and the psychological demands of the reformed faith. [16]

SATAN AND CONFLICT

From the 1520s onwards, the successful establishment of Protestant churches in Germany and northern Europe destroyed the unity of medieval religion. Throughout the Middle Ages, the defenders of the western church had identified heresy as the work of Satan. This tradition continued in the early years of the Reformation, with the leaders of both religious factions condemning their opponents as the Devil's agents; and this rhetoric intensified as confessional warfare engulfed the continent in the second half of the sixteenth century. For Martin Luther, Catholicism was explicitly 'the Devil's church' and the pope was his earthly representative, or Antichrist, while the extremists within his own camp were 'bewitched of the Devil'. In the same spirit, the Roman church and its political allies denounced the satanic origins of all branches of Protestantism. As a consequence, the profile of the ancient enemy increased considerably on both sides of the religious divide. [17]

Historians have speculated about the relationship between this heightened awareness of Satan and the persecution of witches in the early modern age. While the first prosecutions for witchcraft occurred in the late Middle Ages, and the first wave of persecution took place before the outbreak of religious conflict in the 1520s, the intensification of witch trials in the later sixteenth century coincided with the religious instability engendered by the Reformation. It was once argued that the confessional states that emerged in this period waged war against satanic witchcraft, and confirmed their authority in the process; but this view has not survived the discovery that the most intense persecutions were driven by local people acting independently of central governments. A more plausible explanation, advanced strongly by Brian Levack in the context of Scotland and England, is that some zealous Christians came to view witches as a kind of satanic fifth column within their communities. In those regions where witchcraft was perceived mainly as a religious crime, and where legal safeguards against torture were weak, the desire to create a God-fearing society could involve the elimination of witches. More generally, the widespread interest in the crime after 1560 contributed to the intense awareness among Catholics and Protestants of the Devil's presence in the world. [18]

In England, the effects of religious division were complicated by the course of the national Reformation. The Protestant reforms introduced cautiously by Henry VIII, and more aggressively in the brief reign of his son Edward, were swept away by the Catholic Mary Tudor in the 1550s. Mary's reign, which resulted in the execution of nearly three hundred Protestants and the exile of many others, caused later English reformers to identify their faith with persecution and conflict. Following the accession in 1558 of her Protestant half-sister Elizabeth, this perception was expressed most forcibly in John Foxe's *Acts and Monuments* (1563), the contents of which were summed up neatly by its popular title, the *Book of Martyrs*. As Foxe declared in the preface to the 1570 edition, the history of religion was the story of 'what Christian blood hath been spilt, what persecutions raised, what tyranny exercised, what torments devised, what treachery used against the poor flock and church of Christ, in such sort as since Christ's time greater hath not been seen'. This preoccupation with conflict was reinforced after 1588 by the war with Spain, which many Protestants perceived as a struggle against the Roman Antichrist. The view that religion was a kind of warfare was further encouraged by the hostility of many ordinary people to the perceived excesses of Protestant ministers and their supporters among the laity. The most zealous English Protestants, who were derided by their enemies as 'puritans' and known to one another as 'godly' Christians, sought to impose their own model of religious discipline on a largely unenthusiastic population. Their efforts divided many parishes between a minority of 'godly professors' and their more easy-going neighbours. This tendency pre-disposed the godly minority to perceive itself as an embattled vanguard of 'true Christianity'. Thus by the late 1500s, many English Protestants believed that their religion was besieged by enemies at home and adversaries abroad. This perception, in turn, encouraged them to develop an intense awareness of the Devil's power. [19]

Another factor that influenced Protestant perceptions of Satan was the incomplete nature of the Reformation itself. On her accession in 1558, Elizabeth sought to impose an inclusive religious settlement that could satisfy the wishes of her Protestant supporters without alienating the Catholic majority. Like her father, she also favoured the traditional model of church government by bishops, not least because their appointment by the crown tended to secure its authority. Consequently, the Elizabethan church retained much of the administrative structure of its Catholic predecessor, along with a liturgy and style of worship that was in some respects similar to Catholicism. The survival of these 'popish trappings' was resented by a sizeable portion of the Protestant community, which hoped that future concessions from the crown would complete the unfinished business of reform. Such people expressed their views in diverse ways: most accepted the rites of the English church but looked for their eventual amendment, while the more extreme pursued a policy of 'nonconformity', refusing to participate in the offensive rites prescribed in the Book of Common Prayer. More generally, all godly professors favoured a style of worship that focused on preaching instead of ritual. Support for this attitude was indicated in 1603 when the queen's successor, James VI of Scotland, was presented with a thousand-name petition for reform of the church as he travelled south to claim the English throne. The new king considered these proposals at the Hampton Court Conference in 1604, but few significant concessions were made. Subsequently, the Elizabethan settlement remained in force until the 1640s, when it was violently overthrown by the godly supporters of parliament in the civil war.

This environment gave Protestants much opportunity to witness the crafty operations of the Devil, and to observe the extent of his kingdom on earth. While God's hand ensured that his final defeat was inevitable, the many obstacles to the establishment of true religion – both in the hierarchy of the church and the hearts of ordinary people – suggested that Satan's party would outnumber the godly for some time to come. By seeing the Devil's influence primarily in the mind, Protestants could detect his stratagems in a host of earthly agents. More darkly, they could feel his presence in their own spirit and flesh, where he sought to undermine their faith and secure their damnation. In this role the Devil helped to explain – and sometimes to resolve – the doubts and trials that often accompanied the practice of godly religion itself.

THE DEVIL WITHIN AND WITHOUT

In his perceptive and subtle study of the Devil in the English Reformation, Nathan Johnstone relates the Protestant experience of Satan to the practical and pastoral concerns of those it affected. He notes that demonic temptation 'provided a means of understanding very real experiences'. Above all, Satan's wiles explained how apparently God-fearing people could be seduced by the false religion of Rome. As the 'father of lies', the Devil was a master of deception, and popery was his masterpiece. In the words of William Tyndale, the Roman church had 'set up the ministers of Satan, disguised yet in names of and garments like unto the angels of light and ministers of righteousness'. As Johnstone points out, the success of this charade made English Protestants acutely aware of the spiritual blindness that afflicted fallen humankind, and Satan's resourcefulness in exploiting it. This encouraged vigilance against demonic subversions of Christianity that could seduce honest believers if they were off their guard. It was only through careful attention to scripture, aided by sedulous pastors, that Christians could evade the Devil's plausible deceits. [20]

Engagement with Satan also made sense of the spiritual difficulties that Protestants encountered. It helped to explain moments of spiritual failure, uncertainty or despair. Demonic temptation forced its victims to scrutinize their consciences and acknowledge their own sins. The Gloucestershire divine John Sprint offers a good illustration. In 1623 Sprint published a short pamphlet, *The Christian Sword and Buckler*, in the form of a letter to an unnamed friend. The text, which was reprinted ten times before 1650, suggested conventional responses to 'the assaults of Satan' on a sensitive conscience. These included the despairing thought that the reader was unworthy of salvation:

> If he [the Devil] say your sins are many, and more than can be pardoned, tell him, where sin aboundeth, grace over-aboundeth. If he say you are the greatest sinner in the world, tell him it is true, but Christ came into the world to save sinners, whereof I am chief. If he allege the greatness of thy guilt, say, though my sins be as red as scarlet, yet he will make them as white as snow.

Here Sprint's letter acknowledged a familiar source of anxiety among his godly audience: the fear that their sins excluded them from divine mercy. It was the Devil's aim to cultivate this thought;

and its remedy was God's unmerited grace. The whole experience was intensely introspective: both the spiritual crisis and its resolution involved self-examination and the admission of sin. [21]

Such experiences undoubtedly help to explain the importance of Satan in the English Reformation. For Johnstone, the Protestant emphasis on a spiritual Devil entailed vigilance against falsehood and the kind of painful self-scrutiny described in Sprint's letter. Above all, it compelled believers to confront their own fallen natures. Rather than crudely labeling their enemies as the Devil's associates, or attributing their own 'satanic' thoughts and deeds to an external force for which they were not responsible, Protestants searched their own souls for Satan's imprint. This interpretation may be unduly narrow, however. Satan had always served many purposes, and been understood with varying degrees of sophistication. The Protestant Devil was no exception: indeed, the idea of demonic temptation was an exceptionally flexible psychological resource. The potential of this resource was indicated elsewhere in Sprint's text. Most crudely, the enemies of Protestant piety were placed in Satan's camp: the Devil, Sprint observed, was 'called the God of this world because he ruleth in the children of disobedience', who showed their allegiance 'by lying, swearing, and forswearing, deceiving, and oppressing, and such evil courses'. In eschewing the company of such people, the godly implicitly rejected Satan. More subtly, the experience of demonic temptation itself was a potential sign of grace. 'Every temptation of a Christian', Sprint noted, 'is a ground of strong consolation'. This was because 'warriors never besiege nor batter cities they have won, so Satan seeks not the souls he hath devoured'. This idea, which was a commonplace in devotional literature, could transform the anxieties of godly men and women into marks of election, and thereby confirm their separation from an unregenerate world. [22]

While the awareness of the Devil's power could lead Protestants to rake their consciences for signs of sin, it could also provide an explanation for troubling thoughts and feelings. In this context it was possible to attribute 'unnatural' attitudes to Satan, and sometimes to deflect responsibility from the individual to an external power. The philosopher Charles Taylor has argued that a 'porous' conception of the self, in which the mind is open to supernatural agents beyond its control, was a defining quality of the pre-modern world. This outlook was accepted explicitly by Tudor and Stuart theologians, who held that Satan could implant thoughts directly into the human consciousness. Such demonic 'injections' could be identified and repudiated as the work of the ghostly enemy. Again, Sprint hints at this possibility in his description of religious anxiety. He notes that Satan 'tells you that the word of God is false. This is the first lesson that the Devil teacheth'. Here he appears to identify moments of doubt as demonic intrusions to be renounced. More openly, the Oxford theologian Robert Bolton described how his friends found 'great ease and comfort' when they discovered that certain sinful thoughts they had experienced belonged to the Devil. Such attribution was possible when Protestants faced Satan as a tempter, and became grimly explicit in cases of demonic possession. The whole logic of possession – which Johnstone describes as an 'extreme form' of temptation – rested on the belief that the Devil was speaking through the afflicted individual, who was therefore not responsible for the words that he or she uttered. [23]

Thus the Protestant struggle with Satan created diverse possibilities for the individuals involved. His mastery of deceit meant that believers had to watch against seductive falsehoods and submit their consciences to scrupulous self-observation. At the same time, Satan's hold over 'worldlings' set the godly apart from their more carefree neighbours; and the awareness of demonic temptation in itself was a hopeful sign of election. The Devil's wiles could encourage soul searching and the admission of sin; they could also free people from responsibility for inappropriate thoughts and feelings. The autobiographies of godly men and women, which are considered in chapter three, suggest that all these possibilities were realized, and often in the same individuals. It was the very richness of the Devil as an intellectual resource that helped keep him at the heart of Protestant spirituality.

But engagement with Satan was not, of course, confined to the godly. While the reformed services of the church of

The Devil walks the earth, from the title page of *Grand Plutoes Remonstrance* (1642)

England reflected a new attitude towards the ancient enemy, and ministers impressed his power as a spiritual tempter in sermons and printed texts, many older beliefs about the Devil survived long into the eighteenth century. The existence of this wider tradition further extended the role of the Devil in Tudor and Stuart life. It also created tensions and synergies within English culture that reflected the fate of the Reformation as a whole.

THE DEVIL AT LARGE

For most ordinary people the Reformation of the Devil was negative and indirect. During the 1530s the cult of saints, which offered protection against demonic influences, was systematically destroyed; and subsequently the use of blessed water and candles that could ward off unclean spirits was abandoned in the English church. The act of exorcism was removed from the baptism service in 1552, on the basis that Christians would engage directly and continually with the Devil rather than relying on the ritual cleansing performed at the font. At the other end of life, the sacramental blessing and protections of the deathbed were abolished. These reforms were overturned in the brief reign of Mary Tudor, but restored in the Elizabethan settlement of 1559. Thus the religious structures that had defended men and women from the Devil were stripped away in the sixteenth century, and replaced by the English Bible and the ministry of Protestant churchmen. [24]

The effects of this process were predictably partial and mixed. While it is impossible to recover the response of the majority of the population, the evidence of cheap print suggests that Protestant ideas about Satan did not penetrate evenly and deeply throughout English society. Nathan Johnstone suggests that there is 'no real basis to delineate differences between popular and elite conceptions of the Devil so far as they are represented in the written sources'; but this claim requires some modification. The Protestant idea of Satan was certainly present at every level of the print market – from expensive works of devotional literature to broadsheet ballads – but the *range* of representations of the Devil was more extensive in the most widely available texts, such as chapbooks and songs. This suggests that a common culture of images, ideas and expectations of the Devil survived in Tudor and Stuart England, while more committed Protestants concentrated only

on certain aspects of demonic agency. To take one example, the large
collection of ballads published as *Merry Drollery* in 1661 contained
six titles in which the Devil played a prominent role. In one of these
he was an invisible voice, and in another he appeared as the serpent
angling for souls in the Garden of Eden. The other four ballads
presented Satan as a physical being, and their stories emphasized his
fleshly nature. Thus he was castrated by a baker in 'The Gelding of
the Devil', a woman farted in his face in 'A Merry Song', and in 'The
Feasting of the Devil' he enjoyed a banquet of sinners, including 'six
pickled tailors' and a 'bawd and bacon'. [25]

The Devil's role in these texts covered a range of familiar possibilities. He was a tempter, a deceiver and a punisher. He kept company
with well-known villains and consumed them as his prey. As a foil to
wily heroes, he provided challenges to overcome and opportunities
for rough comedy. He was also a dreadful enemy and a rapacious
beast. In some incarnations, his behaviour echoed the themes of
Protestant demonism. *The Devil Transformed*, for example, presented
Satan in a series of disguises by which he intended to deceive the
narrator. These included an ostensibly attractive maiden:

> In woman's attire I meet him most fine,
> At first sight I thought him some angel divine:
> But viewing his crab-face I fell to my trade,
> I made him forswear ever acting a maid;
> Meaw, quoth the Devil, and so ran away,
> And hid him in a friar's old weed, as they say.

Here the theme of demonic deception is clear, and is underscored by
a possible echo of St Paul's warning that 'Satan himself is transformed
into an angel of light' (2 Cor. 11:14). The Devil also retreats to his
natural home in the Roman church. At the same time, the Protestant
elements in this depiction are balanced by other qualities drawn from
a repertoire of traditional ideas. Satan takes physical shape in this
and his other manifestations in the song, and he is defeated by the
hero's own resources rather than the power of God. These themes are
united in the opening verse, in which the Devil, disguised as a ram, is
tied by the horns and stabbed. [26]

As the reformed understanding of Satan was drawn from a larger
body of beliefs that remained in circulation, it was possible for
Protestant churchmen to exploit these wider beliefs in their pastoral

and educational work. Nothing in Calvinist theology precluded the possibility of the Devil taking bodily form, though this was a minor consideration for a creature that made a 'palace in men's souls'. Thus the London minister Vavasor Powell described how Satan 'once like a house stood directly in my way', though the hazards he placed in the pastor's mind were far more dangerous. The Protestant clergy retained the physical Devil in their armoury of weapons against incautious sinners. Thus Thomas Beard included numerous tales of bloody satanic justice in *The Theatre of Gods Judgements* (1597), a text that was frequently reprinted and copied in the seventeenth century. In one example, a 'blasphemous wretch' in an alehouse offered to sell his soul to anyone who would buy him a cup of wine. Beard described what happened after one of the man's companions took up the offer:

> Now Satan himself was there in a man's shape (as commonly he is never far from such meetings), and bought it again of the other at the same price, and by and by bad him [to] give him his soul; the whole company affirming it was meet he should have it, since he had bought it, not perceiving the Devil. But presently he, laying hold on this soul-seller, carried him into the air before them all, towards his own habitation, to the great astonishment and amazement of the beholders.

As Beard noted in the 1631 edition of the book, such incidents showed how God 'useth the ministry of evil angels . . . to execute vengeance upon wicked men'. Tales of this kind also carried risks, however, as they focused attention on the most garish and uncommon of the Devil's exploits, thereby deflecting attention from his more powerful and insidious role as a tempter. This problem came to the fore in cases of witchcraft and demonic possession – which are examined in chapters six and seven – where Protestant demonology interacted most fully with popular beliefs. [27]

The areas of common ground between Protestant demonism and the broader culture of Tudor and Stuart England should not conceal the radicalism of reformed ideas about the Devil. While the theology of the Church of England allowed space – often cautiously – for the physical manifestations of Satan that had been commonplace in the late Middle Ages, it rejected completely the possibility that individuals could defeat the enemy through their own efforts or the intervention of sacred institutions. Only the word of God – unaided by the saints, holy objects or rituals – could free men and women from the prince of this world. Worse still, the canopy of rites and relics that appeared to shield individuals from his power belonged to his devious strategy to subvert true religion. When patients contemplated the painting of judgment in the dying room in St Wulfstan's hospital in 1530, they may have drawn comfort from the image of Mary besting the feeble efforts of the Devil to claim a human soul. Within a generation, her power had been abolished and her cult ascribed to Satan himself. The Devil in the mind may have evoked less obvious terrors than the physical monster familiar from the church paintings that were white-washed in the reign of Edward VI; but his influence on Tudor and Stuart culture was pervasive and profound.

THE DEVIL AND THE
ENGLISH REFORMATION

MEDIEVAL PERSPECTIVES

A 'merry tale' published in 1526 provides a lively illustration of late
medieval attitudes towards the Devil. It tells the story of a Suffolk
man named John who acted the part of Satan in a town play, then
walked home at night wearing the costume he had put on for the
role. His path took him through a wood, where he stumbled on the
activities of a gang of poachers. As he approached in the failing light,
they mistook him for 'the Devil indeed, [and] for fear ran away', aban-
doning their horse and a booty of dead rabbits. When John realised
what had happened, he took the horse with the rabbits hanging from
its saddle and rode to the house of the gentleman who owned the
estate, intending to return his property. This neighbourly act inspired
panic among the gentleman's servants when they caught sight of the
visitor advancing towards them. At John's arrival, the steward informed
his master that the Devil 'is at the gate sitting upon a horse laden all
with souls, and by likelihood he is come for your soul'. Marshalling
the spiritual forces at his disposal, the gentleman called his chaplain
and 'as many of his servants as durst go with him' to the gate, armed
with holy water and a blessed candle. Here the priest confronted the
dreadful rider. He declared 'in the name of the Father, Son and Holy
Ghost, I conjure thee and charge thee in the holy name of God to tell
me why and wherefore thou come hither'. At this, John explained his
intentions and announced that he was 'a good Devil'. The company
recognised his voice, and their 'fear and dread was turned to mirth'. [1]

This tale offers a useful starting point from which to explore late medieval attitudes towards Satan. While it does not encompass every view that was expressed about 'the fiend' in this period, it contains many elements that were common in contemporary descriptions of him. Perhaps its most striking feature was the assumption that the Devil could appear as a physical being. Without this belief, the actions of the poachers and the inhabitants of the house would have seemed unconvincing, and the story would have lost much of its humour. Indeed, the author notes at the end of the tale that sightings of 'spirits and devils' were widely reported and believed. The idea that the Devil could assume a physical form was underlined in a similar story from Germany in the fifteenth century. In this version a stranger arrived at a town during a carnival, just as a man in a Devil costume was chasing an old woman outside the walls. Unaware that the carnival was taking place, the visitor attempted to rescue the woman by attacking her assailant with an axe. His defence at the ensuing murder trial was that he had genuinely believed the performer to be the Devil, and that his actions were intended to save the woman's life. Just as carnival players could be mistaken for the Devil, Satan himself could masquerade convincingly in human form. So realistic were his disguises that English folklore identified tokens, such as the possession of one cloven hoof, by which his counterfeits could be discovered. The author of the fourteenth-century mystical tract *The Cloud of Unknowing* affirmed that the fiend could be detected in any guise by the fact that he 'has never more than one large and flaring nostril'. Such concern for physical details emphasised the bodily reality of the Devil, which appears to have been taken for granted by many people in the late Middle Ages. [2]

Even when the Devil manifested himself invisibly he was generally assumed to occupy real space. The concept of demonic possession, in which an unclean spirit was physically located

Christ performs an exorcism in an illumination from a thirteenth-century Psalter.

A medieval depiction of the jaws of Hell.

inside the body of its victim, was a vivid illustration of this idea. A common treatment for the condition was to beat the possessed individual so the invader was made uncomfortable in its lodgings. Accounts of exorcisms affirmed that bystanders could themselves become possessed when the demon, expelled from the body of one host, fled into another person who happened to be nearby. Such ideas reflected a tendency to view supernatural phenomena in ways which can seem shockingly materialistic to twenty-first-century eyes. The arrival of the Devil at the gates in the 'merry tale' indicated that he intended literally to carry away the gentleman's soul, adding it to the collection of damned spirits hanging from his saddle. Another story from the same collection described a night-time encounter between a priest and a poacher carrying a sheep on his back. When the priest saw the poacher he thought he was 'the Devil with the spirit of [a] dead man on his neck'. The same kind of literalism was apparent in visual depictions of the fiend. A stained-glass window in the parish church of Fairford in Gloucestershire, for instance, shows Satan carting off souls in a wheelbarrow. He is depicted in a carving in Worcester cathedral with a bundle of damned souls trussed up on his back. It is easy for modern observers to mock such concrete representations of the Devil's activity – as did some Protestant writers in the sixteenth century. Nonetheless, the physical depiction of Satan, Hell, and the souls of the damned can be viewed as a logical component of medieval religion, and is perhaps more consistent than the modern tendency to retain such concepts while interpreting them in purely 'spiritual' or metaphorical terms. [3]

Combating the Devil

As well as illustrating the physical reality of the Devil, the story of the Suffolk player indicates the availability of defences against him.

These followed in part from the limitations imposed by his material form, which made it possible for mortals to run away, hide, or even attack him with an axe. When the poachers encountered the fiend in the wood, their immediate response was to run for their lives; later, the inhabitants of the house fended him off by shutting the gates. In the other 'merry tale' about the priest and the poacher, the hero tried to escape

The torments of those guilty of the sin of anger, from the medieval *Vision of Lazarus*.

the fiend by jumping into a ditch. Greater bravery was attributed to St Dunstan who, according to legend, grabbed Satan by his nose with a pair of tongs. The physical vulnerability of the ancient enemy was also depicted in church carvings. In Tewkesbury abbey, for example, the tomb of Robert Forthington, a thirteenth-century abbot famed for his skills as an exorcist, bears a spandrel depicting the abbot thrusting his sword down the Devil's throat. A similar motif is found in wood carvings in Carlisle cathedral and the parish church of St Andrews in Greystoke near Penrith, which show St Michael plunging his sword into the gaping mouth of the fiend. [4]

While Satan's physical limitations made him vulnerable to attack, it was much more common to deploy supernatural weapons against him, such as the candle and holy water employed by the chaplain in the 'merry tale'. Such

The punishments of the proud in Hell, from the *Vision of Lazarus*.

instruments were typical of the 'sacramentals', or consecrated objects, which were recognised in folklore and theology to offer protection against wicked spirits. Similar powers were attributed to certain passages of scripture, such as the story of the annunciation in St Luke's gospel, which were recited or written on paper and placed in amulets to protect both humans and animals from the Devil's assaults. Ultimately, these deterrents relied for their potency on the authority of the church. The church also offered direct protection against Satan through a variety of services dedicated to this purpose, including the baptism of infants and the annual blessing of parishes on the days before the celebration of Christ's ascension. More routinely, many theologians and layfolk accepted that the ringing of church bells could offer protection against flying demons. [5]

The existence of such protections meant that Satan, though fearful, could be defeated by human effort. This was also apparent from the legends surrounding saints such as Dunstan and figures from folklore like John Schorn, who was reputed to have trapped the Devil in a boot. It is possible that Schorn's legend was connected to the practice of burying shoes in the walls and foundations of houses in

The summoning of a demon by a ritual magician. Illustration from the title page of Chrisopher Marlowe, *Dr Faustus* (1636).

late medieval and sixteenth-century England; these artefacts were apparently believed to trap evil spirits which attempted to enter the buildings. In a different context, the resourceful heroes of folk tales also exposed the Devil's limitations by their habit of outwitting or deceiving him. The belief that the Devil could be tricked was illustrated in a remarkable trial from Norfolk in 1465. It was alleged that a weaver, Robert Hikkes, and his accomplice, John Cans, had used 'unlawful arts' to summon up an 'accursed spirit' and asked it to reveal the location of buried treasure. They had enticed the demon to divulge this information by promising it 'the body of a Christian', but deceived the fiend by baptising a cockerel with holy water, killing it and offering its remains 'as a Christian carcass'. The charges against the men alleged that this fraud had succeeded and they had thereby acquired a 'vast treasure'. Such confidence in the ability of mortals to contain and exploit demonic power underpinned the practice of invoking spirits in both learned and popular magic in medieval England. [6]

Comic depictions of Satan

The belief that the Devil could be constrained by human effort helps to explain another feature of the tale of the Suffolk player, which appeared in many other contemporary works. The Devil was presented in a humorous context. While he was not depicted as a figure of fun, he was apparently regarded as a suitable subject for comedy. Thus the revelation that the phantom on horseback was only a man in disguise was an occasion for 'mirth and desport'; the incident was not presented as a warning against sin or a call to virtuous living. The same tendency was evident in another tale published around 1530. This told the story of a man who dreamed one night that he met the Devil, who led him into a field to dig for gold. When they uncovered the treasure the man wanted to take it away, but his companion would not allow it:

> 'Thou canst not carry it away now, but mark the place that thou may fetch it another time.'
> 'What mark shall I make?' quod the man.
> 'Shit over it', quod the Devil, 'for that shall cause every man to shun the place.'

The unfortunate hero took the fiend's advice, and when he awoke he found that he 'had foul defiled his bed'. Undeterred by this catastrophe, he got up and prepared to seek out the riches that had been revealed in the dream. The story ends with a nicely gratu-itous touch: 'he put on his bonnet, wherein also the same night the cat had shit . . . Thus his golden dream turned all to dirt'. Here the Devil's mischief provided an opportunity for vulgar entertain-ment, and no attempt was made to extract a moral from the tale. In a slightly different context, the Devil's name was uttered mockingly in the punch-lines of early sixteenth-century jokes. When a widow discovered that her potential suitor was impotent, she exclaimed that he could 'go to the Devil'. A man condemned to hang was granted one last wish by the aristocrat responsible for his execution, and he requested that the lord should kiss him 'on the bare arse'. To this 'the lord answered: 'The Devil kiss thine arse', and so let him go'. Again, the use of the Devil in these tales was essentially comic, and indicates that he could be treated as a figure of mirth as well as dread. [7]

The scatological humour associated with the Devil in 'merry tales' was also found in some medieval drama. *The Temptation of Christ* in the Chester mystery cycle, for instance, included a passage in which Satan, having been vanquished by Christ, bequeathed his excrement to the audience as his last will and testament. The comic possibilities of the fiend were also explored in some versions of *The Harrowing of Hell*, which featured comedic exchanges between the Devil and his minions before their kingdom was purged by Christ. In this instance, the subject matter of the play, which portrayed Jesus' descent into Hell to free the souls imprisoned there, probably helped to make the fiend a safe target for comedy. The humorous aspect of Satan was also captured in visual images. Perhaps the most striking example is a carving on a choir stool in the priory church of Malvern in Worcestershire, which also neatly conveys the Devil's concrete reality and his limitations. It depicts a monk driving away the fiend by inserting the nozzle of a pair of bellows into the creature's anus. Other grotesque and comic depictions of the Devil have survived in the bosses of Norwich cathedral, while the leering, feline carvings of the fiend on the nave columns of Gloucester cathedral emphasise his comic aspect as much as his malevolence. The same can be said of the mischievous demons which populate the stonework and wood carvings of many parish churches. [8]

How representative was the image of the Devil described so far? The 'merry tales' were probably collected from oral traditions and printed for a literate minority, which then passed them back into oral circulation. The potential market for such work was huge, and most likely encompassed many different social groups. An equally large and diverse audience probably existed for late medieval religious drama, which presented a version of Satan similar to that found in the tales. It appears that devout Christians as well as less pious men and women believed that the Devil could appear in a physical form, though some theologians noted that, as a spiritual entity, he possessed no flesh of his own and needed to compose an earthly body from materials such as mud and dust. The fifteenth-century mystic Julian of Norwich claimed that she was awoken from sleep one night by the Devil in the form of a red-headed man, who clasped his hands around her throat and pressed his face close to hers. Her contemporary, Margery Kemp, experienced frequent visions of Satan before she abandoned her husband to devote herself to piety. Many highly religious individuals also believed that the Devil's powers were strictly limited, and could sometimes treat the fiend with remarkable levity. When Satan first appeared to Julian, she 'laughed so heartily' at his pathetic weakness 'that it made those around me laugh too'; she wished that all Christians could 'have seen what I saw, that they might laugh with me'. [9]

Many late medieval ideas about the Devil survived throughout the sixteenth and seventeenth centuries. Indeed, it is likely that the majority of the population subscribed to similar views in the early 1700s, despite the suppression of many of the ecclesiastical and cultural conventions which had supported them. The continuity of these beliefs will be considered in chapter four. But the rest of this chapter will argue that the introduction of Protestantism challenged traditional ways of understanding Satan, and a different view of the Devil came to be embraced by the minority of men and women who committed themselves devoutly to the new creed. For such people the Devil assumed a new importance in religious life. The reasons for this transformation will be considered below, but first it is necessary to describe the characteristics of Protestant attitudes towards Satan.

THE PRINCE OF THIS WORLD

In his 1530 book *A Werke for Housholders*, Richard Whitford presented a brief exposition of the Lord's Prayer. This was intended as a guide for layfolk to the essential meaning and relevance of the sacred text, and formed part of the author's larger purpose of providing a model for Christian living. His exposition made no reference to the Devil. Even the words of the seventh line, 'Deliver me from evil', were interpreted without mentioning Satan: Whitford read them as a plea to God to 'keep me and all thy people from all sin and offence' and to 'conserve and keep us continually in the state of grace'. It is revealing to compare this work with a commentary on the same text published by the Protestant Thomas Becon some twenty years later. Becon began his interpretation of the second line, 'Thy kingdom come', with these words:

> It is not unknown how great, how mighty, and of what puissance [great power] the kingdom of Satan is . . . There is no ravening wolf that so earnestly seeks greedily to devour his prey as this enemy of mankind, that old serpent, [who] hunts and studies every moment of an hour how he may destroy and bring to everlasting damnation mortal men.

Becon devoted the next two pages to a description of the Devil's 'most ample and populous' earthly kingdom. The fiend's power could be seen in the palaces and armies of his many political allies, in the false church of Rome which had been consecrated for his worship, and, most horribly, in the secret and sinful desires of outwardly pious men and women. Only by reflecting on the terrible extent of Satan's kingdom, Becon asserted, could Christians appreciate the importance of praying 'that the kingdom of our heavenly father may come and rule over us'. This interpretation set the tone for the rest of his work. When he came to the line 'Deliver us from evil', he not only mentioned the Devil but embarked on a lengthy exposition of the various ways in which he assailed the people of God. [10]

Satan's dominion

The work of Thomas Becon was part of a general tendency among Protestants to amplify the Devil's power. Martin Luther described him as 'the prince and God' of the earth, and averred that 'the bread which we eat, the drink which we drink, the garments which we wear, yea, the air, and whatever we live by in the flesh, is under his dominion'. The reformer's opinion was endorsed by English Protestants, who habitually described the Devil as the 'prince of this world'. Luther's position was later elaborated by William Perkins, arguably the most influential English theologian of the late sixteenth century. When the catechist William Chub observed in 1584 that 'the gates of Hell are opened and the floods of Satan hath over-flown the whole world', he was stating an opinion that few devout Protestants would have disputed. This pessimistic outlook was noted by the historian of Satan, Jeffrey Burton Russell, who argued that the emergence of reformed theology entailed a 'vast increase in the Devil's powers'. For committed adherents of the new faith, Satan was transformed from a limited and rather peripheral figure into a central actor in daily life. [11]

The main way in which the Devil's power was enhanced was through a massive extension of his sphere of influence. It was the central idea of Protestantism that men and women could do nothing to earn the love of God: his mercy, together with the promise of salvation, was bestowed purely by His own will, irrespective of the merits of those to whom this gift was offered. Thus all human efforts to obtain salvation were ultimately futile; all one could do was place complete faith in God's goodness and mercy. This apparently benign principle could lead to some alarming conclusions. The bleakest interpretation of the doctrine held that people were incapable of performing any act that was pleasing to God. Most reformers followed Luther in arguing that humans were so deeply stained with sin that they could not, without divine assistance, keep any of the Ten Commandments. For the majority of Protestants, and especially those influenced by the work of John Calvin in the second half of the sixteenth century, this meant that almost all human inclinations were inherently bad. They served the Devil rather than God.

In 1530 Richard Whitford had asserted that only the sins of pride, envy and wrath could rightfully be attributed to Satan. Other sins, such as gluttony, sloth and lust, resulted from the failure of people to live according to God's laws. The English reformers, in contrast, made it clear that the sins of the flesh were directly inspired by the Devil. Many took this idea further by suggesting that human flesh itself belonged to Satan's kingdom. This view was expressed most succinctly in Perkins' catechism of 1590, which stated baldly that 'all men are wholly corrupted with sin through Adam's fall, and so are become slaves of Satan'. All human emotions were the Devil's property: 'the affections of the heart, [such] as love, joy, hope, desire, etc, are moved and stirred to that which is evil, to embrace it, and they are never stirred to that which is good, unless it be to eschew it'. Perkins' catechism was reprinted at least four times in the next decade, and went through several editions in the seventeenth century. It followed from these ideas that the Devil was an intimate, lifelong companion; as a godly preacher put it in the 1630s, he 'builds his nest' in the human heart. Thus the struggle to overcome Satan had to be fought every day, with one's own body and mind enlisted in the enemy camp. In one of his daily prayers, the Protestant martyr John Bradford described his own body as 'a foe to myself' which he could only overcome with the help of God. In 1616 William Gouge, the author of a guide to religious living equivalent to that published by Whitford ninety years earlier, urged all Christians to fight against their own 'flesh and blood, [which] is but Satan's instrument; he is the general, he [is] the captain, he setteth flesh and blood to work'. [12]

The Devil as a tempter and deceiver

Protestants combined the idea that the Devil was the 'captain' of flesh and blood with an emphasis on his role as the source of personal temptations. Satan's most common manifestation was as a tempter who sought to exploit the innate depravity of human beings. He pursued this goal with ferocious relish: as an early seventeenth-century broadsheet warned, Christians should 'be always armed against temptations' which relentlessly assaulted the mind. Since men and women could do nothing to resist this onslaught on their own, the only armour available was prayer and faith in God's mercy. The range of the Devil's temptations was great. One of his favourite enticements was sexual lust, which was so prevalent that it was routinely cited by Protestants as proof of Satan's dominion over the earth. Thus John Olde claimed in 1557 that the satanic nature of the Roman church was proved by its adherents' love of 'whorish women and of filthy and abominable sodomitical lusts'. This claim was repeated countlessly in the second half of the sixteenth century. Another favourite weapon was greed. This point was illustrated in 1569 in the arresting woodcuts created for Stephen Bateman's *Christall Glasse of Christian Reformation*. One of these depicts three riders approaching the Devil, who holds in his hand a net containing earthly riches. The first rider represents 'persons of gentility that are not content with sufficiency'; the second is a papist duped by superstitious promises of wealth; the third is a yeoman who, not content with his lowly station, seeks to rise from 'the dunghill to [become] a gentleman'. Each one is beguiled by the fiend's temptations to ride towards his doom. More luridly, the same point was made by murder pamphlets in the seventeenth century, which described how killers were egged on to their crimes by the Devil, who lured them with promises of financial gain. In the most compendious example of the genre, John Reynolds explained that murder was usually inspired by 'the fiery and bloody darts of Satan's temptations', and cautioned his readers to avoid 'the snares and enticements of the Devil'. [13]

As well as temptations, the enemy deluded Christians with a wide range of 'false' and heretical thoughts. This concept derived from the medieval belief that Satan sometimes deceived men and women with evil ideas disguised as revelations from God. It was well known that the fiend could appear as an 'angel of light'. Protestant divines, with their conviction that human reason was utterly corrupted, were sharply aware of the Devil's capacity to trick people into false beliefs. According to John Olde, the Devil won many followers with 'crafty persuasions, deceitful and false illusions'. In 1601 Arthur Dent likened him to 'a crafty juggler'. Ballads from the same period described Satan simply as 'the liar'. For committed Protestants, the most common example of the Devil's 'illusions' was the false belief that individuals could earn salvation through their own merits. This delusion underpinned the practices of Catholicism and provided further proof that it was a satanic religion; it also dominated the thinking of most ordinary members of the Church of England, whose belief that they could obtain God's favour by doing good works meant that they were only nominal Christians. [14]

At the other end of the spectrum, Satan also tried to deceive godly Protestants into believing that their faith was in vain. Since they were painfully conscious of their own spiritual unworthiness, they were susceptible to the terrible belief, inspired by the Devil, that God had abandoned them completely. Such moments of despair were identified by Perkins as the most subtle and cruel of the Devil's works. This idea was expressed vividly in a godly ballad from 1587, which described how a Christian was tempted to doubt God's mercy when she contemplated the greatness of her own sins. Her agony was relieved by the words of Christ:

> Believe not the Devil, for all his delay!
> For his subtle sleight is to work thy decay.
> Think how I converted my apostle, St Paul,
> By mercy and favour, which I give to you all.

Similar assurances of God's mercy to true Christians were offered in sermons and books of practical divinity throughout the period. While they provide a reminder that Protestant ideas were not unreservedly gloomy, they also indicate the awful pressures that reformed theology could sometimes place on its adherents. [15]

The view that Satan operated mainly through temptation and deceit was exemplified in John Bunyan's biography of an imaginary arch-sinner, *The Life and Death of Mr Badman* (1680). Bunyan's villain commenced his career in wickedness as a child, when his nature was marked by an addiction to lying. This inclination was the fount of all his subsequent misdeeds, and also identified him as a soul lost to Hell. The person who tells a deliberate falsehood, Bunyan observed, 'has lain with and conceived it by lying with the Devil, the only father of lies'. To lie was to commit 'a kind of spiritual adultery with the Devil'. Badman's enslavement to evil, which led him from adolescent dishonesty to a lifetime of deception and theft, was characterised by his unthinking acceptance of the falsehoods that Satan placed in his mind and those of his companions. Bunyan illustrated the essentially intellectual nature of the Devil's ploys in his reflections on the wicked household in which his anti-hero served his apprenticeship:

> Such places are the very haunts and walks of the infernal spirits who are continually poisoning the cogitations and minds of one or another in such families, that they may be able to poison others. Therefore observe it, usually in wicked families some one or two are more arch for wickedness than any other who is there. Now such are Satan's conduit pipes, for by them he conveys the spawn of Hell through their being crafty in wickedness into the ears and souls of their companions.

Thus demonic thoughts spread through a web of social influence. While Satan was sometimes permitted by God to appear directly to sinners, he preferred to exploit their spiritual blindness through these subtle and invisible means. Only divine grace could lift individuals from this mesh of deception, while God abandoned hardened sinners like Mr Badman to their fate. [16]

The Devil's agents

As John Bunyan's fable implied, Satan's invisible power over individuals was combined with immense influence in society as a whole.

Since human nature was fundamentally depraved, all people who lacked true faith in God were the possessions of Satan. William Perkins spelt out the implications of this idea with characteristic bluntness:

> Most of the common people think that good meaning will save them; but a man may profess any religion, and have good meaning, and yet not know one step to the kingdom of Heaven, but remain the vassal and slave of Satan. For a man may have outward civil justice and civil policy, and mean well, yet be the servant of the Devil.

This idea, which was elevated to the status of one of the 'six principles' of Christianity in Perkins' best-selling catechism, enormously swelled the number of the Devil's servants. It was a truism among godly preachers that most of the world was occupied by Satan's forces. In the 1580s George Gifford likened them to a great 'army', and Richard Sibbes later affirmed that Satan 'never yet wanted a strong faction in the world'. Not only were Christians outnumbered by the Devil's allies, but the fiend was constantly rallying his troops against them. As Sibbes explained, there 'hath ever been . . . a continual conspiracy of Satan and his instruments' against God's people, whose fate was to endure the hatred of 'the world'. This sense of persecution shaped the religious experience of many zealous Protestants. The martyr John Bradford advised Christians to pray for protection from 'Satan and his mischievous ministers' whenever they left their homes. The ideal of heroic suffering at the hands of Satan's creatures was exemplified in Foxe's *Book of Martyrs* (1563) and its many imitators in the early seventeenth century. At a more personal level, Elizabeth Grymeston advised her son in 1604 that the profession of Christianity would bring him constant persecution from the Devil's agents, but he could endure it all with the protection of God. This sentiment was repeated in the autobiographies of godly men and women such as Robert Bolton, John Bunyan and Lucy Hutchinson. [17]

Satan's earthly instruments were not a random and uncoordinated force; they were organised into powerful institutions. The most dangerous of these were the false churches established to rival and undermine the true worship of God. Thomas Becon noted that 'the Jews, the Muhammadans, the Anabaptists . . . with all the rabble of heretics and sectaries, have their churches also, but all those churches are the synagogues of Satan, unpure, filthy, stinking, vile, abominable, full of all sin and wickedness'. The most terrible of the false religions, however, was Catholicism. The doctrines and rites of the Roman church were expressly designed to exploit the sinfulness of human nature by promoting idolatry and fostering the belief that individuals could earn salvation by their own actions. Thus the preface to a catechism published in 1586 denounced the former pilgrimage site at Walsingham as the 'proud shrine of Satan'. After his conversion from popery in the 1630s, Richard Carpenter realised that 'the invocation of saints is a by-way which the Devil hath sought and found to divert man from the due and true service of God'. More crudely, the woodcuts that illustrated godly pamphlets often depicted the pope and Catholic priests as demonic figures, complete with horns and cloven hooves. To underline further its satanic origins, Catholicism was routinely associated with an impressive range of immoral and anti-social activities. In 1612 Thomas Adams preached that 'perjury, sodomy, sorcery, homicide, parricide, patricide, treason [and] murder are essential things to the new papacy'. Such claims were apparently so familiar by 1642 that 'popery' could be invoked by both sides in the civil war as a synonym for immorality and evil. [18]

Catholicism's status as a demonic anti-religion was confirmed by its association with the mythical figure of Antichrist. The idea of Antichrist, who was described as the 'man of sin' in St Paul's letter to Peter and the 'beast' in the book of Revelation, had been developed in theology and art during the Middle Ages. According to tradition, he was destined to appear and conquer the world in the period preceding the second coming of Christ. His tyrannical reign would be challenged by the 'two witnesses' named by St John the Divine, who were usually identified with the Old Testament prophets Enoch and Elias. In his final act of persecution, the beast would strike down the two witnesses, but their murder would be followed by the return of Christ, the destruction of Antichrist and the Last Judgment. While theologians were careful to identify Antichrist as Satan's viceroy, rather than the Devil himself, he was always closely associated with the fiend. This tendency was maintained by Protestant divines, who described the beast as 'the Devil's vicar' and the 'master demon'. Protestants diverged from their medieval predecessors, however, by defining Antichrist as an institution rather than a single man. Thus John Foxe argued in his *Meditationes in Apocalypsin* that the beast foretold by St John was not one individual but an anti-Christian organisation, and William Fulke affirmed that Antichrist was 'a whole succession of men, in one state of devilish government'. This refinement allowed them to argue that

Antichrist's kingdom had already been established, and the events preceding its fall were now unfolding, with the reformers themselves cast in the role of the two witnesses. [19]

Most godly divines agreed that the whole Catholic church was a kind of corporate Antichrist. John Olde attested that 'that malignant church and congregation [is] the mystical body of Antichrist', and added that 'the principal minister is called the chief Antichrist, as all other members of the same faction, ministry and office, be also Antichrists'. The same view was taken by John Bale in his account of the examination and death of the Protestant martyr Anne Askew in 1546, in which he described Askew's interrogator as 'a very full Antichrist'. It was more usual, though, to attach this title specifically to the pope. In 1595, Perkins preached a detailed commentary on the book of Revelation which concluded 'that Antichrist should be a Roman, and that the see of his tyranny should be at Rome'. A few years later, a godly ballad urged all Christians to unite against the papacy and 'drag that triple-crowned beast from out [of] his monstrous throne'. Such apocalyptic images of the pope abounded in theological tracts, ballads and woodcuts throughout the seventeenth century. The identification of Catholicism with the Antichrist appears to have served several purposes for devout Protestants. It provided them with a historic role in the struggle against the Devil, together with the certain knowledge that their final victory was assured. This was the implicit theme of the *Book of Martyrs* and an idea developed repeatedly in spiritual autobiographies. Thus Lucy Hutchinson identified herself and her husband with the 'faithful witnesses whom God raised up after the black and horrid midnight of Antichristianism'. She knew that the work begun by the first reformers would shortly culminate in a glorious triumph for God's servants, 'notwithstanding all the attempts of Satan and his ministers'. Such beliefs attached a cosmic significance to the daily struggle against the besieging forces of the Devil, and probably offered a strong inducement to continue the battle despite the hardship it involved. [20]

The rejection of medieval beliefs

The sentiments of Lady Hutchinson and her devout contemporaries left little room for the beliefs expressed in the 'merry tale' of the Suffolk player in 1526. For a start, Protestant doctrines tended to undermine the idea of Satan as a bodily creature. This did not mean that Protestants rejected the belief that the Devil could take physical form: indeed, many godly men and women experienced graphic and terrifying encounters with the fiend. Rather, their conviction that he operated mainly at the level of temptations and 'false beliefs' caused them to internalise their confrontations with him. Even writers such as John Bunyan who described physical encounters with Satan acknowledged that their most intense and frequent battles with the enemy were fought inside their own minds. Similarly, the idea that the Devil commanded a legion of human 'instruments' against the servants of God tended to limit his direct interventions in earthly affairs. In many Protestant texts he was presented as the infernal mastermind behind a vast conspiracy: a potent but generally hidden figure. Samuel Clarke's 1651 work *A Generall Martyrologie*, 'a collection of the greatest persecutions which have befallen the church of Christ from the creation to our present times', began by asserting that 'the first murderer and persecutor that was in the world was the Devil'. But the fiend made no personal appearances in Clarke's history after his initial manifestation in the garden of Eden, preferring to work through an army of infidels, princes and popes. More poetically, Bunyan likened Satan to a spider spinning webs of deceit, whose victims could become entangled without encountering the creature itself. While this interpretation emphasised Satan's power, it also tended to present him as a rather abstract and invisible force. [21]

Protestants also challenged traditional beliefs about the ability of men and women to protect themselves from the Devil. In part, this followed naturally from their view that Satan possessed great powers that could only be overcome by God. It also reflected their conviction that divine mercy did not depend on the performance of rituals or the use of sanctified objects. Many medieval protections against the Devil, such as holy water, candles and Latin prayers, were intimately associated with the Roman church. In the late Middle Ages, there was such demand for blessed candles, which could be taken from parish churches and kept in private houses to afford protection from demons, that the practice was carefully regulated and restricted to special occasions like the celebration of 'candlemass'. Protestants condemned all such beliefs. In 1616 William Gouge castigated 'superstitious papists who think to drive the Devil away with holy water, holy oil, crosses [and] crucifixes'. This sentiment caused some Protestants to oppose parish rogation processions, which continued in a modified form in the reign of Elizabeth and the early seventeenth century. In a similar vein, Protestant exorcists such as John Darrell condemned their Roman counterparts for using holy water and crucifixes to expel demons, while they defended their own methods by claiming that they relied entirely on the power of faith. The same argument was presented in more concrete terms in a pamphlet in 1612, which mocked a company of papists in Antwerp for trying to defend themselves with holy water when the Devil set fire to their church. Such actions were not only ineffective but also harmful. The idea that holy artefacts and rituals could offer protection from Satan was itself diabolical, since it prevented people from placing faith in God and encouraged them to support the false church of Rome, which was the principal representative of the Devil's kingdom on earth. [22]

Finally, Protestant ideas about Satan made it harder to view him as a comic figure. He was no longer a laughing matter. This resulted partially from the removal of the protections against demonic power afforded by the medieval church, which meant that it was considerably less safe to poke fun at the fiend. More importantly, the new theology gave the Devil a prominent and central role in all aspects of Christian life. Once the proposition that all people were by nature 'slaves of Satan and guilty of eternal damnation' was accepted as a core principle, it was difficult to treat the Devil in a trivial manner. William Gouge summed up the views of many Protestants when he condemned 'sottish worldlings' who thought so little of Satan that they made jokes at his expense, and resorted to music, games and laughter to divert themselves from his assaults. Likewise, godly pamphlets and ballads warned of the dire consequences of swearing on the Devil's name or jokingly calling on him for help. By rejecting the view that Satan was a suitable subject for humour, devout Protestants further undermined the medieval ideas described at the beginning of this chapter. Taken as a whole, their understanding of the Devil was darker and more powerful, yet also more abstract, than the one accepted widely in the late Middle Ages. The reasons for this transformation are considered below. [23]

EXPLAINING THE PROTESTANT DEVIL

At the heart of reformed theology were the doctrines of divine grace and the sufficiency of scripture. God and His Word, not the Devil, were the foundations of Protestant thought. The figure of Satan was balanced within this conceptual scheme, just as he had been incorporated within the belief system of the late medieval church. There was no compelling theological reason why he should have loomed larger in the Church of England than its predecessor: indeed, the Protestant insistence on the supreme authority of God could have reduced his prominence and power. If God was responsible for *all* events, what was left for Satan? As Beezaleel Carter observed in *A Sermon of Gods Omnipotencie and Providence* (1615), 'the Devil may go about like a roaring lion, seeking to devour; but God hath the Devil in a chain, and greater is He that is in us, than he which is in the world'. The fact that the Devil continued to exert a powerful fascination on Protestant thinkers – and even extended his influence in earthly affairs – can be explained by a combination of psychological and practical factors. The removal of sacramental means to fend off Satan left believers dependent on the direct protection of God; but faith in divine providence – unlike the intellectual acceptance of the doctrine – was often hard to sustain. Equally, the abundant evils of the unreformed world caused many Protestants to appreciate the might of the Devil's earthly kingdom. [24]

Fearful hopes

Jeffrey Burton Russell has highlighted the tendency of the Reformation to encourage an intensely introspective and personal style of devotion, stripped of the traditional comforts and communal support afforded by late medieval Catholicism. It was within this framework that the Devil emerged as a powerful and terrible force:

> Earlier ages had seen the Devil's opponent as God, Christ, or the whole Christian community. If attacked by Satan, you could at least feel part of a great army upon whose hosts you called for aid. But now it was you versus the Devil; you alone, the individual, who had the responsibility for fending him off . . . Against biology, against the social nature of mankind, against Paul's mystical body of Christ, against the practice of the early Christian community, against centuries of Christian tradition, this individualistic emphasis on self-reliance and competition left the Christian naked on a black heath at night, exposed to the winter winds of evil.

While Russell suggests that this new introspection influenced many sixteenth-century Catholics as well as their Protestant counterparts, he implies that it was particularly marked among the supporters of the Reformation. Those men and women who rejected the invocation of saints, along with the traditional rites and recitations used against the Devil by the medieval church, could find themselves exposed to Satan's power with no support except their faith in Christ. This faith could seem a fragile thing. The lonely struggle against the enemy could be made more fearful by the doctrine of justification by faith alone. Since men and women had no power in themselves to earn salvation, they were forced to rely entirely on God's mercy; they could not trust their own inclinations to help them overcome Satan, and could assume that their own bodies and minds were highly vulnerable to his temptations. Russell's image of the solitary Christian facing the Devil in the dead of night, protected only by the hope of God's mercy, is certainly appropriate to the devout men and women whose experiences are described in chapter three. Indeed, this image describes perfectly the 'night terrors' endured by many English Protestants in the early modern age. [25]

This was only part of the picture, of course. The Protestant emphasis on divine sovereignty also meant that the Devil was ultimately powerless against faithful Christians. In the fourteenth century this view had been expressed in *The Cloud of Unknowing*. After asserting that men and women could do nothing to earn God's mercy, the text observed that a simple faith in His goodness was sufficient to overcome Satan: 'Have no fear, the Devil cannot come near you.' During the Reformation, the balance between divine providence and Satan's dominion over 'natural' men and women was illustrated in Arthur Dent's *Plaine Mans Path-way to Heaven* (1601). Dent affirmed that the greater part of humankind was 'under the very tyranny and dominion of Satan', and God's children could expect to suffer at their hands; but equally, 'there is no affliction or trial which God imposeth upon His children, but if they endure it quietly, trust in His mercy firmly, and tarry in His good pleasure obediently, it hath His blessed and comfortable end'. In this spirit, the pastor Richard Greenham advised a gentlewoman 'troubled in mind' in the 1590s that her trust in God was enough to protect her from Satan's wiles: 'while you are tender of conscience, afraid of sin, reverently persuaded to walk holily with your God, laugh at Satan's accusations . . . and set naught at the terrors of Hell'. Other devotional works affirmed that the faithful would ultimately triumph over the Devil. Stephen Bateman's *Christall Glasse of Christian Reformation* included one woodcut depicting an armour-clad man, representing all 'steadfast believers', standing over the broken body of Satan, 'being overcome by faith in Jesus Christ'. Similarly, devotional tracts describing the deathbed experiences of the faithful always ended with the dying subject triumphing over the Devil, who had sought to steal away their soul. Indeed, the Devil was normally shown as a weak and wretched creature at the climax of such encounters. [26]

Trust in divine providence could also discourage the faithful from active combat with Satan. The call to such combat was certainly prominent in devotional literature, and a central theme in many godly autobiographies; but it was also possible for Christians to avoid the kind of painful self-scrutiny which, as Russell noted, often heightened fears of Satan. Greenham observed that the Devil was happy to exploit excessive introspection by planting 'false and cause-less fears' in the mind to keep Christians 'from the glorious feeling of their redemption'. Since Satan was an infinitely ingenious and deceitful adversary, he suggested that it was often wise to avoid confrontations with him altogether: 'dispute not with God lest you be confounded, nor with Satan lest you be overcome'. Similarly, Elizabeth Grymeston observed in 1604, that 'it is better to flee than to fight with Satan'. In 1621 the physician Robert Burton noted that excessive self-scrutiny had terrified 'the souls of many' by provoking unwarranted despair about their spiritual condition. He cited Luther's advice that individuals should not 'torture and crucify themselves' over the state of their souls, but rather try to cultivate a simple faith in God's mercy. It was, of course, impossible to evade the Devil's snares completely by following this course; but it was equally dangerous and unhealthy to focus intensely on the need to confront and overcome him. [27]

These texts indicate the potential of Protestant doctrines to alleviate fears about the Devil. It is clear that faith in God's mercy could strip Satan of his relevance and power; and spiritual diaries and autobiographies are replete with such conquests of the enemy within. In most cases, however, the men and women who experi-enced such triumphs obtained only temporary relief from the Devil's assaults; nor did they expect anything more. The periodical defeat of Satan through faith merely punctuated an ongoing struggle. As Jeffrey Burton Russell suggests, it may simply have been harder for Protestants to face Satan alone than with the support of the saints and the sacramental protections of the medieval church; and as a consequence the ghostly enemy seemed more entrenched and formidable. The social and political context of the English Reformation also contributed to this effect. This caused its supporters to face the theological 'problem of evil' in a distinctive way which encouraged them to emphasise Satan's status as 'the prince of this world'.

The evils of the unreformed world

The problem of evil is essentially practical. As the theologian Paul Helm has observed, 'it is not the invention of the philosophers or theologians'; rather, it emerges from the lived experiences of men and women. These experiences arise in particular historical situations. For English Protestants in the sixteenth and seventeenth centuries, the task of reconciling God's goodness to the imperfections of the world emerged within a particular set of circumstances; and their conception of the Devil offered a satisfying explanation for the peculiar evils that beset them. These included a pervasive awareness that God's people were surrounded by their enemies, and could expect persecution at their hands. Equally important was the perception, amply documented by historians such as Christopher Haigh, that the great majority of the population were unreceptive to the reformed gospel. The twin experiences of encirclement by hostile forces and the failure of the reform movement were evils that the Protestant Devil was well suited to explain.[28]

The political circumstances of the English Reformation ensured that committed Protestants identified their religion with conflict and the threat of persecution for much of the sixteenth century. The suppression of reformed beliefs in the later years of Henry VIII, exemplified by the execution of Ann Askew in 1546, was resumed with increased ferocity under the Catholic regime of Mary Tudor. Unsurprisingly, the theme of martyrdom was extremely prominent in the devotional and polemical literature of the early Elizabethan church. The widely circulated works of authors such as John Olde and Thomas Becon, alongside posthumous publications by martyrs like John Bradford, espoused a style of religion characterised by heroic suffering and conflict with powerful enemies of the gospel. The Protestant message was often expressed in overtly martial language. John Gough, for instance, addressed his translation of Erasmus' *Enchiridion* in 1561 'to all Christ's soldiers living in the camp of the world'. This literature also exploited the apocalyptic tradition of the late Middle Ages by presenting religious conflict as a sign of the imminent fall of Antichrist. John Foxe concocted these ingredients into the epic narrative of the *Book of Martyrs* in 1563, and his work was subsequently sanctioned as one of the approved texts of the Church of England. The war against Spain probably intensified the idea that true religion involved a struggle with hostile forces, despite the efforts of a minority of pastors who advocated peace. By the early 1600s, it appears that most devout Protestants had accepted the struggle with Spain as a natural expression of their faith. Many would have endorsed the view of the courtier Andrew Marten, who believed that the conflict involved much more than a military struggle: it was a war 'against that horrible beast who hath received power from the dragon, against the princes of the nations which have entered into league with the Whore of Babylon'. Such sentiments survived well into the seventeenth century, and were revitalised by the outbreak of religious warfare in Germany in 1618. Zealous Protestants expressed solidarity with their German fellows throughout the 1620s and 1630s: in the private prayers and meditations of gentry families such as the Newdigates of Nuneaton; in financial collections for the 'distressed ministers of the palatinate'; and in petitions and political campaigns for an aggressively Protestant and anti-Spanish foreign policy. Such activities suggest that the idea of religious warfare continued to shape the thinking and behaviour of devout Protestants in the early Stuart period. [29]

The general perception that religion involved a struggle against hostile forces was reinforced by the personal experiences of many believers. The word 'puritan', which emerged as a term of abuse around 1560 and retained its pejorative sense well into the seventeenth century, was used to ridicule the minority of devout 'professors of the gospel' in many communities. In extreme cases, resentment of 'over-zealous' Protestantism could lead to physical attacks. Thomas Wilson, the godly pastor of Stratford-upon-Avon, was threatened with castration by a mob in 1619. His colleague in the neighbouring parish of Woolston 'walked not abroad without his rapier in his hand' to protect him from members of his flock. Such hostility was not confined to the clergy. As a young man in Wales in the 1630s, Vavasor Powell was assaulted by two former friends when he 'reproved them for sin'; and the zealous constable of Brinklow in Warwickshire received 'sore and grievous blows, thrusts, hurts and wounds' when he sought to reform 'vices and abuses' in his village. While such violence was comparatively rare, it appears to have reflected a widespread popular antagonism towards the perceived excesses of committed Protestants, notably their habit of denouncing the impiety of their neighbours. William Perkins observed sadly in 1605 that the 'contempt' felt by most layfolk for godly ministers was 'too obvious in ordinary experience to need spelling out'. Twenty years later, Ephraim Huitt complained that 'the cause of Christ' was mocked 'in every town if not family'. The reason for this hostility was spelt out poignantly by the celebrated Essex preacher Richard Sibbes: 'Because God will not have his children love the world, therefore he suffers the world to hate them. They are strangers here, and therefore no wonder if they find strange entertainment from them that think themselves at home.' Such rationalisations led devout men and women to regard persecution itself as a sign of godliness. Robert Harris declared in 1631 that 'every man that would be Christ's true disciple must look for persecution'. A godly maxim from the same period affirmed that 'persecution is the bellows of the gospel, blowing every spark into a flame, and martyrs' ashes are the best compost to manure the church'. The prevalence of such attitudes is indicated by the fact that they were parodied in seventeenth-century ballads like *The Mad Zealot*, which mocked an archetypal puritan for glorifying his own sufferings and aspiring 'to be one of Foxe's martyrs'. [30]

The sense of persecution experienced by devout Protestants was probably increased by the failure of much of the population to embrace what they perceived to be the true 'cause of Christ'. Historians of the English Reformation have recently emphasised the inability of the clergy to convert their flocks to the most basic Protestant doctrines. In practice, this meant that many communities came to be divided between a minority of convinced 'professors' and a much larger body of layfolk whose religious convictions were less intense. Understandably, many godly pastors in the late sixteenth century abandoned the hope of converting the whole nation and focused instead on the small groups of 'true believers' within their parishes. This trend was encouraged by the tendency of godly professors to form close networks of friends, often travelling together to hear sermons and meeting informally to discuss the scriptures. The division between the godly minority and the impious masses was a common theme in late Elizabethan sermons and devotional works. George Gifford lamented the woeful inadequacy of 'the religion which is [found] among the common sort of Christians'; and Perkins prefaced his catechism by listing thirty-two 'false opinions' which were commonly believed. At a more personal level, the sense that true Christians constituted a distinct community surrounded by an ungodly world was expressed by godly diarists. Thus Margaret Hoby identified with a small network of pious friends and ministers, and recorded her disapproval of the more 'profane' society outside this circle. Following the successful outcome of a lawsuit against her neighbours in 1602, she noted 'the justice and mercy of God to his servants in manifesting to the world, which little regards them, that he will bring down their enemies unto them'. In the 1630s, similar sentiments were expressed in the journals of Robert Woodford, the constable of Northampton, and the Warwick schoolmaster Thomas Dugard. The close-knit social circles of these godly professors, combined with their distrust of the impious society outside, probably reinforced their view that religion involved a perpetual opposition between God's children and their many foes. [31]

It is in this context that Protestant attitudes towards Satan are best understood. The conflictual world-view of many godly men and women encouraged a preoccupation with the Devil. As Frank Luttmer has observed, such Christians came to view the unreformed majority as 'accomplices in a vast conspiracy of cosmic evil' with Satan at its head. At the level of high politics, the fiend's influence was obvious in the attempts of Catholic forces, both at home and abroad, to destroy the 'cause of Christ'. The papal Antichrist was intimately linked with the Devil, and his supporters were 'like black incarnate fiends'. The cosmic struggle between God's people and the hordes of the beast provided an ideal framework for understanding the religious conflicts of the age. Similarly, Satan's power could be seen in the widespread hostility towards God's servants in their own communities. This point was often made explicit in devotional texts. Ephraim Huitt described scoffers of the gospel as 'vassals of Hell in execution of the Devil's offices', and Protestant autobiographers routinely claimed that their enemies were 'stirred up' by Satan. More generally, godly professors understood that 'as there are many devils that molest the people of God so there are also many men to second them herein', and persecution by such foes was an inevitable consequence and sign of their faith. Such afflictions, indeed, were testimonies of divine favour in 'this raging age of the Devil', as the preacher Isaac Colfe observed in 1592. Satan's power was further demonstrated by the mulish refusal of most people to embrace true religion. Their addiction to falsehood and sin was so strong that it confirmed the Devil's status as the 'prince of this world'. His capacity to stir up the masses to impiety was described memorably by George Gifford in 1584: 'all whoremasters, drunkards, dicers, railers, swearers and such like are the Devil's army, as on the other side such as profess God's word and live godly are his soldiers, and do fight under his banner'. [32]

Military metaphors of this kind abounded in devotional literature. Christ was a 'brave captain' whose soldiers, armoured in faith, marched defiantly against a multitude of foes. Their war was fought publicly against Catholics and 'worldlings' and internalised in the private struggle to overcome temptation and sin, so that religion was 'a daily fighting with inward fears and outward troubles'. This conflict placed the faithful in a harsh but ultimately heroic role: as John Milton affirmed in 1641, they fought for God 'with the unresistable might of weakness, shaking the powers of darkness and scorning the fiery rage of the old red dragon'. This struggle was made endurable by the knowledge that victory was assured. Thus Isaac Colfe offered these words of comfort to God's soldiers in 1592:

> Albeit they are for a season in sorrow and heaviness, in affliction and trouble, having temptation upon temptation heaped on them: yet at the last, if the Lord in His heavenly wisdom see it to be profitable, in the time that he seeth most profitable, he will give unto them a joyful issue out of all their troubles and temptations, wiping all tears from their eyes, and turning their sorrow and heaviness into a most victorious and triumphant rejoicing.

These sentiments recall Elaine Pagels' analysis of the rise of Satan in first-century Christianity. For Pagels, 'Christian tradition derives much of its power from the conviction that although the believer may feel besieged by evil forces, Christ has already won the decisive victory'. Thus the battles of the faithful are never in vain. 'The faith that Christ has conquered Satan assures Christians that in their own struggles the stakes are eternal, and victory is certain. Those who participate in the cosmic drama cannot lose.' The appeal of this world-view in the political and social context of the English Reformation was understandable. But its consequence was to elevate the Devil to the leader of a vast army, whose influence at every level of human experience was a fact of life. [33]

This interpretation suggests an interesting corollary. Many of the conditions that led English Protestants to emphasise Satan's power as a spirit of falsehood were also experienced by Catholics. Like their confessional opponents, devout adherents of the old faith saw abundant evidence of the Devil's ability to deceive: indeed, those who rejected the Church of England viewed it as a triumph of demonic artifice. As the reformers consolidated their position in the later sixteenth century, English Catholics also became an encircled minority in much of the country. This environment may well have encouraged a heightened awareness of the Devil's power, albeit one that was ameliorated by the sacramental protections retained by the Roman church. This possibility awaits detailed research. Such scholarship may demonstrate the existence in England of a Catholic counterpart to the Protestant Devil.

Whether or not this was the case, it appears that the particular circumstances of the English Reformation encouraged godly men and women to emphasise those aspects of reformed theology that amplified Satan's power. This contextual understanding does not, however, mean that the beliefs and fears of these people were not sincerely held. The private writings and autobiographies of those individuals who committed themselves firmly to the Protestant cause suggest that the Devil could be a powerful presence in daily life, whose ability to inflict mental and physical distress was frighteningly real. The experiences of these men and women are considered next.

Living With the Enemy:
PROTESTANT EXPERIENCES
OF THE DEVIL

BELIEF AND RESPONSIBILITY

In 1652 an anonymous woman published her account of a nocturnal encounter with Satan. The visitation occurred as the woman, who called herself simply 'E.C.', was lying in bed and trying to say her prayers. Suddenly she felt 'strange temptations upon me to put God out of my mind, and I could not speak a word, nor scarce think of God'. This sensation was followed at once by a dreadful vision: 'Satan then appeared to me in a most ugly shape, laughing and jeering at me, which did much affright me'. The woman's fear turned immediately to a sense of guilt and the realization that her religion was shallow and false: she was an untrue Christian who lacked faith and 'had played the hypocrite with God'. As soon as this feeling struck her she appealed to Christ for help. She remembered that Jesus had overcome the Devil by his death on the cross, and this knowledge empowered her to rise from her bed to confront the apparition. Strengthened by her newly restored faith, E.C. commanded the Devil to fly from her bedside. The creature was so overwhelmed by the power of God that it 'departed from my sight'. [1]

This encounter, which was described in a collection of 'spiritual experiences' compiled by the minister Vavasor Powell, contains many typical ingredients of a Protestant vision of Satan. The confrontation took place at night, a time when godly men and women were especially aware of the Devil's influence. More significantly, the fiend's appearance was associated closely with the spiritual condition of his victim, who interpreted the episode in terms of her relationship with God. The attack was heralded by E.C.'s failure to compose her prayers, and its most terrible effect was to suggest that her commitment to Christ was weak and 'hypocritical'. It was only when her faith was renewed that she was able to confront and vanquish the demonic intruder, relying entirely on divine power. Thus the incident was both a test of her faith and a demonstration of the Lord's mercy. The same themes were found in many other Protestant autobiographies in the sixteenth and seventeenth centuries. These texts, which were published for the inspiration and instruction of the wider community, tended to present the Devil as a constant companion throughout their subjects' lives, relentlessly trying to exploit their weaknesses and lapses of faith. He was 'that cruel murdering thief, our ghostly enemy who every hour watcheth to take advantage of us, for bringing us to utter confusion'. [2]

How should modern readers understand these encounters? It may be tempting to dismiss them as psychological projections, or even as symptoms of mental disorder; but this temptation should be resisted. It is worth noting that many millions of people today claim to engage personally with supernatural powers through the act of prayer, and such people are not normally regarded as mentally ill. The concept of Satan in Tudor and Stuart England was what some contemporary philosophers describe as a 'background' belief: a core assumption about the world that was almost universally accepted, and which provided part of the intellectual landscape in which people thought and acted. In the language of anthropology, such basic presumptions belong to the 'system of beliefs' by which people understand the world around them. The perception that religious ideas – including the Devil – were the *only* credible way of explaining all the facts of human existence may well be a defining quality of non-secular cultures, as the philosopher Charles Taylor has suggested. [3]

In this context the existence of the Devil helped to make sense of many life experiences, and could sometimes help individuals to deal with them. This certainly applied to the kind of religious anxieties that were described frequently in the 'spiritual autobiographies' of individuals such as E.C. Engagement with Satan could assume many different patterns and result in various outcomes, involving greater or lesser degrees of personal responsibility. At one extreme, men and

women could experience satanic impulses and thoughts that burst
on them like lightning, and which belonged entirely to the Devil: the
phenomenon of demonic possession involved a particularly radical
version of this state. More often, demonic 'assaults' combined the
sinful inclinations of the recipient with the agency of Satan. In the
evocative metaphor of William Perkins, human nature was like tinder
or gunpowder for the Devil to ignite. William Gouge made the same
point in 1622 when he described how the sin of pride issued 'from
the corruption of nature and is daily increased by the instigation
of Satan'. This mixture of human depravity and demonic exploitation allowed individuals to set the balance of responsibility between
themselves and the Devil, with many possible variations. In the case
of E.C., the sudden appearance of 'strange temptations' implied
Satan's direct intervention, followed immediately by the awareness
of her own failings as a Christian. A similar dynamic applied to the
Devil's activity in the social world. Individuals could recognize their
own sinfulness when they faced demonic temptations – effectively
turning responsibility in on themselves – while perceiving their
earthly enemies as demonic agents. Thus the Protestant struggle with
Satan could involve both intense self-scrutiny and the demonization
of others. As William Gouge noted in typically martial language, 'the
forces of the Lord's soldiers' had to fight both 'inward' and 'outward'
assaults from the ghostly enemy. [4]

The writings of English Protestants illustrate the spectrum of
responses to the Devil's intrusions – from sombre self-examination
to the demonization of unwanted thoughts or impious members of
the community. These were described most formally in published
spiritual autobiographies which presented encounters between
believers and Satan as part of the unfolding pattern of Christian life.
The authors of these testimonies may have sometimes exaggerated
the Devil's role for dramatic or didactic effect: after all, the struggle to
overcome him provided a conventional structure for their narratives
and the opportunity to rebut the false doctrines of the 'father of lies'.
As Nathan Johnstone points out, however, these printed accounts also
illustrate the assumptions and expectations of the community they
served, even – and perhaps especially – when they were recorded in
an idealized form. They were also consistent with the unpublished
records of devout Protestants such as the Yorkshire diarist Margaret
Hoby and the Warwickshire lawyer Richard Newdigate. For the
most part, Satan manifested himself in both public and private texts

in the form of invisible temptations, which will be considered in the second part of this chapter. The first part will deal with the less common but more dramatic experiences of individuals such as E.C., whose visions and 'night terrors' provide unusually vivid illustrations of the conflict between Protestants and the Devil. [5]

Godly apparitions

Satan appeared in a remarkable variety of forms in the visions recorded by godly Protestants. Perhaps his most grotesque manifestations were witnessed by the preacher John Rogers, who was tormented by visions of Hell as a young man in the 1640s. The fiend and his helpers presented themselves 'in several ugly shapes and forms (according to my fancies) and sometimes with great rolling flaming eyes like saucers, having sparkling fire-brands in the one of their hands, and with the other reaching at me to tear me away to torments'. Rogers' apparitions recalled the horrors described by the physician Robert Burton in 1621 as symptoms of 'melancholy' induced by excessive religious zeal: his patients had been taunted by the Devil, smelt brimstone and behaved as if they were 'in Hell fire, already damned'. It appears that such experiences reproduced medieval depictions of the afterlife, which had survived in printed woodcuts and godly sermons describing the sufferings of condemned souls. Other writers were apparently influenced by the traditional idea that the Devil could disguise himself in human flesh. When Hannah Allen heard the sound of 'two young men' in the yard outside her chamber one night in 1664 she perceived that they were 'devils in the likeness of men, singing for joy that they had overcome me'. Others encountered the fiend in the guise of a stranger, who tempted them to sin or declared that their souls were lost. Satan could also manifest himself in more ghostly and insubstantial forms. Vavasor Powell recalled a particularly chilling example in his autobiography:

> Being alone in my chamber late at night at prayer, and the door shut, I continued in prayer till the candle went out, and as I went on I sensibly perceived a strong cold wind to blow . . . It made the hair of my flesh to stand up, and caused all my bones to shake, and on the sudden I heard one walk about me, trampling upon the chamber floor, as if it had been some heavy big man.

Powell fled the room and cried for help from the rest of the house-hold. The demonic visitor disappeared, but it continued to 'affright and terrify' him in the weeks that followed, 'not only by secret work-ings in the conscience but by visible representations and outwardly real apparitions'. A similar haunting was recalled by John Bunyan in *Grace Abounding to the Chief of Sinners* (1662), which described how the Devil disturbed the author's prayers by pulling invisibly at the clothes on his back. [6]

Despite the dramatic nature of these events, they were not presented by those who experienced them as particularly exceptional or strange. In part, this can be explained by the tendency of godly narrators to depict their lives as religious *exemplars* revealing the providence of God in every happening, however unpleasant or apparently bizarre. But it also reflects the authors' understanding that physical manifestations of Satan were part of a much wider pattern of religious experience. They were unusually concrete examples of the Devil's influence in the world, which normally expressed itself in more subtle ways. Even the grotesque visions of John Rogers were only one aspect of the spiritual crisis that engulfed him as a young man when he became aware of his own sinfulness. Coming to this awareness, which involved an apprehen-sion of the Devil's sovereignty in the fallen world, was a normal stage in the process of conversion to true religion. Similarly, the torments visited on Powell and Bunyan were an extension of the Devil's usual ploy of disturbing Christians in their prayers. This strategy was described in a guide to the practice of prayer by John Preston in 1629: 'Satan ... knows it is this duty which quickens every grace, it is the greatest enemy he hath, and if he can keep us from prayer he hath the upper hand of us, he hath wrested the weapon out of our hands, he hath disarmed us, and then he may do what he will with us'. Preston assumed that the enemy normally diverted Christians from their prayers with 'fancies' and sinful thoughts, and the writings of Bunyan and Powell confirm that these were his preferred weapons. The physical phenomena they described were simply a variation on the fiend's normal methods, deployed to achieve his familiar goal of unsettling their relationship with God. A similar point can be made about the demonic presence which invaded the bedroom of E.C. In disrupting her prayers and reminding her of her own sinfulness the Devil was only pursuing his usual strategy in an uncommonly direct fashion. [7]

Like the invisible manifestations of Satan, demonic visions prob-ably reflected the tensions imposed by the practice of godly religion.

The introspective nature of devout Protestantism, combined with the assumption that the human mind was innately wicked, could make individuals vulnerable to depression and attacks of anxiety. This danger was particularly marked at those times of solitary prayer and meditation when the Devil's appearances were most commonly reported. In this sense, there may be some merit in Robert Burton's argument that the puritan lifestyle itself was the main cause of 'religious melancholy' and its attendant delusions. Burton was especially critical of those 'thundering ministers' who inspired their flocks with an excessive sense of sin and the horrors of damnation, suggesting that they were the 'most frequent cause of this malady'. It is also possible, as the physician implied, that excessive fasting and lack of sleep might have deceived the senses of men such as Rogers and Powell. Whatever their causes, however, the apparitions were readily explicable within a system of belief that allowed their recipients to treat them as a natural consequence and even a confirmation of their faith. Since these encounters were only an extension of the normal conflict between God's children and the Devil, there was no reason for those who experienced or read about them to question their authenticity. [8]

Night terrors

Protestant visions of Satan were closely related to a collection of phenomena described by contemporaries as the 'terrors of the night'. These phenomena, which ranged from nightmares to nocturnal apparitions and the awareness of spectral presences, were often recorded in godly memoirs as expressions of the Devil's power. As John Bradford observed in the 1550s, the night was a time of particular danger for devout Christians, when they needed to arm themselves against 'the crafts & assaults of the wicked enemy'. This claim was unsurprising, perhaps, as the hours of darkness were particularly propitious for Satan's work. The night was a time for private reflection and prayer, when individuals may have been especially vulnerable to spiritual anxieties. More prosaically, the effects of darkness and shadow made it easier for the senses to be deceived. Unexpected and sinister sights or sounds – which today might be dismissed as 'tricks of the mind' – could be readily explained within a belief system that acknowledged demonic visitations as unproblematically real. [9]

One common form of 'night terror' was the perception, often intense and irresistible, that the Devil was creeping towards the victim's bedside to snatch them down to Hell. As a young man, John Rogers was 'afraid every night lest the Devil should carry me away', and imagined that the fiend 'would tear me a pieces' in his bed. One of the contributors to Powell's *Spirituall Experiences* related that one night she 'was fearful to sleep lest the Devil should fetch me away'. When she awoke, 'the Devil appeared to me and stood before me, and did exceedingly terrify me'. These torments were linked explicitly to 'terrors of conscience' and the fear of damnation, which were part of the Protestant conversion experience. They also recalled the symptoms of a sleep disturbance known to contemporaries as 'the mare'. This was a form of waking dream in which the subject was paralyzed and perceived a malevolent presence bearing down on them. The godly surveyor Richard Norwood recalled his experience of the mare in his journal during the 1640s, and identified its demonic nature. The satanic apparition that afflicted him seemed so real, he wrote, that 'I have sometimes taken a naked knife in my hand when I went to sleep, thinking to strike at it'. [10]

The phenomenon of 'the mare' illustrates the importance of systems of belief in the construction of meaning – both for the people of Tudor and Stuart England and for ourselves. The various symptoms associated with the condition, including paralysis, constriction, and the sense of a menacing intruder in the room, were often attributed to demonic forces in the Renaissance age: these could be direct assaults of the Devil or the work of evil spirits, or 'imps', in cases of alleged witchcraft. Remarkably similar symptoms are still reported today, and are currently related to the medical syndrome known as 'sleep paralysis disorder'. It has been estimated that around a third of the population experience this syndrome to some degree; and its most extreme manifestations can be as terrifying as anything described by pre-modern sufferers of the mare. Modern-day victims may well experience a *frisson* of recognition when they read these earlier accounts: for instance, many will recognize Richard Norwood's description of his waking dreams 'wherein a man is neither quite awake or asleep'. In an insightful study of past and present explanations of the condition, Owen Davies notes how it provides a 'direct and very real link with the supernatural interpretations of past cultures'. Similar physiological experiences have been explained in radically different ways within the prevailing belief systems of different societies: as a medical disorder today and a supernatural event in the past. As Davies observes, the victims of nocturnal demons were 'normal people who experienced something extraordinary but natural, and who made sense of it in the best way they could, based on what they believed and what they thought they saw, heard, and felt'. [11]

While the experience of the mare afforded the most spectacular expression of satanic power, the Devil sometimes chose to appear in ordinary dreams. As a child, John Bunyan was 'greatly afflicted, while asleep, with the apprehension of devils and wicked spirits, who . . . laboured to draw me away with them'. In 1653 Mary Burrill recorded that she 'had in my dreams two terrible conflicts with Satan, by which I have been much assured of God's love, for that I always had the better, the victory'. Nightly battles of this kind were experienced by Thomas Hall, the godly pastor of King's Norton, throughout his adult life:

> His sleep was not rest (many times) but terror . . . He said his bed should refresh him [but] he was scared with dreams & terrified with visions, so he observed Satan's hand helping forward the affliction & distress, for constantly he complained that his nights before the Sabbath or before a fast (though he used all means to prevent it) were his worst nights.

As Hall's interpretation of his afflictions suggests, the 'night terrors' endured by Protestants were an extension of their daily struggle to overcome the Devil's power. Whatever the psychological or medical causes of their experiences, godly men and women assumed that Satan attacked them at night to catch them off guard in their perpetual battle against him. In their waking hours he pursued the same goal in more subtle ways, with falsehoods and illicit desires. Their response to these temptations is considered below. [12]

SATANIC THOUGHTS AND TEMPTATIONS

It is perhaps misleading to suggest that godly Protestants experienced their major conflicts with Satan 'inside their own minds'. This twenty-first-century phrase does not allow for the many ways in which the Devil was believed to affect the mental states of men and women in the Tudor and Stuart age. According to William Perkins, Satan was capable of implanting his *own* thoughts into the mind of a human being. The Oxford pastor and theologian Robert Bolton fleshed out this idea in the 1630s. Bolton argued that satanic thoughts could be 'thrown into our imaginations like a flash of lightning, with such an unavoidable impression that they cannot be prevented by any wit or strength of a man'. He described the experiences of his godly companions whose minds had been 'injected' in this way:

> I have known some which have been fearfully vexed and astonished in heart with horrible and blasphemous thoughts, which were Satan's own immediate injections, and terrors even to nature itself. But when they have been told and taught that [these thoughts] were none of theirs, and that if they did hate, abhor and withstand them as the pure spite and malice of the fiend of Hell, they should never be imputed unto them as their own sins . . . they have received great ease and comfort.

A first-hand account of this phenomenon was recorded in 1643 in an anonymous pamphlet by a London stationer. The author was singing a psalm in church when he was overwhelmed by the desire to blaspheme the name of God: he claimed that Satan impressed this urge 'so vehemently on my mind that I had no power to resist him'. This mental hijacking was followed by a series of temptations which drove their victim to the edge of despair. Similar attacks were described by Bunyan, whose prayers were disturbed when the Devil cast unwelcome thoughts into his mind. As a young girl in the 1650s, Hannah Allen found that 'the enemy of my soul . . . cast horrible and blasphemous thoughts and injections into my mind, insomuch that I was seldom free, day or night, unless when dead sleep was upon me'. Allen claimed that she was comforted during these troubles by reading the works of Robert Bolton, and it is tempting to surmise that the godly author consolidated her belief in the Devil's 'suggestions'. The accounts of Bunyan and Allen suggest a link between the state of temptation, which was experienced by all reformed Christians, and the more extreme condition of demonic possession, in which the subject's whole mind was occupied by the Devil. This connection will be explored further in chapter six. [13]

The belief that satanic thoughts could be planted in the minds of men and women raised the obvious problem of distinguishing between one's own cognitions and those 'injected' by the fiend. This problem was made worse by the assumption that all human faculties, including the mind, were so utterly corrupted by sin that people often succumbed to irreligious ideas without the direct intervention of Satan.

Thus Perkins asserted that wicked thoughts could arise 'either by a man's own conceiving or by suggestion of the Devil'. Bolton suggested that ideas of satanic origin could be detected by the nature in which they appeared: 'sinful thoughts of our own come upon us enticingly, by allurements, baits, and insinuations; but Satan's suggestions rush in violently, forcibly and furiously'. He also implied that the content of these ideas, which were often extremely blasphemous or 'unnatural', set them apart from ordinary cognitions. It appears that these rules were applied by those godly writers who believed they had been visited by satanic thoughts, which usually occurred very suddenly and some-times contained such extreme blasphemy or scepticism that they could only be attributed to Satan. Most authors assumed, however, that such 'lightning flashes' were comparatively rare: they attributed most of their sinful ideas to their own fallen nature, which inclined them to yield to the 'baits and allurements' of the ghostly enemy. [14]

Before considering these 'baits and allurements' in detail, it is inter-esting to note the implications of the belief that Satan could blast alien thoughts into the human mind. This meant that individuals could, in certain circumstances, experience thoughts and desires without perceiving them as their own. They could also express these ideas to an audience that accepted their satanic origin and assumed that their true author was the enemy of everything that their human recipients should properly hold dear. As a result, devout Protestants could safely express fears and anxieties they harboured about their faith in words that denied their immediate responsibility and asserted, in their very utterance, the repudiation of their meaning. This process was apparent in the speech and gestures of some possessed men and women. It was also evident in the accounts provided by some godly Protestants of the mental 'suggestions' they received from the Devil.

Thus Satan's voice could be a remarkably subtle instrument. A striking illustration of this voice was contained in the work of 'M.K.', one of the contributors to Powell's collection of spiritual autobiog-raphies in 1652. Her description of the Devil's 'suggestions' deserves to be quoted in full:

> Fond fool (quoth he) why dost thou trouble thyself? Take thy pleasure, do what thou likest, thou shalt never be called to an account for anything; for as the wise man dies, so dies the fool, and both rest in the grave together. There is no God to save thee or punish thee, all things were made by nature, and when thou dies there is an end of all thy

good and bad deeds. Thou talkest of the scripture, and of a God and of
a Jesus which thou hast heard of there. See thy simplicity now. How
canst thou prove the scriptures to be true? Alas, they were made by
men's inventions, there is no hold for thee to take there.

The satanic ideas recorded by M.K. appear to describe her own doubts
and fears about the Christian religion, which she overcame only after
a protracted and painful struggle. In 1653 another godly woman, Jane
Turner, described how the Devil assailed her with similar doubts
during the process of her conversion: 'Satan was ready to assault me,
and set upon me with this horrid temptation, to question the being of
God; and I remember it usually came upon me when I was alone, but
especially as I was going by myself to hear the minister'. Recognizing
the diabolical nature of this thought, Turner 'did resist and labour
against it, drawing arguments as I went in the fields from the very
works of creation to confirm [to] myself that there is a God, and that
it should not be in vain to serve him'. Hannah Allen was also inspired
by the Devil to have 'hard and strange thoughts of my dear Lord' in
1664, though she demurred from describing the exact nature of these
thoughts in her autobiography. In less extreme cases, the 'suggestions'
of Satan seem to have expressed the feelings of unworthiness experienced by devout Protestants. Thus the pastor Richard Rothwel was
tormented with anxieties about his ministry during an illness in the
1620s: the Devil visited him with the idea that his preaching would be
'the scorn of religion, and every man would reproach it for his sake ...
that he should never preach more, but should blaspheme the name of
God'. It is possible that the attribution of such thoughts to Satan made
it easier for these individuals to express and confront their own deepest
anxieties. At the very least, it allowed them to articulate these thoughts
in a context which absolved them from guilt and emphasized their
own godliness. [15]

The struggle against temptation

While most zealous Protestants accepted that Satan could manifest
himself directly in the mind, it appears that his usual strategy was
to exploit the innate weaknesses of the human body and intellect.
It was a commonplace in sermons and spiritual guidebooks that
human flesh was inclined towards evil. As such, it was one of the
'confederates' of the Devil. In his 1586 catechism, William Chub

expressed the conventional view that it was the natural inclination of men and women to 'fall into all filthy conversation, lewd
lust, abominable sin and devilish desires'. In 1630 the Warwickshire
lawyer, Richard Newdigate, noted the warning of a local preacher
that Christians should be constantly vigilant 'to withstand the Devil',
who took every opportunity to exploit the 'original corruption
whereby our natures are tainted'. It appears that such sentiments
were taken to heart by many godly layfolk. As a young man in the
1640s, Bunyan overheard a group of pious women discuss 'how they
were convinced of their miserable state by nature'. Some forty years
earlier, Elizabeth Grymeston expressed the same thought vividly in a
meditation dedicated to her unborn child:

> What is life but a continual battle and defiance with God? What have
> our eyes and ears been but open gates to send in loads of sin into our
> mind? What have our powers and senses been but tinder . . . to feed
> the flame of concupiscence? What hath thy body been but a stew of
> an adulteress, but a forge of Satan?

As Grymeston implied, the corrupted nature of humankind was
apparent in both the body and the mind. Godly divines identified
the particular temptations to which these two aspects of the human
constitution were especially susceptible. Predictably, the body was
usually associated with the 'fleshly' evils of fornication and adultery,
along with a wide range of illicit urges grouped under the loose
heading of 'sodomy'. Few puritan diarists were prepared to record
their own experiences of sexual temptation, but those who did
tended to ascribe it to a mixture of human frailty and satanic influence. In the early 1660s, Henry Newcombe described how his mind
was 'basely poisoned' by sexual desires which he attributed to the
Devil. The Quaker leader, George Fox, observed in his journal that
sexual dreams were 'the whisperings of Satan to man in the night
season'. The mind, in contrast, was especially prey to the temptation
of pride, and to the deluded forms of mock religion associated with
the Roman church. The only way to escape these inclinations was
through true faith in God. Thus godly preachers likened Christianity
to the 'deliverance' of men and women from the tyranny of Satan, to
whom they would otherwise be enslaved by their natural instincts. As
John Woolton proclaimed in 1576, it was only through God's mercy
that 'Christians are translated out of the power of darkness into the

kingdom of his dearly beloved son'. Similarly, Perkins asserted in 1595 that 'the church of God is a company of men taken out of the synagogue of Satan, the kingdom of the Devil', where their sinful nature had previously bound them as vassals to the evil one. [16]

Unsurprisingly, devout Protestants tended to view the temptations of Satan as weapons in a spiritual war. In 1641 the Catholic convert Richard Carpenter declared that 'when a temptation stands up in arms against me, I will fight valiantly under the banner of Michael the archangel against the dragon'. Similar sentiments were expressed in the godly broadsheet *Stand Up To Your Beliefe* (1640), which enjoined Christians to enter 'spiritual combat' with the fiend:

> First take this shield of faith to arm your hearts,
> And if this quench not Satan's fiery darts,
> (But frequent tempting blows doth crush the shield),
> The Word's a sword, take that, if he not yield.

Despite the availability of these spiritual weapons, the fact that humans were condemned by nature to succumb to temptation meant that one's own body was a potential adversary in the struggle for salvation. Protestant teachers since Thomas Becon had stressed the need to subdue one's own flesh in order to withstand satanic assaults. In 1639, a godly layman noted that his struggle to conquer temptation was constantly hampered by the 'treachery' of his own body, which the Devil 'works upon [for] any base or villainous advantage'. Only the power of God could 'cut off that traitorous corruption of nature' and give him 'strength against the fiery assaults of the tempter'. The belief that one's own flesh was allied with Satan could lead to moments of despair and self-hatred. In 1664 Hannah Allen fell 'under a sad melancholy', and confided in her journal that 'there is such a woeful confusion and combating in my soul that I know not what to do'. Similar agonies were described by Vavasor Powell, while the Warwickshire pastor, James Nalton, was known as the 'weeping prophet' because of the 'violent fits of melancholy' which he suffered throughout his career. [17]

These times of desperation were balanced, however, by moments of confidence in the mercy of Christ. Allen was lifted from her despair by the realization that the Lord would empower her to overcome the Devil and her own treacherous flesh, and Powell and Nalton drew strength from the same source. As a godly pamphleteer declared in 1614,

Satan's powers 'are great [but] the mercy of God is greater, who never faileth to send comfort in temptation if we accept thereof'. The same confidence was expressed by Jane Turner in the preface to her autobiography in 1653. She published the book 'knowing I must expect to encounter with Satan in relation to it [in] several ways, but believing that which way so ever he appears, whether to abase or exalt me in my own thoughts, the Lord will not be wanting with strength to withstand and resist him'. For many Protestants, the conviction that God would give them victory over the Devil's temptations provided the counterpoint to their anxieties about their innate sinfulness. The autobiographies of devout men and women often recorded their oscillation between these two states of mind. [18]

In its most extreme form, this pattern was illustrated in the accounts of suicide attempts recorded in several godly 'lives'. Typically, the subjects were driven to despair by contemplating their own sinfulness and distance from God; this led them to consider taking their own lives, only to be saved by the sudden understanding that Christ would save them despite their unworthiness. Satan sometimes appeared in these narratives as the tempter who told his victims that their lives were irredeemable and urged them to bring them to a violent end, even 'leading' them to places where they could perform the act. This role was hardly surprising, as the Devil was traditionally associated with suicide, and Protestant theologians insisted that his 'policy and practice' was to remind individuals of their degraded nature and persuade them 'that God will forget to be merciful'. In the 1630s John Rogers faced 'the forcible temptations of a furious devil . . . to murder myself', believing that his life was worthless because he was already damned. The fiend told Vavasor Powell that 'the fewer sins I committed in this world, and the shorter time I lived in it, the less would be my torment' in Hell. He was delivered from this temptation by the power of God, but later succumbed to 'great fears as to my eternal condition, being often times tempted by Satan to destroy myself'. In other instances, Satan seized on the guilt felt by individuals when they committed particular sins, using it to remind them of their innate wickedness. One of the contributors to Powell's *Spirituall Experiences* told a lie as a young girl which caused her sister to be punished; she was subsequently oppressed by remorse and convinced by the Devil that God had disowned her. This led her to attempt suicide by swallowing the feathers in her pillow, before she was rescued by her parents. Satan tempted others to end their lives after they succumbed to lustful thoughts or impulses which reminded them of their innately sinful condition, but his designs were foiled when his victims remembered the mercy of God. These experiences were extreme, but they followed the pattern of temptation and disillusionment, followed by the acceptance of God's mercy, which characterized the spiritual 'trials' of most committed Protestants. [19]

If the struggles of John Rogers and Vavasor Powell were violent *exemplars* of spiritual combat, the journal of the Yorkshire gentlewoman Margaret Hoby provides a more domestic account of the Devil's stratagems. Hoby's reflections, recorded every night between August 1599 and July 1605 as part of her daily regime of spiritual devotions, offer an intimate record of one individual's struggle to overcome demonic temptation. Hoby's religion was characterized by the acceptance of her own sinful nature and reliance on the saving power of faith: 'finding my corruption and receiving strength' from God. Satan appears to have played a specific role in this scheme. She always represented him as a tempter, and never mentioned him in the context of her occasional bouts of illness: the sickness which caused her to miss church in July 1600, for example, was recorded as a judgment of God for her transgressions. When the Devil appeared in her journal, he usually assumed the form of a difficult or troubling thought that diverted her from religious duties. On the last Sabbath in August 1599 she noted that 'this day, as ever, the Devil laboreth to hinder my profitable hearing of the word and calling upon God', and prayed that the Lord would 'strengthen his children to resist and overcome' him. During a sermon in July 1602, she 'was provoked to have been disquieted', but God gave her the strength to hear the preacher with 'comfort and profit'; the following week, however, she noted that Satan returned and 'I felt his buffets'. Throughout these trials, Hoby maintained confidence in God's power to overcome her spiritual foe. In May 1602 she reflected that 'howsoever justly God hath suffered Satan to afflict my mind, yet my hope is that my redeemer will bring my soul out of troubles, that it may praise his name, and so I will wait with patience for deliverance'. Elsewhere, she reflected on the providential value of the Devil's temptations: she was comforted in July 1602 by the belief that 'my God will make them in the end profitable to me'. On another occasion, she explained that Christians should 'expect new temptations to humble us for our former negligence'. These sentiments appear to reflect the views of Perkins and the other godly divines whose works provided the basis for her devotional practices. [20]

Hoby's encounters with Satan illustrate the diverse psychological roles that the Protestant Devil could play. While he normally exploited her own fallen nature, and recalled her to the practice of self-examination, he could also act through external agents that were quite literally demonized. When she was obliged to chastise a member of the household in October 1601, for example, she recorded the incident as 'a buffet of Satan's malice'. The Devil's assaults increased markedly in the summer of 1602, during the final stages of her husband's lawsuit against the neighbouring Eure family, who had offended the Hobys with their drunken and 'impious' behaviour two years earlier. Margaret Hoby appears to have perceived the legal conflict with the Eures in terms of her struggle to overcome the evil one, who employed human agents in a second front against her. This perspective was far from unique. A decade later, Lady Anne Newdigate of Nuneaton was faced with 'sundry suits and troubles' concerning the inheritance of her husband's estate. In a letter of October 1617, she expressed the hope that God would protect 'me and mine . . . from the Devil and all his instruments' malice, and give me triumph and victory over my enemies, as he hath done and I trust in Jesus Christ will do'. Similar sentiments were voiced by her son Richard in a prayer composed in 1626. He thanked God for his 'many favours unto me, protecting me in dangers [and] preserving me from Satan's tyranny and the malice of my enemies'. In his assaults on Hoby and the Newdigates, the Devil combined the spiritual weapon of temptation with the less subtle ammunition of his earthly 'instruments', and his victims drew strength from the Lord to overcome them both. Thus Satan sent both 'inward' and 'outward' troubles. The connection between the two was stressed by Vavasor Powell, who claimed that Satan alternated between inner temptations and the work of human instruments in his attempts to destroy him. Thus Powell was first terrified by his own wicked nature and goaded by Satan to attempt suicide, and 'when these temptations failed then he began to raise up persecution against me'. A similar pattern was observed by Samuel Clarke, who suggested in 1642 that 'if we be not encountered with the world's opposition we shall be the more encumbered with the flesh's corruption'. [21]

The Devil at the deathbed

The determination of Satan to torment God's people meant that he not only assailed them throughout their lives, but also visited them

in the hours before they died. The special danger that the enemy
posed at the end of life was noted by Perkins in *A Salve for a Sicke
Man* (1595), which offered spiritual guidance on the art of dying.
Perkins warned that the Devil would make a last assault on the mind
during the pangs of death, and advised his readers to ignore the fiend's
suggestions and 'commend thy cause to God'. Twenty years later, the
English translation of John Gerard's *The Conquest of Temptations* (1615)
offered a fuller discussion of the same theme. The works of Perkins and
Gerard continued the medieval tradition of presenting the deathbed
as a place of combat between God and the Devil for the soul of the
dying Christian, while focusing on the particular 'vexations' of Satan
associated with godly religion. Gerard identified no fewer than forty-
six specific temptations, including 'weakness of faith', 'the want of the
power to believe', and 'the doubting of the application of the benefits
of Christ'. He dealt with each of these separately, concluding each
section by advising the dying person to submit to the saving power
of the Lord: 'it is Christ who fighteth for thee and in thee, believe
the Devil shall not be stronger than he'. The warnings in these books
were apparently vindicated by the deathbed terrors of a number of
godly professors. The Shrewsbury pastor Julius Herring was subjected
to a 'furious assault' from Satan the night before he died in 1644.
Another godly divine, John Dod of Northamptonshire, told one of the
watchers at his bedside in 1645 that he 'had been wrestling with Satan
all that night, who accused him that he neither preached, nor prayed,
nor performed any duty as he should have done'. He died the next day
after winning a 'great victory' over the enemy. Lengthy reports were
published of the deathbed confrontations of godly men and women
with Satan, and at least one such account circulated in the form of
a ballad in the seventeenth century. It is unlikely that such dramatic
conflicts were a common occurrence, but the genre was certainly
popular, with works such as Philip Stubbes' *Cristall Glasse for Christian
Women* republished every few years between 1591 and 1650. Like the
spiritual autobiographies collected by Rogers and Powell, these texts
provided *exemplars* of the fortitude of God's children while reminding
their readers of Satan's presence at every stage of life. [22]

The conflicts between godly professors and the Devil in the last
hours of life centred on the condition of the dying person's soul.
The fiend's usual strategy was to appear to his victims, either physically or in the form of mental 'suggestions', and tell them that they
were so corrupted by sin that God would refuse to receive them

A Renaissance depiction of the 'art of dying'.
The Devil tempts the dying man with riches.

in Heaven. In 1601 Satan reminded Katherine Brettergh of 'the severity of God's justice and the greatness of her sins'. Similarly, he whispered to Elizabeth Stretton of Leicester that 'thy sins will weight thee down to Hell'. Both women responded by asserting the saving power of God despite their sins, a sentiment conveyed in the final verse of the ballad inspired by Stretton's death:

> God's mercy is above my sin,
> Who did protect me from my birth.
> My father knows where I have been,
> Amongst vile sinners here on earth.

The fiend also employed his familiar tactic of disrupting the prayers of his dying victims. Brettergh tried to recite the Lord's Prayer but was 'interrupted' by Satan when she reached the line 'Deliver me from temptation'. She 'showed much discomfort' and cried out to those present that 'I may not pray, I may not pray'. When Katherine Stubbes made a deathbed confession of her faith in 1591 she was suddenly confronted by the Devil, who 'bid her to combat'. The printed

The dying man overcomes Satan's temptations
and his soul rises to heaven. The medieval
tradition of deathbed confrontations with the
Devil was coninued by zealous Protestants in
sixteenth- and seventeenth-century England.

accounts of these struggles suggest that their participants followed
Perkins' advice to place their fate in the hands of Christ, who empowered them finally to vanquish the fiend. Thus Brettergh repelled
the enemy with these words: 'Satan, reason not with me: I am but a
weak woman. If thou have anything to say, say it to my Christ; he
is my advocate, my strength, and my redeemer'. The same approach
apparently worked for Stretton and Stubbes. The final triumph of
the dying professors was revealed by their spiritual rapture at the
moment of death. Samuel Clarke described the blissful appearance of
Julius Herring and John Dod once their struggles with Satan were
concluded. More dramatically, Philip Stubbes recorded the ecstatic
last words of his wife: 'behold, I see infinite millions of most glorious
angels stand about me, with fiery chariots ready to defend me . . .
These holy angels, these ministering spirits, are appointed by God to
carry my soul into the kingdom of Heaven'. [23]

Perhaps the most striking feature of these confrontations was the
martial tone in which they were presented. The language and imagery

of the battlefield was especially pervasive in the deathbed narratives of Katherine Stubbes and Katherine Brettergh. At the end of her conflict with the Devil, Stubbes addressed him as a 'cowardly soldier', and commanded him to 'remove thy siege and yield the field won'. She declared that if he did not flee 'I will call upon my grand captain Christ Jesus, the valiant Michael, who beat thee in Heaven and threw thee down to Hell with all thy Hellish train and devilish crew'. As the fiend retreated, she turned to those at her bedside and asked: 'do you not see him fly like a coward, and run away like a beaten cock?' Likewise, when Brettergh overcame the ghostly enemy she announced that 'my warfare is accomplished and my iniquities are pardoned'. Despite their extraordinary context, the words of both women reflected the conventional belief that Christianity was a kind of combat, and their deathbed experiences can perhaps be viewed as an extension of the normal principles of godly Protestantism. The idea of Christian warfare was taken still further in the published account of Brettergh's death, which presented her experience as a vindication of God's people in their struggle against Antichrist and popery:

> It must needs be a divine religion, and a truth coming from God, that thus can fill the heart and mouth of a weak woman at the time of death with such admirable comfort. And a wretched conceit, and mere Antichristian is that religion which so hateth and persecuteth this faith, which is thus able to lead the true-hearted professors thereof with such unspeakable grace unto their graves.

The author contrasted Brettergh's triumph over Satan with the fate of Catholics 'who have died most fearfully indeed', suggesting that they 'showed manifest signs at their deaths that their popish superstition was the condemnation of their souls'. Thus her final encounter with the Devil was related explicitly to the wider conflict between God's children and the Roman church, which itself was regarded as a demonic institution. [24]

While the dramas of the godly deathbed offered comfort to the faithful, the deaths of the reprobate could illustrate the horrors awaiting those whom God abandoned to Satan. In a *Swoord Against Swearyng* (1579), Edmond Bicknoll described the bleak end of Arthur Miller in 1573. A 'common swearer and blasphemer of Gods name', Miller felt unable to pray for God's grace as he entered his last sickness. Instead, he told the witnesses at his bedside that he felt the Devil clasping his hand; and 'crying for help only upon the Devil, he most miserably ended his most wretched life'. John Bunyan depicted the last moments of other hardened sinners in *The Life and Death of Mr Badman* (1680). In one account a woman spent her last breath on a dreadful confession, which was followed swiftly by the Devil's appearance at her bedside:

> I was once in the presence of a woman, a married woman, who lay sick of the sickness whereof she died. And being smitten in her conscience for the sin of uncleanness, which she had often committed with other men, I heard her, as she lay upon her bed, cry out thus: 'I am a whore, and all my children are bastards! And I must go to Hell for my sin. And look! There stands the Devil at my bed's feet to receive my soul when I die.'

Bunyan described other unredeemed men and women who caught the scent of brimstone in their last moments, and went 'roaring out of this world to their place'. But while some individuals went screaming to damnation, others were so deadened to their sins that they slipped quietly to their fate. This was the case for Mr Badman himself, who closed his eyes softly and opened them in Hell. [25]

The experiences described in this chapter suggest that devout Protestants often viewed themselves as an embattled minority, assailed by 'inward' temptations and the more obvious hostility of the impious world. To some extent this perception was accurate. The demanding nature of their religion meant that it could only appeal to a relatively small number of men and women; and the widespread denigration of 'puritans' in early modern England implies that the Protestant understanding of sin and grace made only a superficial impression on many ordinary people. It is hardly surprising, then, that reformed ideas about Satan were not wholly accepted by the majority of the population. Instead, it appears that many medieval attitudes towards the fiend persisted in folklore and cheap literature throughout the sixteenth and seventeenth centuries, though these were intermingled with aspects of reformed theology. The result was an interesting mixture of Protestant ideas and older beliefs concerning the Devil, an outcome which probably typified the wider achievements and limitations of the English Reformation. This is considered in the next chapter.

The Devil in
Popular Culture

THE SURVIVAL OF TRADITIONAL BELIEFS

Two Elizabethan texts on the doctrine of providence illustrate the difference between academic theology and the beliefs and fears of ordinary people. In 1572 the Oxford professor of divinity Edward Cradocke published *The Shippe of Assured Safetie*, a treatise on God's 'marvellous and unspeakable way' of ordering earthly events for His purposes. Cradocke placed both good and bad angels within the compass of providence, though he devoted relatively few pages to Satan's role as God's instrument. When he addressed this theme, he noted how God sharpened the faith of Christians by allowing them to be exposed to demonic temptations: 'if we should have no ghostly enemies that would stand against us, there could not then, I say, be any . . . rewards laid up for the overcomers, nor the kingdom of Heaven be provided for them that have the upper hand'. A decade later, the godly preacher George Gifford expounded the same theme to a different audience. The opening pages of his *Catechisme Conteining the Summe of Christian Religion* (1583) described the doctrine of providence to plain readers seeking 'to enter the pathway to salvation'. Gifford explained that 'the actions of the Devil . . . are measured and directed' by God's hand for the good of his children. In the practical context of a work of religious instruction, he also found it necessary to comment on popular beliefs about Satan. Thus he reproved the 'common opinion' that 'the Devil doth raise up great winds with tempests and thunders' – an opinion that was 'contrary unto the faith

which we must have in God's providence'. While Gifford concurred
with Cradocke on the effects of providence, his treatment of the
subject reflected his readers' concerns. He addressed a community
in which the Devil was very familiar, but was perceived as a threat to
physical wellbeing at least as much as a spiritual tempter. [1]

A vignette from the seventeenth-century Oxford historian John
Aubrey sheds further light on popular demonology. Aubrey described
how two housemaids mistook a pocket watch for the Devil. The
incident took place in Herefordshire around 1620, when the mathematician Thomas Allen was visiting his patron John Scudamore.
Allen left his watch, a machine which was then a 'rarity', in his
room window before the maids came to make the bed. The women,
'hearing a thing in a case cry *tick, tick, tick*, presently concluded that
it was his Devil, and took it by the string with the tongs and threw
it out of the window into the moat (to drown the Devil)'. Aubrey
claimed that the string on the watchcase caught on the branch of
an elder tree, 'so the good old gentleman got his watch again'. The
lucky preservation of the timepiece, however, only convinced the
maids of the object's supernatural qualities and 'confirmed [to] them
that 'twas the Devil'. This tale reflects the tendency of learned men
to mock the beliefs of uneducated people in Stuart England: the
author characterised the outlook of the maids as 'ignorant', and criticised Allen himself for 'imposing on the understanding of believing
people'. If true, the story also suggests a gap between Protestant
teaching and popular ideas of the Devil. The maids' belief that the
fiend could assume the form of a small object on a window ledge,
and their attempt to drown him in the moat, had little in common
with reformed doctrines about the 'prince of this world'. [2]

This chapter will argue that much of the English population
retained essentially medieval beliefs about Satan throughout the
Tudor and Stuart period. As Gifford and Aubrey indicate, the
Devil was widely perceived as a source of physical danger rather
than a 'ghostly enemy' within the human heart; he was frequently
viewed as a corporeal being; and his incursions could be repelled by
human efforts. These attributes belonged to the stock of medieval
beliefs about Satan that was winnowed by Protestant reformers in
the sixteenth century, but persisted in popular culture. Traditional
attitudes towards the Devil not only survived but flourished,
influencing the depiction of new figures in popular literature like
Faust and Mother Shipton. The vitality of these ideas suggests that

Protestant demonism was embraced by only a minority of the English people. This was not the whole story, however. The second half of this chapter will argue that Protestant ideas and the beliefs of the 'common sort of Christians', though different in many ways, were rather less polarised than godly contemporaries imagined. Protestants were prepared to exploit medieval traditions about Satan despite the compromises this involved, and some aspects of reformed thinking were absorbed into popular culture. The partial assimilation of reformed doctrines meant that a diverse and ambiguous set of beliefs about Satan came to be accepted by much of the English population by the end of the seventeenth century. These beliefs were partly 'Protestant', but they fell woefully short of the expectations of many divines. Before describing this process, however, it is necessary to consider the persistence of older conceptions of the Devil in the sixteenth and seventeenth centuries.[3]

The Devil as an animal

One of the most striking features of the Devil in popular literature was his tendency to appear in the form of an animal. This characteristic was almost entirely absent in godly autobiographies, where his physical appearance was normally that of a man or a monstrous beast. In contrast, the first English edition of the Faust legend in 1592 depicted Satan as a squirrel with 'his tail turning upwards on his back'. When Faust visited Hell he encountered demons 'in the form of insensible beasts, as swine, bears, wolves, apes, goats, antelopes, elephants, dragons, horses, lions, cats, snakes, toads, and all manner of ugly, odious serpents and worms'. Likewise, a ballad published in 1661 described the fiend's manifestations as a calf, a pig, a woman and a Catholic priest. The idea that the Devil could assume animal form was not confined to fiction. When Satan was mentioned by witnesses in witch trials he was often described as an animal: a deposition from Essex in 1565 recorded his appearance as 'a great dog', and 'an evil favoured dog with horns on his head'. Similarly, when a young girl was asked to describe the Devil in 1574 she replied that he was sometimes like 'a man with a grey beard, sometimes like five cats, sometimes [like] ravens and crows'. Two years later, a pamphlet announced the appearance of the fiend in the 'hideous and Hellish likeness' of a monstrous dog in a Norfolk parish church:

The devil-dog, from *The Examination and Confession of Certaine Wytches at Chensforde* (1566).

> There appeared in a most horrible similitude and likeness to the congregation . . . a dog, as they might discern it, of a black colour, at the sight whereof, together with the fearful flashes of fire which there were seen, moved such admiration in the minds of the assembly, that they thought doomsday was already come. This black dog, or the Devil in such a likeness . . . running all along down the body of the church with great swiftness, and incredible heat, among the people . . . passed between two persons as they were kneeling upon their knees, and occupied in prayer as it seemed, wrung the necks of them both at one instant clean backward, insomuch that even at the moment where they kneeled, they strangely died.

Similar visitations were reported in the seventeenth century. In 1614 the Devil appeared in Somerset as 'a strange thing like unto a snail', and then transformed himself into a bear. The patients of Richard Napier in the 1620s reported sightings of the fiend in the shape of dogs, wolves, and swarms of insects. The precise origins of these beliefs are obscure, but the general reluctance of Protestant writers to embrace them suggests that they emerged outside the influence of the Reformation. Equally, their persistence throughout the period indicates that they were largely untouched by the arrival of Protestantism. [4]

The belief that the Devil could appear as an animal was probably linked to the idea that he always possessed cloven hooves when he took human form. Again, this notion was mostly absent from Protestant descriptions of Satan, and such a trivial and arbitrary limitation of his power was certainly inconsistent with reformed theology. In 1624 Elizabeth Jocelyn noted that 'the common people believe the Devil cannot alter the shape of one foot' despite his ability to appear in various human and animal disguises. This belief surfaced occasionally in depositions and confessions from witch trials. A 'cunning man' from Dorset claimed in 1566 that he had summoned up an evil spirit 'something like a man in all proportions, saving that he had cloven feet', and the Devil assumed the same appearance when he presented himself to witches in Suffolk in the 1640s. In the late seventeenth century the possession of cloven hooves signified the demonic origins of figures in cheap literature like Mother Shipton. The persistence of this belief was demonstrated by its frequent appearance in collections of folklore compiled in the nineteenth century. A typical tale from Lincolnshire, recorded around 1880, described how a 'gentleman' asked a tailor to make him a suit on the Sabbath, only to reveal a cloven hoof as the unfortunate man was taking his measurements. Again, the longevity of this tradition suggests that it was largely unaffected by Protestant conceptions of the Devil. [5]

The power of Satan

The existence of different views concerning the physical appearance of Satan was less important than the issue of his power in the world. On this subject, it seems that committed Protestants were at odds with much of the population. In 1971 Keith Thomas argued that popular religion in Tudor and Stuart England was based on assumptions and practices that were largely independent of official Christianity. Thomas' interpretation has been keenly debated, with historians questioning both the distinction between popular and 'elite' culture and the supposed gulf between the religious practices of ordinary people and the activities of the church. Nonetheless, a consensus has emerged that many layfolk accepted the existence of a variety of supernatural entities, including fairies, imps and ghosts,

A witch and familiar spirits, from a manuscript
of 1621.

as well as the orthodox figures of God and the Devil. All of these
beings were capable of influencing human affairs for good or ill.
Thus the cunning man who confessed to calling up the fiend in
1566 also described his dealings with fairies, and the deposition of
a Leicestershire woman accused of witchcraft in 1619 described
the activities of both fairies and the Devil. Richard Napier treated
many patients who were 'haunted with fairies' and imps as well as
those who reported encounters with the fiend. Towards the end
of the seventeenth century, the prevalence of fairy beliefs among
the 'common sort' was noted by Joseph Glanvill and John Aubrey.
It seems reasonable to assume that the acceptance of such beings
diluted the power of Satan by placing him alongside a host of other
supernatural creatures. Indeed, it was even possible for the fiend
himself to be relegated to the status of an 'old subtle elf', as he was

described in a ballad printed in 1665. The concept of the Devil as a single, powerful entity was also compromised by popular beliefs about individual demons and wicked spirits. While Protestant writers tended to attribute the actions of demons to the Devil himself, folk traditions continued to invest individual demons with distinct personalities and a degree of autonomy. This was most evident in depositions in witch trials, which focused on the activities of apparently demonic 'familiars' rather than Satan himself. [6]

While the existence of fairies and elves appears to have been widely accepted, it was common for devout Protestants to dismiss them as 'old wives' tales' or reinterpret their activities as the work of Satan. This tendency was illustrated neatly in a godly meditation published in 1639. The author described how he was nearly killed as a baby by trapping his head between a bedframe and a wall, but was rescued when his parents heard him screaming. He later discovered that some local 'gossips' had interpreted this incident as the work of fairies. In their version, he had narrowly escaped being abducted by the creatures, who had planned to leave 'some elf or changeling (as they call it) in my place'. This explanation was derided by the pious author, who argued instead that the assailant had been the Devil: 'that attempt of stealing me away as soon as I was born (whatever the midwives talk of it) came from the malice of that arch-enemy of mankind, who is continually going about seeking whom he may betray or devour'. As this vignette suggests, Protestants tended to explain those aspects of popular supernaturalism that did not conform to reformed Christianity by extending the work of Satan. Conversely, the continued acceptance of beings such as fairies and elves outside godly circles meant that the Devil's power was balanced by the influence of these other supernatural entities. [7]

Satan's status as the 'prince of this world' was further challenged by beliefs concerning his physical limitations. The medieval idea that he could be bound by physical constraints appears to have survived throughout the early modern period. In 1574 a possessed woman claimed that the fiend had been trapped in a bottle before he took over her body. As some Protestant contemporaries observed, the concept of possession itself seemed to impose an arbitrary restriction on the Devil by placing him in the body of a single victim. Other ideas apparently limited his activities to certain times and places: it was often reported, for example, that the evil one was most active at night and haunted the sites of gallows and crossroads. The idea that the Devil possessed physical weaknesses was presented most strikingly in popular fiction. One particularly robust tale from the late sixteenth century described how Satan, taking the form of a horse, attempted to carry a woman away to Hell. His intended victim so 'kicked and pricked' his body that he had to cry out for mercy, and he finally abandoned the mission when 'she drew her knife and gave his ear a slit'. A ballad printed in 1661 described how a baker castrated the fiend, and another from the same collection related how the Devil, disguised as a calf, was slaughtered and sold 'for excellent veal'. Satan's vulnerability was exposed less violently in other compositions which described how he broke his horns or choked on pieces of meat. Several tales also suggested that the Devil could be deceived. Typically, these stories began with the evil one presenting himself to a potential victim and offering to make a bet: the mortal would receive earthly riches as long as he or she performed a certain task, but the fiend would claim the person's soul if this task was not completed. The hero would then accomplish the feat by some ingenious means and escape from the bargain. One seventeenth-century ballad told how a poor man made a bet with Satan that he could find an animal that had never been seen before. After enjoying the 'cattle and corn' that the fiend delivered as his part of the deal, the man dressed his wife 'in feathers and lime' and pretended she was a strange beast. Satan was fooled, and the man 'went home with his wife, and they lived full merrily'. Similar stories of 'the Devil outwitted' were popular well into the eighteenth century. [8]

The fiend's power was also limited by the belief that he could harm only those who led outwardly wicked lives. This idea was linked to the common-sense assumption that individuals could escape the torments of Hell by practising good neighbourliness and trying to keep the Ten Commandments. In 1592 Perkins repudiated the idea that 'if a man be no adulterer, no thief, no murderer and do no harm' he would be safe from the Devil, insisting that all those who held such beliefs were unwitting slaves of Satan. But this position appears to have won little support. Arthur Dent acknowledged this frankly in his book of religious instruction 'for the better understanding of the simple', *The Plaine Mans Path-way to Heaven* (1601). In a dialogue between a godly divine and three archetypal characters, Dent presented both the core teachings of reformed Christianity and common responses to them. When the divine asserted Satan's command over all 'natural men', one of his companions observed that 'few will be persuaded of that: they will say, they defy the Devil, and thank God they were never troubled with him'. His instructor agreed, noting that Satan 'possesseth the very hearts and entrails of thousands which say they deny him'. After a further exposition of the Devil's deception of such people, his companion reiterated that 'few will believe this to be true'. A survey of popular literature suggests that this assertion was well founded. The victims of Satan's power in cheap print were almost invariably guilty of anti-social or immoral behaviour: they were liars, hypocrites, thieves or cut-throats, or simply 'ill-livers' who mistreated their neighbours. Thus a landlord who stole from his guests was devoured by the fiend in a tale published in 1642. A chapbook from 1684 described how Satan murdered an avaricious money-lender, while a text from 1701 reported that he appeared to a 'lewd, notorious and wicked' prosti-tute, 'dragging her out of her bed and beating her black and blue all over her body'. [9]

As these examples suggest, the Devil could execute dreadful punishments on wrongdoers. Popular literature tended to empha-sise his physical attacks rather than the assaults he inflicted in the mind, and stressed his capacity to destroy sinners in this world as much as the next. Even when malefactors were condemned to Hell, they were usually dragged there physically, like the Coventry woman who was seized by two demons on her wedding day because she had broken her vow to marry someone else. In a nasty variation of the same scenario, another woman who promised to marry a poor man and then left him for a wealthier suitor was punished when her first child was carried away by the fiend. It was more usual, however, for the Devil to murder his victims or treat them to horrible beat-ings. A ballad based on the Faust legend in the 1590s ended with the discovery of the magician's hideously mutilated corpse: his 'brains were cast against the wall', and the rest of his body was 'in pieces torn'. A slightly less gory fate befell a London wool spinner who attempted to defraud her employer: she was 'thrown down' by the Devil in the shape of a man and then murdered in her bedroom. Another ballad, *Strange and True News from Westmoreland*, described how Satan ended the 'wretched life' of a murderer by snapping his neck. Each of these texts made it clear that the fiend's victims had brought about their own demise by their wicked behaviour, and presented the Devil as a kind of supernatural avenger. Such depic-tions were, of course, consistent with the providential understanding of Satan as 'God's hangman'; but by focusing exclusively on the fate of obvious wrongdoers they obscured the Devil's more insidious power in the hearts of all 'natural' men and women. [10]

Comic Devils and scenes from Hell

Despite Satan's horrible punishment of wrongdoers, the relative safety of those who led apparently good lives made it possible to present him in a humorous context. A light-hearted publication in 1606 described the fiend as 'that great tobacconist, the prince of smoke and darkness', and joked that he was illiterate despite attending 'all the universities in Christendom'. In one early seventeenth-century ballad, 'old Beelzebub merry' visited earth to win the souls of gullible mortals by promising them eternal life. His plans were ruined, however, when he encountered the fishwives of London, who were so boisterous and noisy that they scared him away, vowing never to 'have dealing 'mongst women again'. While these texts mocked the fiend's limitations, others poked fun at the deserving victims of his wrath. The jocular ballad *The Feasting of the Devil*, which circulated in at least two different versions in the seventeenth century, described the scene at a satanic banquet. The Devil's table was laid with such delicacies as 'a puritan poached' and 'a lawyer's head and green sauce', which he devoured with great relish. In one version, the meal ended with a dreadful 'fart from the Devil's arse', likened to the stench of tobacco which 'hath foully perfum'd most part of the isle'. [11]

As this example indicates, comic tales about Satan continued the medieval tradition of scatological humour. This was prominent in the tale of a baker who 'gelded' the Devil on his way to Nottingham market. To revenge himself of this outrage, the fiend promised to castrate the man if he ever returned to the town. With typical resourcefulness, the baker's wife put on his clothes and met the Devil in his place, telling him that 'I was gelded yesterday'. When he demanded proof, she lifted her coats and 'let go a rousing fart'. A similar wit characterised the late seventeenth-century tales of Mother Shipton, in which the Devil punished the heroine's enemies by replacing their hats with chamber pots and making them break wind 'for above a quarter of an hour'. In a slightly different vein, another ballad expressed the cheerful sentiment that 'when the Devil comes for you, you need not care a fart'. The Devil also appeared in the punchlines of jokes. A jest printed in 1607 observed that the

Left: The punishments of Hell, from *St Bernard's Vision* (*c.* 1640).

Right: The torments of witches and a catholic priest in Hell, from *The Most Wonderfull and True Storie of a Certaine Witch Named Alice Gooderidge* (1597).

Punishments of the damned, from *A Booke Declaringe the Fearfull Vexation of one Alexander Nyndge* (1574).

fiend was an 'ass' for failing to punish lawyers for their manifest sins, and the phrase 'Go to the Devil' was aimed at lawyers, churchmen and unruly women in cheap print throughout the period. [12]

The same qualities that characterised popular images of the Devil also flavoured descriptions of Hell. In cheap literature the infernal region was usually populated with men and women who had committed terrible sins on earth, and was not regarded as a place where all people were ordained to suffer unless they were saved by the mercy of Christ. The sufferings of the damned were depicted in intensely physical terms. Ballads reported the 'howling and yelling' of the fiend's victims and described the ingenious tortures they had to endure. The relationship between unneighbourly behaviour and damnation was emphasised by the specific torments designated for particular crimes. Thus adulterers were tied to beds while their skin was flayed off with 'whips of glowing fire', and liars had molten lead poured down their throats. Usurers, thieves and murderers could all expect appropriately customised forms of torture. In 1596 the possessed youth, Thomas Darling, received a vision of 'the place of torments, where drunkards are hanged by the throats, swearers and filthy talkers by their tongues'. Most of these horrors were taken from medieval depictions of Hell, and the influence of pre-Reformation traditions was also apparent in pictorial representations of the after-life. Seventeenth-century woodcuts often showed condemned souls trapped in the gaping mouth of a dragon, an image derived from medieval mystery plays. The assumption that most well meaning people would escape the pains of Hell made it possible to depict the place, like its ruler, in a comical fashion. Thus Thomas Decker joked in 1606 that Hell is 'exceeding rich, for all usurers, both Jews and Christians, after they have made away their souls for money here, meet with them there again'. He suggested that Satan allowed no poets in Hell because they would write libels against him, though he tolerated some 'ballad-makers' because their work was too poor to give offence. Decker's light-hearted approach was much closer in spirit to the 'merry tales' of the early sixteenth century than the doctrines advanced by Protestants like William Perkins, who, according to one seventeenth-century admirer, pronounced the word 'damnation' in his sermons with such emphasis that it 'left a doleful echo in his auditors' ears a good while after'. [13]

Illustration from *The Strange and Wonderful History of Mother Shipton* (1686).

The 'Merry Devil' and Mother Shipton

Perhaps the best evidence for the vitality of the attitudes described so far was the emergence of new stories about the Devil which contained non-Protestant elements. The first English version of the Faust legend reflected traditional beliefs by locating the hero's initial encounter with the fiend at 'a crossway' in a wood at night, and included comic touches that were closer to folklore than reformed theology. The story of Faust was imported from Germany, but other tales about Satan developed in Reformation England. The legendary medieval scholar and magician Roger Bacon emerged as a literary character in the sixteenth century, and was presented as a 'brave necromancer' in Robert Greene's play *The Honorable Historie of Frier Bacon and Frier Bongay* (1594). A collection of stories about the magician, *The Famous Historie of Fryer Bacon* (1627), described his ability to outwit the Devil. In one tale Satan made a pact with an impoverished gentleman in order to win his soul, but was rescued when Bacon spotted a loophole in the contract. [14]

The adventures of Roger Bacon may also have inspired *The Merry Devil of Edmonton*, a play first staged around 1604 and subsequently reworked in cheap print. This described the exploits of 'the renowned scholar' Peter Fabell, nicknamed the 'Merry Devil' because of 'his fame in sleights and magic'. Like Bacon, Fabell was a necromancer

Witches and demons from *The Strange and
Wonderful History of Mother Shipton* (1686).

who used his skills to perform 'pleasant pranks' and assist people in
trouble. In a chapbook version of the story in 1631, Fabell made a
pact with Satan but retained his soul through a series of ingenious
ploys. When the fiend came for him one evening, Fabell promised
he could take his soul as soon as the candle in his study burned out.
The Devil assented and sealed the pact with an oath:

> As I hope to draw down [a] thousand souls to the deep abyss (the
> place of my abode), I will forbear [to take] thee till that candle is
> burned. Then Master Peter, presently after his Hellish protestation, put
> the candle out and into his pocket. Look here (quoth he), till this is
> burnt thou mayest not claim my soul. I'll keep this safe enough from
> burning out ... When the Devil saw he was so cunningly deceived by
> Master Peter, with many bitter execrations he left him.

Unlike Faust, Fabell was not cast into Hell at the end of the story.
He promised the Devil his soul if he was buried 'either within the
church, without the church, in the church porch, churchyard, street,
field or highway'. The magician escaped the fiend's clutches by
arranging for his body to be interred in one of the church walls.
Needless to say, the story of the 'Merry Devil' owed little to the
Protestant concept of Satan, yet it emerged and flourished at the
same time that this concept was being developed. [15]

The limited impact of Protestant ideas about the Devil was demonstrated further by the emergence of the Yorkshire prophetess, Mother Shipton, as a popular figure in seventeenth-century literature. Like Friar Bacon, Shipton was based originally on a folkloric character who predated the Reformation, and the demonic aspects of her personality were added as her story was developed in print. The first version of Shipton's prophecies was published in 1641, and this basic text was augmented by the 'discovery' of new prognostications over the next thirty years. It was not until 1667 that Shipton emerged as a character in her own right, with a new edition of her works including the story of her nativity and the events surrounding her predictions. This text claimed that she was literally the daughter of Satan, who had taken her mother Agatha as his wife. Shipton's diabolical nature was confirmed in the following year, when a chapbook reported that she had cloven feet. The acquisition of these features did not, however, turn the prophetess into a wicked or frightening figure. On the contrary, the author of the 1667 tract claimed that she was held 'in great esteem' by everyone who met her, 'and her memory to this day is much honoured by those of her own county'. In an arresting reversal of the Protestant insistence that Satan was the 'father of lies', Shipton's reputation rested on the truthfulness of her prophecies. Her alleged epitaph was 'Here lies she who never lied'. As well as her ability as a seer, the later editions of Shipton's life focused on the 'merry pranks' she played on her neighbours. These were often accomplished by diabolical means. In one story, she visited a mayor's banquet only to be ignored and insulted by the other guests. In retaliation, she 'run'd into the middle of the hall and shrieked out aloud, whereat a whole legion of devils instantly rose among them with terrible thunder and lightning, who seized on every dish of meat and, walking orderly out of the hall with Shipton before [them], at the gate all vanished'. A tract from 1686 described how 'her father the foul fiend' visited Shipton as an infant and played tricks on her nurse. These tales were presented as 'pleasant exploits' in which the Devil was playful rather than malevolent. [16]

The adventures of Friar Bacon, the 'Merry Devil' and Mother Shipton indicate the strong appeal of Satan as a character in popular fiction. It appears, indeed, that the fiend became more commercially attractive in the course of the seventeenth century, since the earliest stories about the Yorkshire prophetess included few references to her satanic connections. The success of these characters also suggests the persistence of folkloric ideas about the Devil. Satan was gullible and limited in the tales of the magician of Edmonton, and he assumed a playful and comic role in the Mother Shipton stories. Strikingly, an attempt in 1670 to recast Mother Shipton in a more orthodox religious context appears to have failed. Thomas Thomson's play *The Life of Mother Shipton* borrowed freely from earlier writers, and retained folkloric elements that sat uneasily with Protestant doctrines; but it also concluded with Shipton repenting her sins and renouncing her demonic allegiance. The prophetess was released from Satan's grip through the mercy of God. 'All your temptations', she tells the defeated Devil at the climax of the play, are 'too weak to besiege my fortified soul'. This version of Shipton's narrative spawned no imitations, however, while texts depicting her as Satan's merry and impenitent daughter were reprinted and elaborated until the end of the century. [17]

The success of such publications makes it easy to understand why godly pastors routinely castigated the ignorance and 'superstition' of ordinary people. It would be misleading, however, to assume that Protestantism and popular culture were always in conflict. Protestant proselytisers were prepared to exploit traditional images of the Devil in order to reach a wide audience. This caused them to emphasise certain ideas more than others, and to play down some of the more difficult aspects of their theology, with results that were often ambiguous and occasionally misleading. At the same time, ordinary layfolk were capable of appropriating aspects of reformed religion, notably the link between popery and the Devil, while ignoring the harsher and more demanding ideas propounded by men like William Perkins. Both of these processes are considered below.

TRADITIONAL IDEAS IN PROTESTANT TRACTS

It is tempting to view the English Reformation as a revolution 'imposed from above', in which an elite minority sought to refashion the beliefs and practices of the rest of society. This interpretation is valid in many respects. Almost certainly, the establishment of Protestantism owed more to the decisions of the crown than to a popular clamour for reform, despite the shortcomings of the late medieval church. It would be a mistake, however, to assume that the relationship between the new faith and popular culture was only a one-way process, in which traditional attitudes were gradually reshaped by the teachings of godly divines. On the contrary, it appears that the Protestant message was often modified in order to meet the needs of a popular audience. In part, this reflected the willingness of reformers to exploit traditional themes and images for their own ends, despite the compromises this involved. It also demonstrated the problems inherent in translating difficult theological concepts into popular media. These problems were exacerbated by the fact that much of the population was semi-literate, which meant that the tenets of reformed theology had to be communicated in pictures as well as words.

Picturing Satan

A woodcut printed in 1569 contained one of the most bizarre portrayals of the Devil in the sixteenth century (see plate). It depicted the fiend as a bird-like creature with a peacock's tail, holding a gun in one of its misshapen hands. A stream of crucifixes and rosary beads issued from the gun's barrel, which was apparently aimed at a sword-bearing angel standing in the monster's path. The illustration was included in Stephen Bateman's *Christall Glasse of Christian Reformation*, a collection of annotated images intended to express the core themes of reformed theology. A brief text under the woodcut explained that 'the monster with the gun signifieth all popish ceremonies', while the angel represented 'god's wrath against all such persecutors of his people'. The woodcut illustrates some of the obvious limitations of pictorial images in conveying the message of reformed Christianity. While it succeeded in linking the Roman church with the Devil, it failed to explain that popery was satanic because it taught that salvation could be achieved through human actions. Indeed, it is difficult to imagine how this concept could have been conveyed effectively in pictures. The rosary-firing gun was an ingenious attempt to illustrate the satanic nature of 'works-based' religion, but the awkwardness of the image only indicates how difficult it was to communicate the idea in a picture. [18]

This problem was encountered by all Protestant teachers who attempted to convey their message in print to a large audience. In his ground-breaking work on popular propaganda in sixteenth-century Germany, Bob Scribner showed that the earliest reformers relied heavily on pictorial images to reach the non-literate majority of the population; he suggested that this material was enormously effective at exploiting grievances against the medieval church, but was ill-suited to communicate more complex and positive doctrines. Luther and his supporters plundered a range of familiar images and media to promote their agenda, but this process imposed inevitable limitations on the propaganda they created. A similar process has been documented in England by Tessa Watt, who found that traditional imagery and genres were appropriated by Protestants in their campaign to re-educate the population in the sixteenth and seventeenth centuries. Again, the use of traditional forms meant that certain ideas could be expressed more successfully than others, and the purity of the original message was sometimes lost. Protestant attempts to promote a new understanding of the Devil followed this general trend. Propagandists for the new faith inherited from the medieval church a fund of powerful and familiar images of the evil one, and the centrality of Satan to their belief system meant that they were bound to exploit them. The use of these images, however, imposed subtle restrictions on their work. [19]

This difficulty was exemplified in Bateman's *Christall Glasse*. Fourteen of the book's forty woodcuts contained images of Satan, and he was a central figure in seven of these. These representations drew heavily on traditional images: the fiend often possessed cloven hooves and horns, and Hell was depicted as the jaws of a dragon. Other figures were taken from popular drama: the first tableau, for instance, presented a man dressed as a carnival fool confronting the Devil, who was tempting him with a bag of money. These symbols were employed to create some arresting and memorable scenes. In one, the Devil in the shape of a friar watched approvingly through a doorway as a monk and a nun engaged in fornication. Another picture depicted two women, one riding a goat while the other held its beard and led it after a flying demon. Bateman's text pointed out that 'the goat signifieth lechery, the woman whoredom, she who leadeth the goat by the beard is . . . the bawd, and the Devil [is] a blind guide or deceiver'. A later woodcut in the series represented the triumph of faith over temptation. An armoured man, holding a sword and shield, stood on the crumpled body of the Devil. As the author explained, the figure 'signifieth all steadfast believers of the verity, being armed with constant zeal of Christianity and weaponed with the shield of lively faith . . . The Devil under him is temptation, being overcome by faith in Jesus Christ'. [20]

In some ways, these images were strikingly effective. They under-lined the demonic nature of Catholicism and highlighted Satan's delight in sins such as lechery. But in other respects they were potentially misleading. By focusing on men and women engaged in specific sins, the woodcuts tended to support the view that only obvious wrongdoers were in thrall to the Devil. While the identification of particular sins was essential for the pictures to make an impact, it also made it virtually impossible to convey the message that *all* people were slaves of Satan by virtue of their fallen nature. Equally, the pictorial representation of the Devil emphasised his role as a physical threat rather than a source of temptations. Again, this problem was probably unavoidable. It is hard to imagine a visual depiction of the defeat of temptation through faith more effective than the one in Bateman's book; nonetheless, the picture does not really convey the daily struggle to overcome Satan's influence in the mind. It was partly for this reason, presumably, that Bateman supplemented the woodcuts with brief texts explaining their meaning. These tended to reinterpret the concrete images as abstract signs, and always presented the Devil as a source of temptation rather than a physical creature. It is impossible to know how the *Christall Glasse* was received by its audience, but the work does reveal the problems involved in translating Protestant ideas into a medium suitable for a largely illiterate population.

The same limitations were evident in other Protestant woodcuts produced in the sixteenth and seventeenth centuries. These illustrations were generally successful at linking Satan with popery and specific sins, but failed to communicate the idea that he was the 'prince of this world'. Pictures of priests, cardinals and monks were often embellished with horns and cloven hooves, while the pontiff himself was commonly placed on the back of the dragon from the Book of Revelation. In 1616 the fiend appeared 'in Jesuited-angel shape', complete with cloven feet, on the title page of William Gouge's *Whole Armour of God*. Later woodcuts showed him blowing instructions into priests' ears with a pair of bellows, and offering 'popish trinkets' to his earthly disciples. In some cases, these images reinforced the more detailed content of the texts that accompanied them; but often they did little more than assert that Catholicism was the Devil's creed without explaining why. Protestant propagandists also followed Bateman in linking Satan to specific sins: woodcuts depicting the Devil encouraging blasphemy and fornication continued to circulate well into the eighteenth century. Likewise, Protestant illustrations of the afterlife tended to populate Hell with obvious criminals, usually including a contingent of cardinals and priests. More generally, all pictures of the Devil tended to emphasise his physical presence rather than his role as a tempter. This could lead to some bizarre images. In 1683, for example, a godly broadsheet warning against the temptation 'to neglect learning and follow pastimes' was illustrated by a picture of Satan playing tennis. [21]

Satanic retribution

The problems of communicating reformed ideas in pictures were probably greater than those posed by the exploitation of other media. Nonetheless, the attempts by Protestants to employ the conventions of story-telling also led to some interesting compromises. The idea that the Devil would punish men and women for particular sins had an obvious appeal to godly churchmen, who could use it to inspire fear in those layfolk who resisted their ministry. The career of Hugh Clarke in Northamptonshire offers a good illustration. Clarke's seventeenth-century biographer described the fate of a group of Sabbath-breakers in his flock in the 1580s:

> In the night, when they were retired to their several homes, there was heard a great noise and rattling of chains up and down the town, which was accompanied with such a smell and stink of fire and brimstone that many of their guilty consciences suggested unto them that the Devil was come to fetch them away quick to Hell. This so terrified and wrought upon them that they began to give better heed to the ministry of God's Word, and to break off their profane courses for the greatest part, so that there was an eminent reformation wrought amongst them.

It appears that news of this event was actively disseminated by the minister as a warning to other malefactors. The impact of the tale is impossible to know, but the narrative itself did nothing to challenge the popular wisdom that the Devil troubled only those who were guilty of particular sins, just as God rewarded those who tried to keep His commandments. This problem was probably unavoidable. It was very difficult to describe the punishment of sin by the fiend without identifying individuals guilty of specific crimes, but this tended to undermine the idea that all people were by nature 'servants of Satan'. [22]

Equally, tales of 'exemplary punishment' relied for their impact on the sudden physical appearance of the Devil rather than his insidious presence in the mind. These limitations were evident whenever Protestants used the threat of the Devil to promote moral reform. The sin of blasphemy, for instance, was often cited as the occasion for satanic retribution. A tale from 1631 related how a blasphemer was killed by the Devil in the shape of a black dog. A tract from 1642 described how a drunkard made a toast to the fiend and invited his companions to join him in the 'damnable' oath. When they refused, he called on Satan 'to come and do it himself', and was visited by a dreadful stranger who left him insane. In a similar vein, the Gloucestershire minister Walter Powell appended a story about a 'ruffian' who drank a toast to the Devil to his treatise against ungodly oaths, *A Summons for Swearers* (1645). The unwise young man dared the Devil to come and 'pledge' him when he made the toast, with predictable consequences:

> The rest of his companions (as it was high time) hasted out of the room, and presently after, hearing a hideous noise, and smelling a stinking savour, the vintner ran up into the chamber, knowing that such a guest was there. But coming in, he missed his guest, and found the window to be broken, and the bar in the same to be bowed, with blood on the said bar.

Powell noted that this episode reached his attention as his book was being printed, and he felt impelled to add it to underline God's heavy judgments against cursers. But its message was ambiguous at best. From a theological perspective, such tales presented the Devil as the providential agent of divine justice; but they failed to communicate his dominion over fallen humanity as a whole. [23]

A similar problem occurred in some Protestant texts describing Satan's dealings with papists. One remarkable example, published in 1612, told how the Devil exacted punishment on a Catholic church in Antwerp. The author began by noting the altars, images and 'other idolatrous and superstitious relics' that adorned the building, and then described how the fiend appeared on the steeple and caused fire to rain down on the rest of the church. Holy water and crucifixes proved useless against the demonic arsonist, who proceeded to rampage through the church's interior. The fiend paid particular attention to an idolatrous picture hanging over one of the altars, which he 'spoiled and defaced . . . with his wicked nails and claws,

[so] that he almost tore the same quite down to the ground'. The moral of the story was made plain: 'God sendeth such . . . messengers unto the places wherein idolatry and superstitious ceremonies are daily used, thereby to give them warning to amend and leave all such wickedness and abomination'. In a reversal of conventional Protestant thinking, this tale portrayed Satan as the punisher of idolatry rather than its promoter. The same apparent contradiction was found in other anti-Catholic works. *A Relation of a Strange Apparition* (1641) described how the Devil disrupted the prayers of a group of Irish Catholics in a London alehouse. Here he took 'the shape of a monster, all as black as pitch, [and] as big as a great dog', and proved impervious to his victims' attempts to defend themselves with the sign of the cross and other 'popish customs'. As late as 1729, a ballad described how a papist was murdered by the Devil for committing blasphemy 'and worshipping of stone'. The fiend declared that he would carry the man to Hell to 'save the priests the trouble', and then left him dead on a muckhill with his head 'turn'd behind, his eyes sunk in [and] his tongue swell'd out'. Again, tales of this kind did little to challenge the idea that Satan attacked only obvious wrongdoers, even when his victims were members of the Roman church. [24]

Protestant murder books

While tales of satanic retribution for impious behaviour had limited value as Protestant propaganda, another popular genre appeared to be better suited for the task. This was the murder pamphlet, one of the staples of cheap literature in the sixteenth and seventeenth centuries. Works in this genre, which were the precursors of modern 'true crime' books and magazines, were written in grisly and sensational language and often accompanied by lurid woodcuts depicting murders and executions. Their appeal to Protestant proselytisers was that they offered an opportunity to depict Satan as a tempter, exploiting the weakness of human flesh to persuade men and women to commit terrible acts. Murderers could be presented as extreme examples of the depravity of human nature, and a warning to others to resist the ever-present temptations of the fiend. This message was spelled out in 1595 in the preface to *A Most Horrible & Detestable Murder Committed by a Bloudie-Minded Man Upon his Owne Wife*:

> How many most execrable murders have there been done of late time,
> which hath been published for our example to the world, thereby to
> put us in mind of our duties to God and withhold us from like trespasses
> . . . But so rageth the enemy of mankind, day and night, restlessly with
> his temptations, that he ceaseth not still to urge us to all mischief.

In an exemplary statement of reformed faith, the author enjoined
his readers to take 'such firm hold on that anchor of faith, Christ
Jesus, that neither pope nor Devil may have power to harm us'.
The rest of the book described how a Sussex miner was led by 'the
ancient enemy of our salvation' to cut his wife's throat and leave
her 'weltering in her own gore', only to be caught and hanged for
the outrage. Three years later, a similar publication described how
Satan seduced a fisherman from Rye into poisoning his wife with
rats-bane. In this case, the fiend exploited the man's desire to leave
his spouse and begin a new life abroad, and lured him with the
false hope that his crime could not be detected, 'till by his devilish
practices he had brought him to the gallows'. The Devil's role as a
master of deceit was underlined in a passage describing the fisherman's interrogation. When he claimed that he had bought the poison
for the innocent purpose of killing rats, his examiner retorted that
'the Devil is the father of liars, and I fear thou art his son'. The text
concluded by entreating God to allow others 'to withstand Satan's
temptations and eschew his subtleties, that they be not led by his
allurements nor entrapped by his snares'. [25]

Perhaps the most complete depiction of the Protestant concept
of Satan in a murder pamphlet was inspired by the case of Elizabeth
Caldwell, who was hanged for killing one of her servants in 1603. A
year later Gilbert Dugdale published a 'true discourse' on the crime,
including Caldwell's letter to her husband from prison and the
confession she made on the gallows. Assisted by her lover and two
accomplices, Caldwell had attempted to poison her husband with
rats-bane in oatcakes, but the food had been accidentally consumed
by one of her maids. She confessed to the crime and implicated
her partners, and then experienced a conversion to true religion in
the months before her execution. The beauty of this story was that
it provided a first-hand account of the Devil's temptations and their
appalling results, together with an affirmation of the saving power of
God's grace. Dugdale stated at the outset that the case was a warning to
others to guard against 'that ugly fiend (ever man's fatal opposite)', who

had exploited the 'corruptible lives' of the protagonists. He noted that only Caldwell herself had been delivered through faith from Satan's dominion, while her accomplices remained his servants. In her letter to her husband, the murderess explained how the Devil had taken advantage of her own wicked nature by sending 'his Hellish instruments' to work on her mind, 'until they made me yield to conspire with them [towards] the destruction of your body'. The rest of her letter was an appeal to all worldly people to admit their transgressions and fall on God's mercy. Caldwell expressed particular revulsion at the sin of Sabbath-breaking, which was the 'certain badge and livery' of all 'servants of the Devil'. The same preacherly tone pervaded her scaffold confession. After attributing her crime to her 'own filthy flesh, the illusions of the Devil and those Hellish instruments which he set on work', she exhorted her audience to keep the Sabbath and resist the lure of adultery, asserting that these were her 'chief and capital sins', although the world regarded them as 'a small matter'. [26]

The propaganda value of murder stories ensured that the form remained popular with Protestant educators in the seventeenth century. In 1657 a pamphlet described how a London apprentice was convicted of cutting the throat of one of his workmates and then experienced a conversion to true faith before he was hanged. A similar tract from 1668 recorded the 'wicked life and shameful-happy death' of another penitent killer. Like Dugdale's account of Elizabeth Caldwell, these texts focused on the pious deportment of the felons after their crimes, and presented their experiences as dramatic examples of Christians 'delivered out of Satan'. Other works concentrated on the Devil's role as the instigator of murder. The most extensive publication in this tradition was John Reynolds' *Triumphs of Gods Revenge Against the Crying and Execrable Sinne of Willful and Premeditated Murder* (1635), which gathered together murder stories from the whole of Europe. Reynolds' preface explained that these tales were intended as warnings against 'the snares and enticements of the Devil', though their lurid content meant that they probably attracted an audience much wider than the normal readers of pious literature. One typical story told how a French innkeeper conspired with a priest to poison a wealthy guest. The men were spurred on to the crime by Satan, who exploited their covetousness and turned their 'uncharitable contemplation into bloody actions'. The crime was eventually exposed by divine providence: God sent a wolf as 'a minister of his sacred justice and revenge' to dig up the victim's body from the innkeeper's orchard, making sure that the beast 'never touched any part of his face' for the purposes of easy identification.[27]

Stories of this kind were perhaps the most effective genre for presenting Protestant ideas of Satan to a general audience. They offered a racy and sensational context for the depiction of the Devil as the source of temptations, and could even incorporate conversion narratives similar to those found in spiritual autobiographies. Nonetheless, the genre imposed certain limitations. By their very nature, murder pamphlets implied that the fiend had a special interest in the most extreme and violent forms of wrongdoing. This tended to negate the message that humans were condemned by their fallen nature to the Devil's service. This problem was reinforced by the tendency of many writers to depict murderers as unusually sinful before they committed their crimes: most were characterised by extreme covetousness or lust, and in some cases they were identified as papists. Thus it was difficult to avoid the impression that only the most obviously wicked individuals were likely to fall prey to the Devil's wiles. In practice, many authors quietly dropped the idea that all people without faith were unwitting 'servants of Satan', or relegated it to a slightly incongruous passage outside the main body of the text.

Satanic murder in Coventry

Despite their tensions and ambiguities, Protestant murder books and tales of satanic retribution suggest the willingness of their authors to exploit popular themes for religious purposes. In 1642 this process was exemplified by Lawrence Southerne's *Fearefull Newes From Coventry*, a reworking of the ideas behind the stories of Faust and Peter Fabell. The tale described how a musician was visited on his deathbed by a handsome stranger who turned out to be Satan. The fiend murdered the man and vanished, leaving his widow to discover a chest full of gold that 'fell to dust' when she touched it. It transpired that this false treasure was the prize for which her husband had 'sold himself to the Devil, with whom he had made a contract for certain years'. Southerne's unpleasant tale re-affirmed many of the stereotypes of popular works on the same theme. The pretend gold was a motif in broadsheet ballads about the Devil in the early seventeenth century, and recurred later in tales about Mother Shipton. Similarly, the fiend's appearance was heralded by a 'mighty and tempestuous' storm like the one described in early versions of Faust. The tract also stressed the material presence of Satan in its grossly physical depiction of the musician's death: his carcass was found 'in his bed with his neck broken, to the terror of the beholders'. [28]

These themes were combined, however, with a Protestant message. Although the title page stated that the man arrived at his fate 'through covetousness and immoderate love of money', Southerne pointed out that the true cause of his damnation was his infidelity to God. He presented his fate as a warning to others to fall on the mercy of Christ. At the conclusion of the story, he also introduced the sombre doctrine of 'double predestination', which held that the elect and the damned had been chosen by God from the beginning of time. To press home this message, the tale ended with a meditation on the torments of condemned souls in Hell:

> Oh! The heavy doom of the just judgment of Almighty God, who as he hath not limited his mercies to his elect, so he hath not set or appointed an end to the punishment of the reprobate, but so far is their misery from ending that it is ever but beginning. Now then, let those damned soul-selling witches, conjurers and such like consider the miseries of eternal death. Consider it, I say, all you that forget God, lest suddenly his wrath break out upon you and he tear you in pieces.

Southerne's pamphlet represents a sophisticated attempt to marry traditional ideas about Satan with reformed theology. But it is impossible to know how such publications were received. Protestant arguments presented in popular forms could be easily misinterpreted or only partially understood, not least because of the ambiguities they inevitably contained. There was a danger that traditional beliefs would be overlaid with a veneer of Protestantism which was not fully accepted or understood. This may help to explain the emergence in popular culture of an eclectic and inconsistent set of beliefs about Satan in the course of the English Reformation. The rest of this chapter will consider this interesting *melange*. [29]

POPULAR BELIEFS AND THE PROTESTANT DEVIL

Two ballads inspired by particularly nasty murders in the reign of James I illustrate the role of demonic temptation in popular literature. *The*

Wofull Lamentation of William Purcas, composed around 1620, described
how a man cut the throat of his own mother in a 'drunken fit'.
In the other ballad, entitled *A Warning for All Murderers*, two brothers
conspired to kill their uncle in order to inherit his property. Both texts
assigned a prominent role to Satan. He was portrayed as a tempter
who exploited the particular weaknesses of the murderers and goaded
them to commit their crimes. Thus he enticed the two brothers 'to
murder, death and blood, thereby to purchase to themselves their long
desired good'. He took advantage of William Purcas' drunkenness
to persuade him to take his mother's life. To reinforce this message,
both ballads were accompanied by woodcuts depicting the fiend at
the scene of the crime. In this respect, these works were similar to the
Protestant murder pamphlets described earlier; but there is no reason
to assume that they were written as religious propaganda. Neither
of the ballads took their bloody subject matter as the starting point
for a wider discussion of the Devil's temptations. It appears, rather,
that the fiend was introduced simply to provide a motive for the kill-
ings. Moreover, *A Warning for All Murderers* was primarily a revenge
story rather than a religious tract: much of the text was devoted to
an account of the killers' capture by their uncle's son, who was born
shortly after his father had been slain. It appears that these ballads were
not composed for the purpose of religious instruction, but they nonetheless presented Satan in a typically Protestant role. This role, it seems,
reflected popular expectations. [30]

The Devil appeared as a tempter in many other secular works
produced for a general audience. A song from 1632 described how
he enticed an apprentice to speak disrespectful words about the king,
an act that caused the poor youth to be hanged for treason. In a later
ballad, he persuaded a woman to defraud her employer by claiming
she had spun eight pounds of wool when she had only done six.
The fiend's 'subtle cunning game' led to the woman's death. A more
cheerful song, entitled *Fayre Warning*, called on men and women to
resist the temptation to cheat or slander their neighbours, and promised happiness and prosperity to all those who took this advice. Its
chorus enjoined people 'to shun Satan's charms'. The Devil's love of
deception was acknowledged in other ballads that referred to him
simply as 'the liar'. All of these texts presented the fiend as a tempter
and a deceiver, but they did not develop this theme at any length or
link it to any wider religious message. It seems, rather, that the ballad-
makers simply assumed that Satan was the originator of temptation

and falsehood, and expected their audience to recognise him as such. This suggests that at least one aspect of Protestant demonism enjoyed widespread acceptance, and existed alongside a stock of other popular beliefs about the Devil. [31]

This impression is confirmed by other ballads and tales. In one striking example, probably composed around 1620, a poor man from Essex met the Devil disguised as a tall stranger wearing 'coal-black' garments, and was tempted to accept from him a purse of gold. When he returned home he discovered that the purse contained nothing but 'oaken leaves'. In despair, he returned to the stranger and fell into conversation with him. This time he was presented with a more dreadful temptation: the fiend told him to murder his 'children young and miserable wife' and then take his own life. The man ran home 'raging mad' and intent on bloodshed, but was prevented by one of his neighbours, who tied him to his bed and relieved his family's poverty 'with meat and money'. This narrative resembled folk tales about the Devil that had been in circulation since the Middle Ages: it included a typical meeting between a mortal and the evil one, and the promise of riches followed by disappointment. But it also echoed contemporary crime pamphlets that identified Satan as the source of murderous thoughts. Interestingly, it combined the idea that the Devil was the father of temptation with the popular convention of depicting him in bodily form. The belief that the fiend appeared physically to tempt people was also recorded in other contexts. In 1600 a victim of witchcraft in Norfolk claimed that she was visited by 'a little black boy with glistening eyes, tempting her and speaking to her'. The demonic apparition tried to persuade her to drown herself. The patients of Richard Napier described similar experiences. In August 1601, for example, Stephen Rawlings complained that 'the Devil tempteth him often in his sleep and appeareth to him'. These episodes resembled the encounters with Satan described in godly autobiographies, but recast him as a corporeal being rather than a presence in the mind. [32]

While the idea of satanic temptation appears to have been widely accepted in Stuart England, it is hard to know if this was the result of Protestant teaching. The Devil had been depicted as a source of impious thoughts and desires before the Reformation, though his importance in this role was increased by Protestant doctrines. It seems reasonable to assume that reformed sermons and printed propaganda reinforced the idea that Satan was a tempter, without convincing the majority of the population that his power was as ubiquitous as theologians claimed.

The presence of demonic temptation in popular texts that ignored other aspects of the Protestant Devil tends to support this view. Thus Satan could appear as a physical creature – a handsome stranger or an animal – in order to tempt or deceive unwary mortals. The source of temptation was externalized and placed within a familiar folkloric context, and the central Protestant assumption that the Devil reigned in the hearts of all 'natural' men and women was discarded.

At best, such representations involved only the partial assimilation of Protestant doctrines. A similar process was evident in other areas where reformed ideas about the Devil challenged traditional beliefs. The concept of ghosts provides an interesting illustration. As Peter Marshall has shown, English reformers denied the possibility of spirits returning from the grave, as this belief was closely linked to the discredited doctrine of purgatory. The souls of the dead were wholly separated from the living: as the Elizabethan preacher Henry Smith made clear, the dead 'hath no more society with them that live upon the earth'. Reports of ghostly visitations were therefore attributed to the Devil, and less frequently to angels. Popular literature sustained a lively interest in appearances of the dead, however. Seventeenth-century ballads such as *The Disturbed Ghost* and *The Suffolk Miracle* described the intervention of spirits in the lives of their surviving families, and implied that the dead retained ties to those they had loved or wronged on earth. Such spirits were depicted as ghosts rather than demons. In some cases, however, reports of ghosts were presented with satanic trappings. In *A Godly Warning for All Maidens*, a woman was plagued by the spirit of a spurned lover who hanged himself on her wedding day. One night she vanished from her bed: the apparition had taken her 'to what place no creature knew, nor to this day can tell'. The illustration that accompanied the tale depicted the dead lover in a winding sheet at the woman's bedside; behind him, the Devil clasped her and carried her away. Here it appears that Satan's role as a deceiver was yoked to traditional ideas about the returning dead, and the outcome was ambiguous at best. [33]

If the impact of the Protestant Devil is hard to measure in many aspects of popular culture, in one area it was obvious and direct. This was the demonisation of the Roman church. In their campaign to vilify popery, it appears that Protestant propagandists enjoyed remarkable success in exploiting and adapting traditional ideas. In particular, they managed to promote the view that the Catholic church was the instrument of Antichrist. According to one godly observer in the 1640s, it was 'now so evident and notorious' that the pope was Antichrist 'that almost every child is able to assert it'. This belief was closely linked to the assumption that popery was connected to the Devil, an idea that appears to have been equally widespread in Stuart England. [34]

The Roman Antichrist

The biblical figure of Antichrist, the beast that would rule the earth for a thousand years before the second advent of Christ, was deeply rooted in late medieval religion. Derived originally from the Book of Revelation and the letters of Paul, the creature had become the subject of a rich collection of legends during the Middle Ages. In popular mythology, it was generally assumed that when Antichrist appeared he would be intimately related to the Devil; some traditions predicted that he would be the offspring of Satan and a human bride, probably a prostitute. Medieval theologians, in contrast, assumed that he would be an uncommonly wicked man who would act as the Devil's earthly regent. English Protestants challenged both traditions by arguing that the beast was an institution rather than an individual, and asserting that this institution, the Roman church, had already reigned on earth for nearly a thousand years. Despite

The conception of Antichrist, assisted by demons, from a German pamphlet *Der Entchrist* (1475).

these revisions, however, they tended to support the popular view that Antichrist was inseparable from Satan. Thus John Olde declared in the 1550s that popish beliefs were 'the doctrines of devils', and the pope himself was 'the Devil's vicar and successor, or else the Devil himself'. Likewise, John Gough asserted in 1561 that 'the Devil now so rageth for that he seeth his kingdom and his eldest son (Antichrist of Rome) like to be overthrown'. The Protestant insistence that Antichrist was an institution was often blurred in sermons and tracts that referred to the pope as if he was the physical incarnation of the beast. This tendency was probably encouraged by the demands of popular propaganda, since it was easier to present the pope himself as Antichrist, or indeed the Devil, than to explain the Antichristian nature of the whole Roman church. [35]

The identification of the pope with Antichrist was set out in a wide range of popular publications. A play by Nathaniel Woodes in 1581 had the Devil refer to the pope as 'my eldest boy, in whom I do delight', recalling the traditional idea that Antichrist was Satan's offspring. A ballad from 1606 depicted the pontiff as 'that triple-crowned beast', assisted by fiends from the 'deeps of sulphur-flaming Hell'. In the following year, a chapbook account of a flood in Coventry included references to the machinations of the papal beast, who presided over 'false prophets, false prophecies, false miracles and false deceivers'. The outbreak of the civil war was accompanied by a deluge of cheap propaganda from both sides, much of which restated conventional views about the satanic nature of the papacy. In one satire from 1642, the pontiff addressed the Devil as his 'partner in my see of Rome'. Other texts purported to be letters from Satan to his papal viceroy, disclosing his latest plans for the spread of wickedness and superstition. A parliamentarian ballad from 1645 asserted that Catholics in the king's army were fighting under the banner of Antichrist. In the same period, the assumption that the pope was one of the monsters described in Revelation 12-13 provided the basis for a series of printed prophecies. One of the best-sellers in this genre, *The Bloody Almanack: To Which England is Directed to Fore-Know What Shall Come to Passe* (1643), offered an interpretation of the struggle between God's people and the Roman beast, which had commenced when the Lord raised up 'his first ministers and servants, Luther, Calvin, Melancthon and others, to preach out . . . the gospel publicly, which before was hid and obscured under the Antichristian reign'. The author described the defeat of 'the Antichristian and Spanish fleet' in 1588 as one of the 'marvellous indices' of Christ's imminent return. The same themes were recycled in prophecies printed throughout the rest of the century, which generally assumed that the Last Judgment would be preceded by the fall of the 'beast of Rome'. [36]

Anti-popery and the Devil

As well as the papacy, the whole Catholic church was routinely linked with the Devil in popular literature. At its crudest, this involved the depiction of Satan as a member of the Roman clergy. In the earliest version of the Faust legend, the Devil first appeared 'in the manner of a grey friar'. Subsequently, the magician instructed him always to assume this guise, 'that he might know of his certain coming'. The motif of the Devil as a friar recurred in seventeenth-century ballads. In *The Devil Transformed*, for example, the fiend took on a series of shapes before finally disguising himself 'in a friar's old weed'. In a variation on this idea, another ballad described a meeting between a friar and the fiend, in which they discussed which of them was the most wicked. The friar admitted that the fiend was his father, and described himself as 'a doctor of evil'. The relationship between priestcraft and Satan was reinforced by claims that papists delighted in trafficking with demons. Elizabethan chapbooks affirmed that priests excelled in witchcraft and sorcery, and the legend that Pope Alexander VI had sold his soul to the Devil was the subject of stage plays in the early seventeenth century. This theme was revived in a bizarre chapbook in 1652. Purporting to be the confession of the murderer Giles Fenderlin, 'who killed his wife and sold his soul to the Devil', this tract suggested that Fenderlin's crimes were initiated by a Jesuit, who persuaded him to make a compact with Satan in return for special powers. The priest 'drew up a covenant and delivered it to him in Latin', together with a magical ring which allowed him to travel invisibly over great distances. Unfortunately for Fenderlin, these powers lasted for only five years, and when they expired he was unable to renew his arrangement with the diabolical priest. He subsequently killed his wife and was committed to gaol, where he was tormented by the Devil 'in the perfect shape of a bishop'. [37]

   As these illustrations suggest, it was more common for the popish clergy to be vilified in this way than the community they served. On some occasions, however, the entire Catholic population was depicted as satanic. Such allegations usually coincided with news of popish insurrections or threats from abroad. The defeat of the Armada and the discovery of the gunpowder plot were celebrated in anti-popish ballads, chapbooks and drama, which tended to emphasise the diabolical nature of the whole popish community. The latter event was commemorated with feasts and bonfires on the 5th November, with Romish trinkets and effigies of the pope burned alongside those of the Devil in some parishes. In the wake of the Irish rebellion in November 1641, which was accompanied by rumours of particularly vicious atrocities against the Protestant settlers, a series of tracts declared the rebels' allegiance to 'his Hellish majesty'. In one pamphlet, papists were described as 'obedient and well-affected children' of the Devil, who took great care to preserve 'their church and ceremonies'. Another text included a lament from Satan that 'the God the English serve' was too powerful for the rebels to overcome, and 'their beads and holy water can't protect them'. [38]

It is striking that many of the anti-Catholic references in popular literature appeared in works that were not written primarily as attacks on the Roman church. The appearance of Jesuits as devils or black magicians was often incidental to the stories in which they occurred. The role of popery in the tale of Giles Fenderlin, for example, was peripheral to the main narrative of his crimes. Equally, demonic friars often had little more than walk-on parts in ballads and chapbooks, which were composed mainly as entertainments rather than anti-Roman propaganda. This suggests that the satanic nature of Catholicism was sufficiently well known to be taken for granted: the theme could be dropped into popular texts of all kinds without any need for explanation. It is also notable that attacks on popery as 'the Devil's creed' often appeared in works that displayed little sympathy for zealous Protestantism. Some of the pamphlets that described the Irish rebels as Satan's army also mocked the excesses of 'puritan' religion. This was exemplified by *A Disputation Betwixt the Devill and the Pope*, which contained the following report from the Devil to the pontiff on the state of England in 1642:

> There all your books and beads are counted toys,
> Altars and tapers are pulled down by boys . . .
> The clean washed surplice which our priests put on
> There is the smock of the Whore of Babylon . . .
> There, pope, you must expect a certain loss,
> A tailor must not sit with legs on cross,

But straight he's set by th'heels, (It is a sign
Of ceremony, only not divine).

This text poked fun at the excessive zeal of puritan reformers – who supposedly condemned leg-crossing as an ungodly 'sign of ceremony' – while affirming that the Roman church belonged to the Devil. Such publications suggest that both moderate and 'zealous' Protestants accepted the kinship between popery and Satan by the middle years of the seventeenth century, and the idea was established as a motif in popular culture. [39]

This did not mean, of course, that ordinary people accepted the Protestant concept of Satan in its entirety. It appears, rather, that one aspect of reformed thinking was assimilated into a pre-existing set of beliefs, which remained otherwise remarkably unchanged. This led to some fascinating contradictions. In some cases, popular texts combined the idea that popery was satanic with folkloric traditions about the Devil. The ballad *The Devil's Oak*, for instance, began with the meeting between Satan and a friar that was described earlier; but its last verse described how the fiend was deceived by a crafty tinker, who caused him to fall down and break his horns. Another song told how the Devil was subjected to a series of humiliating assaults before he ran away in the shape of a friar. Both these works presented the fiend as a subject of comedy rather than a powerful and terrible force, but they also accepted the diabolical nature of Catholicism. In a rather different vein, the chapbook version of *The Merry Devil of Edmonton* (1631) combined anti-popery with profoundly non-Protestant sentiments. After making his pact with the Devil, the magician Peter Fabell proceeded to mock the hypocrisy and greed of the Roman church. In one story, he came upon a lecherous friar who had abandoned his 'book and beads' to fornicate with a young woman. Fabell disguised himself as an angel and commanded the couple to perform a penance or 'live in despair and die [as] damned wretches'. This passage recalled the escapades of Marlowe's Faust, who also used demonic powers to play tricks on papists; but unlike Faust, Fabell repeatedly outwitted the Devil and escaped damnation at the end of the story. The same elements were combined in an early eighteenth-century ballad, *The Wonder: or The Devil Outwitted*. In this text a 'lover in distress' entered a pact with a demon in order to win the heart of a young woman. In return, he was obliged to keep the creature constantly occupied with tasks; if it ever fell idle he

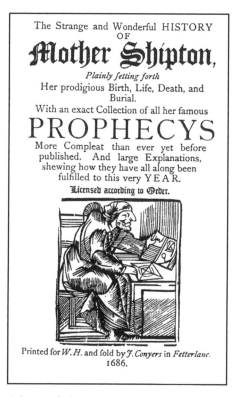

Title page of *The Strange and Wonderful History of Mother Shipton* (1686).

would lose his soul. The man sent the demon on a series of improbable missions, all of which were completed at lightning speed. He then sent it to Rome in the hope that it would be overwhelmed by 'holy water and the pope', but the creature returned swiftly to mock him with a parcel of useless 'bulls and pardons'. Eventually, the man's dilemma was solved by his resourceful lover, who gave the demon the never-ending task of looking after her hair. Like *The Merry Devil*, this ballad mixed anti-popery with a comic depiction of Satan and the belief that he could be outwitted. [40]

Perhaps the most curious example of the combination of anti-popery with popular beliefs was provided by Mother Shipton. Despite her close acquaintance with the Devil, the Yorkshire seer was credited with a series of robustly anti-Roman prophecies in the second half of the seventeenth century. According to a tract in 1667, she successfully foretold the sufferings of Protestant martyrs 'under the bloody hands of Bonner, bishop of London'. She also predicted the defeat of the Armada, 'a victory so remarkable that [neither] time nor age will ever wear the remembrance thereof away'. As the same text affirmed, these landmarks in England's Protestant history were foreseen by a woman who was fathered by Satan and widely regarded as a witch, despite the 'great esteem' in which she was universally held. It was noted earlier that the demonisation of Mother Shipton showed the continuing vitality of medieval attitudes towards the Devil; equally, the anti-popish elements in her legend suggest that hatred of Catholicism had struck deep roots in English culture. This peculiar outcome tends to support the conclusions of research on the English Reformation as a whole. Christopher Haigh has argued that the majority of churchgoers were not converted to Protestantism by the end of the sixteenth century, but they could not be defined as Catholics either: they were 'de-Catholicized but un-Protestantized'. In a similar way, it seems that traditional attitudes towards the Devil were overlaid with anti-Roman sentiments in the Tudor and Stuart age. The set of beliefs that emerged from this process was neither wholly Catholic nor Protestant, but a *melange* of apparently incongruous ideas. The mixing together of traditional assumptions and Protestant teaching has been noted by another historian of the Reformation, Tessa Watt. She has advised historians to be mindful of the capacity of cultures 'to absorb new beliefs while retaining old ones, to forge hybrid forms, to accommodate contradictions and ambiguities'. By the end of the seventeenth century, it appears that a diverse and contradictory collection of ideas about Satan was accepted by most of the English population. These ideas might have made little sense to Protestant theologians, but they apparently met the needs of ordinary men and women. [41]

5

WOMEN AND THE DEVIL

According to legend, St Margaret of Antioch was devoured by
the Devil in the form of a dragon. The monster's meal was ill-
chosen, however: its body dissolved into air once the saint had
been consumed, leaving her standing unharmed in a sea of celestial
light. St Margaret's narrow escape illustrates the gendered nature of
late medieval depictions of encounters with Satan. Margaret's role
was essentially passive, and her triumph was accomplished entirely
through divine intervention. The contrast with St George, another
dragon-slaying saint celebrated in medieval religious culture, was
clear: while George attacked and destroyed the beast through
martial force, Margaret was consumed and rescued by a miracle.
Both saints were agents of God's earthly power, but they expressed
this power in ways that reflected conventional assumptions about
gender in medieval society. [1]

   While the Reformation diminished the status of the saints,
Protestant representations of the Devil remained strongly gendered.
The reception of Protestant ideas depended largely on pre-existing
assumptions, and these ensured that perceptions of Satan reflected
the pervasive influence of male beliefs about female nature. Equally,
the Protestant Devil was adapted to the particular life experiences of
early modern women. It is beyond the scope of this book to account
for the variety of religious experiences available to women in
Elizabethan and Stuart England, and any generalisations about them
must be advanced with a good deal of caution. Nonetheless, there is
sufficient evidence to suggest that women's perceptions of the Devil
were distinctive in several ways: they tended to focus on traditional
female 'weaknesses' such as vanity, and were often connected with
domestic relationships. For Protestant women, moreover, the 'voice
of Satan' could express the anxieties and temptations which often

arose from the practical circumstances of family life, and which were otherwise denied any legitimate expression. [2]

The first part of this chapter deals with contemporary perceptions of the relationship between women and the Devil, and draws largely on literature produced by men. These perceptions, which combined traditional assumptions with the insights of reformed theology, provided the context in which many women conceived of the evil one. The power of these ideas is apparent in the writings of godly women, which are considered in section two. These suggest that many conventional assumptions were internalised by female authors, giving a distinctive flavour to their conflicts with Satan. Their references to the Devil also indicate the tensions which could emerge between wives and their husbands, and show that religion could offer a psychological resource for coping with these problems. The final part of the chapter considers the impact of the Reformation on 'charismatic' women, who claimed to possess special gifts from the Holy Spirit. It argues that the claims of these women were normally rejected by Protestant churchmen, who preferred to understand their behaviour as symptoms of demonic possession. This tendency effectively suppressed a tradition of female spirituality that had flourished in the late Middle Ages, and placed visionary women under the control of men.

REPRESENTATIONS OF WOMEN AND THE DEVIL

An anonymous tract printed in 1655 carried the enticing title *The Reign of the Devil*. This was not, as one might expect, another Protestant commentary on the depraved state of humankind under the earthly rule of Satan, but a description of the unruly behaviour of women. The 'Devil's reign' of the title was illustrated by a series of grisly domestic murders committed by women, and explained by the volatile and treacherous nature of the female mind. A few years later, another pamphlet warned men against a different but equally terrible threat posed by the opposite sex: 'the pox' or venereal disease. This depicted the female body as one of the snares of Satan, and delighted in the title *The Devil Incarnate*. As these texts suggest, the connection between women and the Devil was well established by the middle of the seventeenth century. It was even possible to depict Satan himself as a woman, particularly in the guise of the whore of

Babylon, who combined the traditionally feminine traits of 'proud attire' and sexual lust. The proliferation of such imagery was hardly surprising in the context of English Protestantism, with its emphasis on the innate sinfulness of human desires. It appears that many godly men identified the demonic temptations of the flesh with a rapacious model of female sexuality, epitomised by the image of the 'Romish whore'. The fear that lustful women could entice men to Satan was summed up by Nicholas Breton in 1616: 'a wanton woman is the figure of imperfection, an ape in quality, a wagtail in countenance, a witch, and in condition a kind of devil: her beck is a net, her word a charm, her look an illusion, and her company a confusion'. [3]

In the light of such publications, it is hard to dispute Jerome Friedman's observation that discovering seventeenth-century texts that castigate women 'is only a little more difficult than finding shells at the seashore'. It may be surprising, therefore, to find that the Protestant theology of Satan was not entirely hostile to women. Indeed, it actually provided a theoretical argument for equality between the sexes. This argument, which proved to be limited in practice, will be considered below, followed by a more general discussion of the representation of women and the Devil in popular literature. [4]

Satan and the social role of women

The Protestant argument for sexual equality was based on the bleak premise that men and women were so utterly depraved by sin, and enthralled by nature to the power of the Devil, that there was no spiritual difference between them. Luther himself argued that Adam and Eve were equally culpable in the fall of humankind; and this idea was taken up by several English theologians under Elizabeth and the early Stuarts. Some writers, such as the Catholic convert Richard Carpenter, went so far as to argue that 'the greatest fault' should be attributed to Adam, since he was persuaded to disobey God by a mere mortal, whereas Eve had been deceived by the more formidable powers of Satan himself. These rather esoteric ideas were complemented by a more practical consideration: reformed religion obliged both sexes to join in 'spiritual combat' with the tempter. According to William Gouge, 'neither ministers nor people, poor nor rich, male nor female' were exempted from this duty. This presumption was reiterated in his best-selling guide to 'domestical duties', which insisted that both 'husbands and wives ought to be careful to keep one another from

the temptations of Satan, that is, from sin, whereunto all his temptations tend'. In extreme situations, this obligation could even be used
to justify wifely disobedience: Gouge asserted that women should
defy their husbands if they asked them to commit obvious sins, such as
visiting the theatre or going 'garishly and whorishly attired'. [5]

There is some evidence that these ideas created opportunities for
women to escape from the social conventions that normally restricted
their behaviour. Certainly, it appears that godly women among the
gentry were prepared to condemn the actions of impious or 'superstitious' men. During a visit to York in 1600, Margaret Hoby noted in
her diary that one of the town's beneficed ministers had preached
'false' doctrine; on another occasion she expressed her distaste for the
views of Thomas Bilson, the anti-puritan bishop of Winchester. For
women such as Hoby, the reformed faith entailed an involvement in
the kind of theological and political debates that were traditionally
reserved for their male superiors. The implications of this were most
obvious during the fierce religious disputes of the early 1640s, when
many godly women were outspoken supporters of the campaign to
'purify' the English church. In her autobiography, Jane Turner recalled
that she was repelled by what she regarded as the quasi-Catholic
'innovations' promoted by Charles I in the 1630s, and driven by her
religious convictions to support the parliament at the outbreak of
the civil war. Writing to her daughter in 1640, Anna Temple rejoiced
that the parish churches of Warwickshire were being stripped of their
popish trappings, and looked forward to the abolition of 'idolatry and
superstition' throughout the land. To Temple, the campaign for church
reform appears to have been a natural extension of her faith: she
concluded her letter by noting that 'sin was grown to a great height,
but let it be our care to keep our hearts close to God in the use of his
ordinances, and to avoid every sin, and seek to him to keep us from
the temptations of Satan'. Since educated and reasonably wealthy
women such as Turner and Temple were able to leave their own
records, their political activities are relatively easy to reconstruct. It is
much harder, however, to discover the practices of godly women from
lower social ranks. There is a clue, perhaps, in the fact that women
generally outnumbered men in the religious sects that emerged in the
1640s and 1650s. At least one woman, Martha Simmonds, assumed a
prominent role among the early Quakers, and appears briefly to have
challenged the position of George Fox as the leader of the movement.
The prominence of women within the sects suggests that the concept

Consumed by vanity, a woman is unaware of the trap laid by the Devil. From the English edition of Sebastain Brant, *The Ship of Fooles* (1570).

of spiritual equality could sometimes overcome traditional assumptions about female inferiority, and implies that this phenomenon was not confined to members of the gentry.[6]

Despite these considerations, however, there are good reasons to assume that the Protestant theory of sexual equality was strictly limited in practice. First, committed Protestants made up a minority of the population, and most people were probably untouched by the theological arguments developed by men such as William Gouge. Secondly, English divines were careful to limit their arguments for equality to the spiritual sphere. Thus Stephen Geree asserted in 1639 that women were equal to men in matters pertaining to salvation, for 'grace makes men and women excel'; but in all other respects they were inferior to men. Other English divines followed Luther in arguing that women were inferior by nature: they had been created by God for the purposes of child-raising and home-making, and were constitutionally incapable of more manly pursuits. In practice, this allowed writers like Stephen Bateman, Philip Stubbes and Gouge to re-affirm the traditional female weaknesses of vanity, inconstancy, and intellectual dullness, while preserving the idea that women were spiritually equal to men. Bateman characterised the sin of pride as a peculiarly feminine trait, while Stubbes devoted a whole chapter of his *Anatomie of Abuses* (1583) to 'a particular description of the abuses of women's apparel'. He noted that face paints were 'the Devil's inventions to entangle poor souls in the nets of perdition', and observed that looking glasses were 'the Devil's spectacles to allure us to pride'. Likewise, Gouge argued that the natural limitations of women meant that they should normally be subject to their husbands' will.[7]

The distinction between 'natural' and 'spiritual' qualities was a helpful device for preserving male authority, but it was a rather ambiguous and difficult position to maintain. On one hand, it was not easy to draw the line between spiritual and secular affairs, particularly given the Protestant insistence that religion should be paramount in all areas of life. This left open the possibility that women could assume a leading role in the religious duties of the household, and even participate in public controversies when these touched on matters of faith. On the other hand, some thinkers were tempted to assume that women's natural limitations could affect their relationship with God and the Devil. Stephen Bateman, for instance, illustrated the sin of pride with a woodcut depicting a woman holding a looking glass, resting one foot on a skull, while the Devil stood behind her and mocked her vanity. His text explained that 'the woman signifieth pride, the glass in her hand flattery or deceit, the Devil behind her temptation, the death-head which she setteth her foot on signifieth forgetfulness of the life to come, whereby commeth destruction'. The implication of the print was that women's natural weaknesses made them more vulnerable to the fiend. The same tendency was apparent when Protestant authors addressed the tricky subject of witchcraft. In theory, both sexes were equally subject to Satan's influence, but the predominance of women in witch trials led some theologians to claim that they were especially susceptible to the Devil's wiles. Most famously, James I argued that 'that sex is frailer than man is, so it is easier to be entrapped in these gross snares of the Devil'. Similar views, including the belief that women's vanity and lust made them easy prey for the tempter, were repeated in religious texts throughout the Tudor and Stuart period. [8]

The careers of godly women reflected the ambiguous and limited opportunities created for them by Protestant ideas. Margaret Hoby and Jane Turner were prepared to express strong views on issues of religious controversy, but also acknowledged the 'natural' frailties of their gender and generally deferred to their husbands in secular matters. Hoby privately condemned the falsehood of anti-puritan preachers, but appears to have confined her own evangelising work to the servants in her kitchen. Turner defied the religious censorship of the 1630s to track down godly books that had been condemned by her parish minister, but she delayed the publication of her autobiography in 1653 because she feared that Satan would use it to 'exalt me in my own thoughts'. Similarly, the sectarian women of the 1650s rarely emerged as religious leaders in their own right, and even Martha Simmonds had been marginalised by the male hierarchy of the Quaker movement by the end of the decade. It was, of course, always unlikely that Protestant doctrines would undermine deeply entrenched conventions of sexual inequality, even among those most committed to the reformed faith. They appear to have made even less impact on the population at large, where cheap literature routinely challenged the view that men and women were equally sinful before God. This literature is considered below. [9]

Women and the Devil in cheap print

Encounters between women and Satan were one of the staples of popular literature in the sixteenth and seventeenth centuries. The most common accounts can be divided roughly into three types. The first genre was 'judgment' tales, which focused on the supernatural punishment of individuals guilty of particular sins. Despite their salacious and unpleasant content, these stories often purported to convey a serious religious message, which made them a useful medium for the kind of Protestant propaganda described in the previous chapter. The second genre was accounts of witchcraft, usually precipitated by actual cases and drawing to some extent on the records of trials. Finally, comic stories depicted meetings between resourceful women and the fiend, normally framed within the conventions of folklore and presented in merry ballads. Each of these genres tended to emphasise the traditionally feminine qualities of pride, inconstancy and sexual desire, though the comic tales also presented women as guileful actors who were capable of outwitting the fiend.

A typical judgment story, published in 1600, related the sad experiences of an unnamed 'young maiden' from Colwall in Herefordshire. She pledged to marry a youth from the village but broke off the engagement, and then 'fell a lusting' for one of her cousins with whom she worked as a servant in her uncle's house. As a result of their illicit union, she gave birth to a 'monstrous' child that died soon after its delivery. The role of the Devil in this tragedy was made clear at each stage: first, it was 'Satan, the enemy of all goodness, [who] by his instigations and instruments wrought so in the mind of the maiden' that she broke off her match; subsequently, he 'so blinded the eyes' of the woman and her new lover 'that they lay together and she was gotten with child by him'. The author also noted that the woman's natural weaknesses made her peculiarly vulnerable to the snares of the fiend:

> Such is the lightness and inconstancy of a great number of this sex . . .
> [that] they are many times in extremes: for, either they will not at all be
> ruled by their parents and friends in marriage, or else, when with their
> parents' and friends' consent, they have assured themselves, and entan-
> gled the minds of young men, yet upon some sinister course they will
> flit off again; yea, and sometimes get a great belly by some such match,
> and so break off, with all the shame that may be.

While the tract offered a brief warning to young men that they
could also expect punishment from God for fornication, it made no
reference to the fate of the cousin and failed to link his sin to the
'inconstancy' of his gender. The tale concluded by enjoining young
women to practice 'fasting, prayer, modesty in apparel, looks, gesture
and countenance'. [10]

The same didactic tone was adopted in another tale about a
'monstrous birth', *God's Handy-Worke in Wonders* (1615). This
unpleasant text concerned the benighted relationship between a
woman and her debauched husband. When she found herself to be
pregnant, she begged her spouse 'to tarry at home' and abandon the
company of prostitutes and his wicked friends. He refused to do so
and cursed her, causing her to exclaim that she would rather give
birth to 'the Devil of Hell' than continue to live in the 'woe and
misery wherewithall thou dost so vex me'. Having thus sealed her
fate, she gave birth to a hideously deformed child. Again, the author
depicted the woman's sin as typical of her gender, and hoped that
her fate 'may be a looking glass unto every wedded woman, whereby
to refrain [from] casting out such unadvised words'. The tract
entreated wives to have patience with their husbands 'and commit
all matters to almighty God'. A similar message was conveyed in *A
Good Warning for all Maidens*, a broadside ballad telling how the Devil
deceived a young woman into betraying her lover, and then stole
away her child on the 'woeful night' that it was born. Tales of God's
punishment of evil women were particularly abundant in the decade
after the civil war. In one well publicised incident in 1645, the birth
of a deformed child in Leicestershire proved not only the immorality
of the unfortunate mother but the wickedness of the whole region,
since 'no other part of England hath had so many witches'. The ultimate cause of such judgments was spelt out in a pamphlet in 1653,
which observed that women were the 'instruments and immediate
causes of murder, idolatry and a multitude of other heinous sins'.

They were, the author concluded, faithful servants of 'their great lord and master, Lucifer'. [11]

The image of evil women presented in judgment books was complemented by cheap tracts about witchcraft. The role of women in English witch trials has been the subject of intense debate. James Sharpe has argued that women played an unusually active role in the prosecution of witches: they furnished allegations against suspects, appeared as witnesses in trials, and sometimes acted as searchers for incriminating marks on the bodies of the accused. This interpretation has been challenged by Clive Holmes, who suggests that men normally took the lead in initiating prosecutions, with women providing only supporting evidence. Whichever of these views is correct, there can be little doubt that women were more likely than men to appear as defendants in these cases. They were also far more prominent in popular accounts of the crime. Even fictitious female characters such as Mother Shipton were sometimes transformed into witches as their stories were elaborated in successive editions. The assumption that witches were usually female was also noted by sceptical observers of the beliefs of the 'common sort of people'. Reginald Scot, for instance, observed in 1584 that those most often suspected of the crime were 'women, which be commonly old, lame, blear-eyed, pale, foul, and full of wrinkles'. That this cultural assumption was influential in the prosecution of real witches is suggested by a list of 'presumptions against witches' drawn up for Yorkshire JPs in the 1590s: the first presumption was that 'they are most commonly weak women'. [12]

While it is easy to demonstrate that ordinary people regarded witchcraft as a typically female vice, the connection between witches and the Devil is more problematic. Many historians now dispute the view, set out in the pioneering work of Alan Macfarlane and Keith Thomas in the 1970s, that accusations of witchcraft in England lacked the elements of diabolism that characterised allegations in Scotland and mainland Europe. The nature of the Devil's relationship with English witches was highly complex, however, and the subject will therefore receive more detailed consideration in chapter seven. For now, it is sufficient to note that popular accounts of witchcraft frequently linked the crime to the Devil. In 1566 the first printed description of the trial and execution of a witch claimed that the accused woman had named her familiar spirit 'Satan'. A chapbook report of a witch trial in Windsor in 1579 claimed that the accused had performed magic with the help of 'a wicked spirit' and 'the Devil'. Ten years later, another pamphlet described a witch 'invocating upon Satan' and offering her soul to the fiend. In *A Newe Ballad of the Life and Deaths of Three Witches* (1589), three women hanged for witchcraft in Chelmsford were described as 'Satan's fiends', who 'cried the Devil's name'. The satanic nature of witchcraft had become a commonplace in cheap print by the middle of the seventeenth century. In 1653 a chapbook recorded how Ann Bodenham, a witch from Salisbury, caused her followers to write their names in blood 'in the Devil's book'. Later that year, another pamphlet reported that a Cornish witch was obliged every month 'to send the Devil on some destructive errand'. By this period, the links between women, witchcraft and Satan were entwined in the fantasy that the fiend enjoyed sexual intercourse with his female disciples. As a newsbook explained in 1645, 'the female being the weaker sex, and the inclinations of the flesh being prone unto lust, the Devil maketh choice by that way most to oblige his servants, which by nature most they are addicted to'. [13]

A much lighter and slightly more positive portrayal of women was offered in comic ballads describing the Devil's misadventures on earth. Typically, these songs described how the fiend's plans to destroy some unfortunate man were thwarted by the unexpected intervention of a woman. In *The Devil Gelded*, for instance, a quick-thinking baker's wife saved her husband from being castrated by Satan, while the heroine of *The Wonder* prevented her young lover from losing his soul to a demon. In these and other tales, women rescued men from apparently hopeless situations in which they had trapped themselves, normally by making foolish bets with the Devil. It is tempting to view these ballads as celebrations of the intelligence and courage of their female protagonists, but this would probably be a mistake. First, it is quite likely that the strong roles given to women in these tales were intended for comic effect: they represented a jocular reversal of normal social expectations, and served to underline the haplessness of the male characters. Viewed in this way, the ballads actually reinforced conventional assumptions about women. Secondly, the female characters in comic ballads often defeated the Devil by behaviour that was perceived as typical of their sex, and was regarded as a vice rather than a virtue in most other contexts. Thus a ballad from the 1620s described how the fiend was driven from London by 'the poor women that cry fish and oysters', whose sharp tongues and unruly conduct were more than he could endure. Similarly, the fiend was overwhelmed by the unquenchable vanity of the heroine of *The Wonder*, and ended the tale working as her hairdresser. Finally, the punch-line of some 'merry tales' was that women were actually *worse* than the Devil. This was exemplified by a sixteenth-century ballad about a man who was so abused by his wife that he asked Satan to take her away. The fiend accepted his offer, but returned her after she had given him more pain than 'a hundred years in Hell'. In sum, it seems that comic depictions of women and the Devil did not really challenge prevailing ideas about the weaknesses of the 'fair sex', and probably confirmed many conventional beliefs about female behaviour. [14]

THE PERCEPTIONS OF GODLY WOMEN

The cultural assumptions described above provided the context in which religious women experienced 'spiritual combats' with Satan. The idea that women were particularly sensitive to the presence of the Devil pre-dated the Reformation, and was apparently confirmed by the mystical experiences of pious women in the fifteenth century such as Julian of Norwich and Margery Kempe. The opening pages of Kempe's *Book*, which is generally regarded as the earliest autobiography in the English language, describe her encounters with the fiend and tempestuous visions of Hell, where she saw 'devils opening their mouths all alight with burning flames of fire, as if they would have swallowed her in, pawing at her, sometimes threatening her, sometimes pulling her and hauling her about both night and day'. [15]

Kempe's acute awareness of the Devil was echoed by many women in the Tudor and Stuart age. During the 1630s, John Bunyan overheard some 'poor women' in Bedford describe their own less dramatic, but equally intense confrontations with Satan. His account presents a remarkable vignette of the beliefs of ordinary women committed to the reformed faith, and deserves to be quoted at length:

> They talked [of] how God had visited their souls with his love in the Lord Jesus, and with what words and promises they had been refreshed, comforted, and supported against the temptations of the Devil; moreover, they reasoned of the suggestions and temptations of Satan in particular, and told each other by which they had been afflicted, and how they were borne up under his assaults: they also discoursed of their own wretchedness of heart, of their unbelief, and did condemn, slight and abhor their own righteousness, as filthy and insufficient to do them any good.

Bunyan's text suggests that the Protestant theology of Satan provided some women with a framework for understanding and describing their spiritual experiences, and shows that these experiences could be the topic of lively discussions amongst them. Frustratingly though, it reveals nothing about the content of the Devil's 'temptations', and offers no clues that they were significantly different to those endured by men. It is possible, however, to discover the nature of Satan's 'assaults' in the numerous spiritual autobiographies and meditations composed by women in the seventeenth century. These suggest that Protestant women internalised conventional assumptions about the limitations of the female mind, and perceived them-

A late fifteenth-century depiction of Satan seducing a woman. The idea that the fiend seduced his female disciples resurfaced in English witch trials in the 1640s.

selves to be especially vulnerable to demonic attempts to exploit these weaknesses. They also show that women often experienced their most intense struggles with the spiritual enemy in the context of difficult family relationships. It seems that Satan was most likely to intervene when women were unhappy with their domestic circumstances, and their efforts to overcome him can be viewed as attempts to come to terms with the practical frustrations of their lives. [16]

Satan and the sin of pride

The tendency for women to internalise the idea that they were particularly vulnerable to the sin of pride was not confined to the godly. Margaret Cavendish, the fiercely anti-puritan duchess of Newcastle, wrote in 1653 that vanity was 'so natural to our sex' that it would be abnormal if she did not suffer from it. At the opposite end of the social spectrum, a woman executed for murder in 1655 ignored the chaplain who entreated her to repent before she went to her death, but 'only cried out against pride, saying that that was the cause that brought her to this miserable end, and desired that all women take warning by her example thereof'. Similar sentiments were expressed in the confessions of female witches in East Anglia in 1645. Thus Ellen Driver and Elizabeth Warne confessed that 'pride was the cause' of their witchcraft. [17]

For women intensely committed to the reformed faith, however, the daily struggle to overcome the Devil's temptations meant that the conquest of pride assumed particular importance. In an essay on the 'puritan deathbed', Ralph Houlbrooke has observed that dying women were more likely than men to engage in lengthy combats with the Devil in their final hours, and speculates that their heightened awareness of his presence was 'because of the impression made on them by Eve's fall'. This point can be taken further, perhaps, since it appears that many of these women believed themselves to be especially guilty of the original sin of pride. This was most explicit at the deathbed of Katherine Brettergh, who 'accused herself of pride, that she had delighted too much in herself and her beauty'. She exclaimed that she 'wished that she had never been born, or that she had been made any other creature, rather than a woman'. Despite her acute sense of her own vulnerability, Brettergh overcame Satan by telling him 'to reason not with me' but with Christ, who intervened to save her from the fiend. The belief that women had a peculiar susceptibility to pride was also expressed by Elizabeth Jocelyn in *The Mother's Legacie* (1624), a collection of spiritual advice addressed to her unborn child. Jocelyn implored her offspring to shun the vanity of 'new fangled fashions' in dress, 'whether thou be [a] son or daughter'. She added, however, that 'if a daughter, I confess thy task is harder because thou art weaker, and thy temptations to this vice greater'. For Jocelyn, this meant that her daughter would be more exposed to the temptations of the enemy, who 'is always busy and ready at hand to draw thee away from God'. [18]

It is, of course, impossible to know how women's awareness of pride affected their daily lives, but a tantalising clue is provided in the diary of Lady Margaret Hoby. In January 1600 Hoby chastised herself for speaking 'of something not so as I ought', and resolved to be 'more watchful hereafter that I so grossly offend not my God'. The next day she was assaulted by the 'malice' of Satan, but found comfort in her private prayers and the devotional writings of Thomas Cartwright. Three weeks later, another entry in the diary hinted strongly at the nature of her previous sin: she had spent the afternoon discussing parish affairs with her husband and the minister, Mr Rhodes, 'yet though I were with all the company, it pleased God to free me from sundry temptations wherunto I had before been subject'. It appears that Hoby had suppressed her desire to speak inappropriately in the presence of her husband and the minister, and that she had previously succumbed to a similar temptation. If this interpretation is correct, it is reasonable to assume that her earlier struggle with the Devil had been occasioned by her proud behaviour in speaking 'not so as I ought', and her victory over temptation had prevented her from committing the sin again. Hoby's diary provides an insight into the social pressures that shaped the religious experiences of godly women, and suggests that satanic temptations could arise from the practical limitations imposed on their lives. In turn, the conquest of these temptations could restore women to their 'proper' role within the household. This process was demonstrated most explicitly in situations of extreme domestic tension, which are considered below. [19]

Satan and the troubled household

The connection between Satan and domestic strife was not invented by the Reformation. Some of the most memorable passages in Margery Kempe's autobiography described how her 'combats' with the Devil arose in the context of her troubled marriage, which ended when she admitted that she 'would rather have eaten and drunk the ooze and muck in the gutter' than have sex with her husband. Many more accounts of this kind were written, however, by Protestant autobiographers in the Tudor and Stuart period. A small number of godly men linked Satan's temptations with their anxieties about domestic life, such as the London apprentice who noted in 1643 that 'Satan followed me and suggested unto me that it were best for me to leave my wife and children'. But it was more common for women to describe the work of the tempter in this way, a fact that probably reflected their greater investment in family life and the particular restrictions that it imposed upon them. [20]

Unsurprisingly, the Devil made his most dramatic appearances at times when wives were very unhappy with their spouses. In 1652 a woman described as 'M.K.', one of the anonymous contributors to Vavasor Powell's collection of 'spiritual experiences', told how her husband disported himself 'with some company which did not only cause much time to be spent in idleness, but almost all of our means'. After he befriended a particularly offensive drunkard, M.K. implored him tearfully 'to refrain [from] that man's company, or at least not to suffer him to come so often home to our house'. Her entreaties failed; and this point 'the Devil set his foot into my heart' by suggesting the murder of her husband's friend. She was immediately overwhelmed by guilt, and managed to defeat the temptation through strenuous prayer. In the days that followed, however, she was assailed by satanic thoughts and visions of Hell, imagining that demons 'waited in every corner, and behind every door to snatch me away'. Her torments reached a climax one night when a 'little dog' jumped on her bed and she 'thought it was the Devil who was come to take me away'. This episode was apparently the catalyst for her spiritual recovery: it forced her to throw herself on the mercy of Christ, who empowered her to resist the fiend's temptations and patiently accept her lot. A similar pattern was evident in the brief memoir of Mary Burrill published in 1653. Burrill confessed that 'I have been infinitely troubled by my marriage to my second husband, and have been afflicted in conscience about it very much, till my Lord gave me comfort within that my sins were forgiven me'. During her period of affliction, Burrill experienced in her dreams 'two terrible conflicts with Satan', which ended in her victory over the enemy through the power of 'God's love'. [21]

As well as overt conflicts between wives and their husbands, periods of frequent or prolonged absence between spouses could create tensions for the Devil to exploit. In the most spectacular, if not the most typical case of this kind, Elizabeth Caldwell succumbed to the fiend's temptation to kill her husband in 1604. In a letter to her intended victim written after her conviction for attempted murder, she invited him to 'remember in what a case you have lived, how poor you have many times left me, how long you have been absent from me, all which advantage the Devil took to subvert me'. She described how Satan 'continually wrought upon my weakness, my poverty, and your absence', until she was driven to contemplate murder. Less dramatic but probably more common was the experience of Hannah Allen, who recalled how 'the Devil had the more advantage' of her during her marriage in the 1650s, 'occasioned by the oft absence of my dear and affectionate husband, with whom I lived present and absent about eight years'. Allen was afflicted with further 'great strugglings' with the Devil after her husband's death at sea in 1663. For

1. The Roman Antichrist, *c.* 1640.

2. The scene of judgment, from the dying room of St Wulfstan's monastic hospital in Worcester. The scene portrays archangel Michael and St Mary tipping the balance in favour of mercy. (*Courtesy of Worcester Museum Service*).

Of Faith.

The signification.

T'He man in armour signifieth all stedfast beleuers of the veritie, being armed with constant zeale of Christianitie, and weaponed with the shielde of liuely faith, the spere of continuaunce, and the sworde of the word of God: The Diuil vnder him is temptation, being ouercome by faith in Christ Iesus.

M.iiij.   Faith

---

3. The triumph of faith over Satan, from Stephen Bateman, *A Christall Glasse of Christian Reformation* (1569).

Of Enuie.

{ To Serpent like I may compare : those greedie wolues that lambes deuoure:
Awayting still to catch in snare : all such as gette they may by power.

¶The signification.

THe Dragon signifieth the enemie to all that professe the worde of God : the Cardinall persecution, or a persecutor of the same : the Fryer murther : the sheepe which are a killing, signifieth the professours of Christ, from the beginning of the worlde to these present dayes.

Hist.   Enuie

4. The persecution of 'all that professe the worde of God', from Stephen Bateman, *A Christall Glasse of Christian Reformation* (1569).

True and Wonderfull.

A Difcourfe relating a ftrange and mon-
ftrous Serpent (or Dragon) lately difcouered, and yet
liuing, to the great annoyance and diuers flaughters
both of Men and Cattell, by his ftrong
and violent poyfon,

Jn Suffex *two miles from* Horfam, *in a woode*
called S. Leonards Forreft, and thirtie miles from
London, *this prefent month of Auguft.* 1614.
With the true Generation of Serpents.

Printed at London by *John Trundle.*

5. A 'monstrous serpent' reported in 1614. The text likened the beast to
the dragon described in the Book of Revelation, and warned that 'from the
monsters of our sinnes, the monsters of our punishment increaseth'.

The Miracle, of Miracles. 44

As fearefull as euer was seene or heard of in the memorie of M A N.

Which lately happened at *Dichet* in Sōmmersetſhire , and ſent by diuers credible witneſſes to be publiſhed in L O N D O N.

Alſo a Propheſie reuealed by a poore Countrey Maide, who being dead the firſt of October laſt, 24. houres, 1613. reuiued againe, and lay fiue *dayes weeping, and continued propheſying of ſtrange euents to come, and ſo died the 5. day following.*

Witneſſed by M. *Nicholas Faber*, Parſon of the Towne, and diuers worthy Gentlemen of the ſame countrey. 1613,

With Lincolneſhire, Norfolke, Suffolke, and Kent their Teares For a great deluge, in which fiue Villages were lamentably drowned this preſent month.

T. I.

At London printed for I O H N T R V N D L E : and are to be ſold at

6. The devil as a headless bear, from *The Miracle of Miracles* (1613).

The Witch of Edmonton :

A known true S T O R Y.

Compoſed into

A TRAGI-COMEDY

By divers well-eſteemed Poets ;

William Rowley, Thomas Dekker, John Ford, &c.

Acted by the Princes Servants, often at the Cock-Pit in *Drury-Lane*,
once at Court, with ſingular Applauſe.

Never printed till now.

London, *Printed by* J. Cottrel, *for* Edward Blackmore, *at the* Angel *in*
Paul's *Church-yard.* 1658.

7. Title page from *The Witch of Edmonton* (1658).

Sith witles braines doth alwayes frowne : and folishe errours will defend:
Such monster Satyre shooteth downe : all popishe relickes without end.

¶ The signification.

*T*He monster with the gunne, signifieth all Popish ceremonies : he which sitteth on horsebacke is mainteynance of
the same : the horse swiftnes : and his sworde persecution :
the Aungell standing with a burning sword, signifieth Gods
wrath agaynst all such persecutors of hys people.

                                        I.i.   **Be**

8. The demon with a gun firing popish trinkets, from Stephen Bateman, *A Christall Glasse of Christian Reformation* (1569).

¶The description of

Couetousnes.

Ariftotle. { To delight in treafure, is a daungerous pleasure,
Seneca.   {   In a lyer doubtles, there neuer was goodnes.

¶ The signification of the picture.

*T*He deuil is Enuy, the fwords in his hand betokeneth
mifchief, the purfe couetoufnes, the globe the world,
the man in fooles weede fignifieth careleffe couetoufnes,
a man being ouercome with Enuy and couetoufnes, may
be likened to a foole that is not able to rule himfelfe, and
fo the ende is death. B.i.

9. The fool confronts the devil, from Bateman's *Christall Glasse* (1569).

The deſcription

Great griefe aſſailes the Lecherous minde : of ſuch as doth the youth alure:
More worſe then beaſtes I do thē finde : ſuch youth to lechery to procure.

¶The ſignification.

T He Goate ſignifieth Lechery : the woman Whoredome:
ſhe which leadeth the Goate by the beard is *meretrix*, the
baude : and the deuill *Nicticorax*, a blinde guide or de-
ceauer.

Lechery

10. The devil leads the way to sin, from Bateman's *Christall Glasse* (1569).

11a. The pope's reward in hell, from the seventeenth-century ballad *The Great Assize*.

11b. The fiend encourages William Purcas to murder. From the ballad *The Wofull Lamentation*.

ANTHONY PAINT[

THE

Blaspheming Caryar.

Who sunke into the ground up to the neck, and there stood two day
two nights, and not to bee drawne out by the strength of Ho[
or digged out by the help of man: and there dyed the
3. of *Nouember.* 1613.

Also the punishment of *Nicholas Mesle* a most wicked blasphemer,

Reade and tremble.

Published by Authoritie,

> Thou art mine.

> I am Damn'd.

At London printed for *Iohn Trundle* : and are to be sold at
Christ Church Gate. 1614.

12. The devil claims a blasphemer, from *Anthony Painter* (1614).

STRANGE

Newes from *Antvvarpe*, which happened the 12. of August laſt paſt. 1 6 1 2;

FIRST PRINTED In DVTCH
at Bergen ap Zoame by Ioris Staell and now tranſlated into Engliſh by I. F.

¶ At London printed by Ralph Blower. 1612.

13. Satan attacks a catholic church in *Strange Newes from Antwerpe* (1612). (*Opposite top*) 14a. The pope as Antichrist from a 1642 pamphlet. (*Opposite bottom*) 14b. Archbishop William Laud as Antichrist, from a 1642 pamphlet.

Of Pride.

When daintie dames hath whole delight : with proude attyre them selues to ray:
Piramos shineth in the sight : of glittering glasse such fooles to fray.

¶ The signification.

¶ He woman signifieth pride : the glasse in her hand flattery or deceate : the deuill behinde her temptation : the
death head which she setteth her foote on, signifieth forget-
fulnes of the life to come, wherby commeth destruction.

H.iij.   **Take**

15. Satan exploits the female sin of pride, from Stephen Bateman, *A Christall Glasse of Christian Reformation* (1569).

16. Familiar spirits depicted in the illustration from Matthew Hopkins, *Discovery of Witches* (1647).

A

Timely Warning

To Rash and Disobedient

CHILDREN.

Being a strange and wonderful RELATION of a young Gentleman in the Parish of *Stepheny* in the Suburbs of *London*, that sold himself to the Devil for 12 Years to have the Power of being revenged on his Father and Mother, and how his Time being expired, he lay in a sad and deplorable Condition to the Amazement of all Spectators.

EDINBURGH: PRINTED ANNO 1721.

17. An eighteenth-century warning of the dangers of Satan.

Allen and some other godly women, the death of a spouse appears to have occasioned a spiritual crisis, accompanied by particularly vicious assaults from the Devil. This experience was described vividly in 1647 by a woman who agonised over the fate of her husband's soul, and her own responsibility for his possible damnation. She wondered 'what would become of me that had made him worse by my perverse words to him, when he was faulty'. Her sufferings culminated one morning when she awoke to a terrible vision: 'I suddenly flew out of my bed into the midst of the room; and a voice said within me to my heart: 'Thou art damn'd, thou art damn'd.' I felt the smell of brimstone.' In this case, the tormented widow found some solace in the unconventional ministry of the prophetess Sarah Wright, who assured her that Christ would 'show mercy'. [22]

Other domestic situations could also create feelings of intense guilt, which left some women vulnerable to Satan's malice. A particularly dramatic and tragic case, recorded by the physician Richard Napier in 1602, concerned a woman who confessed that she had helped one of her serving maids to terminate an unwanted pregnancy. Napier observed that she was overwhelmed by guilt and 'distracted of her wits'; she wanted 'to kill [and] make herself away, being tempted (as she sayeth) thereunto by the tempter'. It appears that the Devil could also exploit family conflicts between women. In 1634 Napier's nephew described how one of his patients, Joan Fellow, was afflicted with 'night terrors' during a dispute with her mother-in-law, who 'hath used her very unkindly'. He noted that Fellow had slept badly for nine nights, 'and in her slumbers fears somebody will kill her'. The exact nature of the conflict between the two women was not recorded, and one can only speculate about the psychological pressures that caused Fellow to experience these nocturnal visitations. It seems reasonable, however, to accept the doctor's assumption that they were linked in some way to tensions within the household. [23]

Most of the women described in this section experienced feelings of temptation or guilt arising from domestic situations that were largely beyond their control. They appear to have understood these feelings as the 'buffets' of Satan, which had to be endured and overcome through Christ before they could be restored to spiritual health. The implications of this belief were deeply conservative: it encouraged women to concentrate on defeating the Devil within them instead of attempting to change their material circumstances. Even Elizabeth Caldwell ended her life as a penitent sinner on the scaffold, publicly renouncing her proud and lustful behaviour and imploring others to resist Satan's snares. The conservative consequences for women of belief in the Devil can be shown in another, very different area of religious experience. By emphasising the power and ubiquity of the ghostly enemy, English reformers effectively suppressed a tradition of female mysticism that had thrived in the late Middle Ages and the first part of the sixteenth century. This process is considered below.

THE END OF PROPHECY

The Italian historian Ottavia Niccoli has described the suppression of religious visionaries by the Counter Reformation as 'the end of prophecy'. Until about 1530, she argues, prophetic visions were accepted at all levels of Italian society, and the recipients of these revelations, most often women, were treated with admiration and respect. From the 1530s, however, this situation was transformed. Faced with the challenge of Protestantism, the Roman church adopted a much more sceptical attitude towards ecstatic religious experiences, believing that they could give encouragement to the kind of heresy that was flourishing in Germany. Subsequently, women who claimed to receive revelations from angels or saints were subjected to a regime of close examination by their confessors, who sought to persuade them that they were deluded or, worse, the victims of demonic possession. Niccoli cites the case of one woman, Christina della Rovere, who was so affected by this pressure that her rapturous visions of 'a most handsome young man with blond hair, dressed in white', were replaced by apparitions of a monstrous, fire-breathing dog. More generally, she argues that 'women who seemed to enjoy particular charismatic gifts' were often accused of delusion or 'affected sanctity', arising from their pride and hypocrisy or the seductive wiles of the Devil. These conclusions have been confirmed by research in other European countries, which suggests that similar pressures were responsible for transforming women's visionary experiences into cases of demonic possession. [24]

There is reason to assume that a similar process was encouraged by the English Reformation. As Niccoli's study suggests, the theology of Protestantism itself was not primarily responsible for the suppression of visionary women, just as the doctrines of sixteenth-century Catholicism did not lead inevitably to this outcome. Rather, the interests of the crown and the clergy created a situation in which all forms of charismatic religion were treated with scepticism. Like the papacy, the English crown was inclined to take a dim view of any activities that threatened to promote heresy. This concern was heightened by the creation of the Church of England, which made any open expression of religious dissent a potential challenge to the state. Equally, Protestant pastors had good reason to be cautious about claims of divine inspiration: not only were they anxious to avoid the promotion of unpredictable and potentially heretical 'fanatics', whose actions could discredit God's people, but they were wary of sanctioning sources of religious authority that could undermine their own leadership. These interests were complemented perfectly by the emphasis on the power of Satan that characterised English Protestantism: since the enemy delighted in falsehood and sought constantly to undermine the true church, it was only to be expected that he would assail God's people with false prophets who appeared as 'angels of light'. While a number of male visionaries were cast in this role, the effects of the new climate of scepticism were felt most strongly by women: the experience of divine inspiration was a traditional aspect of female piety, reflecting the conventional belief that women's passivity made them unusually receptive to the power of God. This tradition of female spirituality was effectively suppressed by the second half of the sixteenth century. As a result, women who attempted to take on the role of prophets were usually dismissed as charlatans or hysterics, or presumed to be possessed by the Devil. [25]

From prophecy to possession

The prohibition of women's visionary experiences was illustrated neatly in a case from Huntingdonshire in 1629. This concerned the activities of Jane Hawkins, a self-proclaimed prophet from the village of St Ives, who experienced religious ecstasies and 'uttered verses in rhyme' during a period of prolonged illness. Her revelations were apparently accepted as genuine by some members of the local community, and were recorded in a book by the curate. When news of these events reached the Bishop of Lincoln, John Williams, he instigated an investigation which concluded that Hawkins was a fake: her performance was 'stark juggling' that abused the name of God, 'as if those notions came from God which came from fraud, and from Satan'. The parish minister was obliged to denounce the prophet from the pulpit, and to apologise for endorsing her exploits. In a later account of the story, John Hacket offered an explicit acknowledgement of the political motives behind the bishop's move: Hawkins' verses were 'full of detraction and injury to the authority of the bishops, to the church-way of England in the liturgy, and not sparing some occurrences of the civil government'. It is impossible to test this assertion against Hawkins' own words, since Williams' intervention proved so successful that no copies of her work have survived. Whatever their content, Hacket had no doubt that they had a wide appeal 'among the rural hobs'. He noted sadly that they 'would have spread into fairs and markets, and been sung by fiddler's boys, if it had not been prevented'. [26]

While the Devil was implicated indirectly in the ecstatic experiences of Jane Hawkins, he was given a leading role in the story of other women who attempted to play the role of religious visionaries. In 1621 Helen Fairfax, the eldest daughter of a gentry family from Fuyston in Yorkshire, fell into a series of trances in which she received visions of the Devil and local women believed to be witches. Her condition was accepted as a genuine case of possession by her father Edward, who later wrote an account of the episode, and the godly clergy in the region. After a few weeks, however, the symptoms of Helen's condition changed dramatically, and she began to receive heavenly visions conveying messages from God:

> She fell into a trance in the hall, and then one in bright clothing appeared to her, a man of incomparable beauty, with a beard, and his apparel shining: upon his head [was] a sharp high thing, from which, and from his mouth, and from his garments, streamed beams of light, which cast a glorious splendour over him. He spake unto her and said that he was God, come to comfort her; that the Devil had troubled her by God's sufferance, but she was so dearly beloved of God that he was come to comfort her.

Helen engaged in conversation with the apparition, which promised to relieve her afflictions and assured her of a place in Heaven. She joined it in reciting the Lord's Prayer. When the spirit departed, 'she was persuaded [that] this was God or some angel sent to comfort her', and would probably have persisted in this view had it not been challenged by her father and his friends. Despite her strong opposition, they were convinced that the vision was a subtle attempt by the Devil to seduce her mind. According to Edward Fairfax, they spent the rest of the night trying unsuccessfully to convince her of this, 'but next morning, with some difficulty, we persuaded her . . . by such reasons and scriptures as our small knowledge could afford'. The effect of this intervention was dramatic. Three days later, Helen fell in a trance and 'saw the same glorious apparition again'. This time, however, she confronted the angelic figure with her knowledge of its true identity, declaring that 'God did not reveal thee unto me, and will rebuke thee for taking his name upon thee'. At this, 'she saw many horns begin to grow out of his head, and his beauty and glorious light were gone, and he changed into a most terrible shape'. [27]

Like the Italian visionary Christina della Rovere, Helen Fairfax appears to have abandoned her claim to divine inspiration in the face of persistent male scepticism, and convinced herself that her ecstatic experiences were demonic. One can only speculate about how her condition might have developed in a more sympathetic context, but her initial refusal to accept that her angelic visitor was the Devil suggests that she would have continued to receive heavenly revelations. The crucial role played by social factors in shaping the experiences of charismatic women was shown after the civil war, when the collapse of the church courts and the proliferation of religious sects created an atmosphere much more receptive to the claims of 'inspired' individuals. In these new circumstances, visionary women such as Anna Trapnel and Sarah Wright were freed to pursue brief careers as prophets. In a striking reversal of the experience of Helen Fairfax, Trapnel admitted in 1654 that she had once suspected that her visions were signs of demonic possession, but later decided that this was 'but a fancy'. Despite these new opportunities, however, women who displayed signs of inspiration still came under intense pressure to accept that they were really possessed. Around 1645, Joyce Dovey of Bewdley in Worcestershire was affected by convulsions and 'fits' after attending a sermon. These symptoms, which were 'observed especially to take her in the time of private prayer or performance of pious duties', were consistent with the signs of the Holy Spirit; but this possibility was closed by the intervention of an army chaplain who 'strongly imagined that she was possessed'. Subsequently, Dovey began to manifest the conventional symptoms of demonic possession, which reached a climax when the fiend seized control of her voice to declare that 'my power is over all the world, and my kingdom is the greatest'. [28]

Satan and female authority

One of the consequences of the suppression of divine inspiration was to deny women the respect and power that traditionally accompanied the role of prophet. But while this option was largely closed off in the period before the civil war, some women managed to exploit other extreme spiritual experiences to assert a measure of authority that would normally have been denied them. The most obvious examples occurred in cases of demonic possession. In 1593 Joan and Jane Throckmorton, the daughters of a gentry family from Huntingtonshire, were possessed by evil spirits that caused them to suffer convulsions and experience terrible visions. Towards the end of their ordeal, however, the girls were allowed to deliver religious speeches to the adult members of the household. According to one observer, 'the heavenly and divine speeches of these children' were such 'that if a man had heard it he would not have thought himself better edified at ten sermons'. These performances, which were presumably attributed to the Holy Spirit, allowed the Throckmorton girls to enjoy some of the privileges of divine inspiration without relinquishing their role as victims of the Devil. An alternative way for women to express spiritual authority was by confronting and overcoming the Devil in public, an opportunity normally associated with the Protestant deathbed. Thus Katherine Stubbes assumed the manner of a preacher as she addressed her ghostly foe in front of the audience gathered to witness her last hours:

> But what sayest thou now Satan? Dost thou ask me how I dare come to Him for mercy, He being a righteous God, and I a miserable sinner? I tell thee, Satan, I am bold through Christ to come unto Him . . . Christ's arms were spread wide open, Satan, upon the cross (with that she spread her own arms) to embrace me and all penitent persons: and therefore, Satan, I will not fear to present myself before his foot-stool, in full assurance of His mercy, for Christ His sake.

This kind of behaviour went beyond the passive submission to Christ recommended in Protestant guides to dying, but was apparently accepted by Philip Stubbes, Katherine's husband and biographer. The privileges of the deathbed were exploited more ostentatiously by Sarah Wright in 1647. At the age of sixteen, Sarah took to her bed with a mysterious and apparently terminal illness, which left her blind, deaf and unable to eat. During her sickness she embarked on an epic struggle with Satan, who fought with her 'as he did with Michael and the angels'. She periodically interrupted this conflict to offer words of religious comfort and advice to the audience at her bedside; and eventually, when she had overcome the final onslaughts of the fiend, she devoted herself entirely to this more tranquil role. After spending several weeks in the role of a semi-conscious spiritual advisor, Sarah recovered her health and retired to Highgate. [29]

As these accounts suggest, it was possible for women to exploit religious experiences involving the Devil to express the kind of authority traditionally associated with female mystics. Such opportunities were limited, however, and they imposed severe restrictions on the individuals involved. Even in the relatively favourable circumstances of the 1640s, Sarah Wright was obliged to endure a lengthy and debilitating illness for her prophetic status to be acknowledged; and she relied heavily on the support of a Baptist minister, Henry Jessey, to authenticate and publicise her experiences. Other women, such as Katherine Stubbes, enjoyed their brief moment of preacherly authority only at the very end of their lives. For the victims of possession, the conventions surrounding the condition imposed strict limits on their behaviour and made the expression of divine inspiration extremely problematic. The 'inspired' experiences of Helen Fairfax and Joyce Dovey were denied by their male interpreters, while the 'heavenly speeches' of the Throckmorton children were accepted only at the end of their affliction, when the Holy Spirit was working to free them from the Devil's grip. Moreover, the logic of possession dictated that its victims would eventually be restored to health through the ministry of godly men, who thereby asserted their own authority over religious affairs. This was, perhaps, one of the factors that encouraged many Protestants to accept the existence of demonic possession and the practice of exorcism. This subject is considered in the next chapter.

POSSESSION AND EXORCISM

THE POSSESSION EXPERIENCE

No manifestation of Satan's power in Tudor and Stuart England was more wrenchingly physical than demonic possession. Accounts of possessed individuals – or 'demoniacs' – presented wicked spirits in arrestingly concrete terms. A pamphlet describing the condemned witch Alice Samuel, who was hanged at Huntingdon assizes in 1593 after allegedly sending demons into the bodies of five young girls, provides a vivid illustration. During her interrogation, Samuel asserted that the demons had fled her victims and entered her own body instead: they were 'now in the bottom of her belly, and make her so full that she is like to burst'. She claimed that these spirits 'caused her to be so full that she could scant lace her coat, and that on the way as she came [to be questioned], they weighed so heavy that the horse she rid on did fall down and was not able to carry her'. [1]

Graphically physical accounts of this kind were by no means uncommon; nor were they confined to the most sensational cases of witchcraft. During the possession of Edward Dinham of Somerset in 1621, witnesses described something 'beat up and down in his stomach and belly'. Jane Slade, a patient of the physician Richard Napier in 1635, claimed to feel 'something stir in her body with a rising up and down'. In the same year, another of Napier's patients was 'conceited that there is something within [him], which came into him on Whitsun's eve in the night'. The physical location of the possessing demon was some-times revealed when it spoke from the body of its victim. According to Stanley Gower in 1651, the spirit possessing a man in Nottingham was heard 'with an audible voice in him, which seemed sometimes to be heard out of his belly, sometimes out of his throat, and sometimes out of his mouth, his lips not moving'. Less dramatically, it was commonly claimed that possessed men and women spoke without moving their lips, with the words issuing from the upper part of their body or the back of their throat. [2]

The physical nature of possession was underlined by accounts of how unclean spirits invaded their hosts. As Kathleen Sands has observed, 'it was generally presumed that possession could occur only when Satan entered a human body through an orifice, such as a nostril, an ear, a wound, or a skin pore'. In a well publicised case from Lancashire in 1596, Edmund Hartley was accused of breathing demons into the mouths of five children and two housemaids when he kissed them. It appears that this procedure was essential for the possessions to succeed, since Hartley failed to infect one of his intended victims, Joan Smith, when she avoided his attempts to kiss her. A similar technique was described in Leicestershire in 1618, when a witness at a witch trial described how a 'spirit' had been blown into her mouth. The belief that a demon needed to be in close proximity to its potential host meant that observers at exorcisms sometimes perceived themselves to be in danger. During the dispossession of Thomas Darling of Burton in 1597, for example, some of the spectators were alarmed when one of the demons inside the boy threatened to 'enter into some of these here'. The concrete reality of unclean spirits was further emphasised when the victims of possession claimed to have actually seen the creatures as they entered or departed from their bodies. Thus Darling attested that a devil had come out of his mouth in the shape of a mouse. His claim was apparently confirmed by some of the witnesses at his exorcism. A similar belief was expressed by the accused witch, Margaret Mixter, who claimed that Satan 'came like a mouse' to possess her in 1645. She thanked her examiners for forcing the creature from her body. [3]

There are, of course, many reasons to question the accuracy of these accounts. Leaving aside twenty-first-century scepticism about the existence of demonic powers, the confessions of Alice Samuel and Margaret Mixter were obtained under psychological duress in response to their accusers' leading questions. Moreover, Marion Gibson has shown that printed narratives of possession cases reflected the political and family interests of those who produced them. The original circumstances of many cases of possession will inevitably remain elusive. Despite this, however, the consistency of descriptions of the phenomenon testifies to widely shared assumptions about it.

Indeed, the reports that survive were often tailored to persuade a large audience of their plausibility, and assumed their readers' knowledge of the signs of 'authentic' possession. Both sceptics and believers acknowledged that the condition involved the physical manifestation of the Devil in the victim's body, though they might disagree about the genuineness of the symptoms in specific cases. Similarly, popular accounts tended to emphasise the corporeal presence of the Devil or demons in the body of the afflicted person. [4]

The grossly material accounts of demonic possession in Tudor and Stuart England departed significantly from the usual Protestant understanding of the Devil. As English divines regarded Satan mainly as an invisible spirit of temptation, one might have expected them to view the phenomenon skeptically. Lyndal Roper has argued that this was the case among German reformers in the sixteenth and seventeenth centuries. She notes that German Protestants 'denied that divine forces could be captured in the physical', and were therefore often dismissive of possession. The situation in England was more complex, however. Many committed Protestants accepted the reality of possession, while opposition to the concept was strongest among those churchmen who objected to the supposed excesses of the 'puritan' ministry. Thus the more zealous English Protestants tended to advocate the practice of exorcism – or 'dispossession' – despite the intensely physical manifestations of the Devil that this involved. Indeed, Protestant clergy were associated with many of the cases of possession described above. [5]

Why was this so? First and most generally, Protestant Biblicism confirmed the possibility of demonic possession. The account of the demoniac cured by Jesus in the land of the Gadarenes (Mark 5:1-15, Luke 8:26-36) proved the ability of unclean spirits to occupy the flesh. The scriptures also supported the casting out of devils: indeed, Christ described the ability to do so as a sign of the true church (Mark 3:15). Secondly, the practice of reformed religion could make its adherents, and those living under their influence, particularly susceptible to the affliction. The reasons for this are explored later in this chapter. Finally, the performance of dispossession provided valuable opportunities for pastors to advance their ministry, despite opposition from the leaders of the late Elizabethan and early Stuart church. Once such ministers were prepared to embrace the concept of possession, and to practice the casting out of demons, they were inevitably influenced by traditional beliefs and conventions associated with the phenomena.

These conventions are explored in the first part of this chapter. The second part will consider the experience of demonic possession and exorcism within the Protestant community.

The symptoms

Historians have often noted the theatrical elements in cases of demonic possession. Apart from the obvious trappings of the stage, such as the presence of large audiences at some of the more famous incidents, it seems that both the possessed and their spiritual doctors were acting out socially determined roles. These roles, which they performed either consciously or unconsciously, had the effect of confirming the legitimacy of the victim's affliction. In the earliest stages of the drama, both sides relied on a standard repertoire of symptoms and responses, and the behaviour of either party could determine the eventual diagnosis. It appears that the assumptions of those around a potential victim could shape their perception of their own condition, causing them to accept it as a 'natural' illness, a religious experience, or a true case of demonic possession. In the 1620s John Hall, a physician from Stratford-upon-Avon, treated a woman who had fallen suddenly into 'a grievous delerium' and 'was most angry with those that formerly she most loved, yet her talk was very religious'. Though her condition displayed some of the signs of possession, Hall regarded it as a physical malady. As a result of the doctor's attentions, 'she was happily cured' in the space of a few days. In other cases, the initial assumption that patients were suffering from 'natural' disorders was revised when their symptoms grew worse or they failed to respond to medical treatments. Both Thomas Darling and the Throckmorton children were diagnosed with physical ailments before the supernatural cause of their suffering was identified. Even when patients were convinced that they were possessed, the true nature of the invading spirit was sometimes unclear, and the behaviour of those around them could determine whether they believed themselves to be divinely inspired or possessed by the Devil. As the previous chapter showed, both Helen Fairfax and Joyce Dovey were persuaded by others that they were the victims of demonic possession, despite their initial conviction that they were inspired by God.[6]

Once a case of possession was recognised, the repertoire of symptoms was remarkably consistent. The demoniac almost always showed physical signs of the Devil's presence, often in the form of swellings around the throat. Thus Catherine Wright was so afflicted in 1586 that 'her body and neck were swollen twice as big as they were wont to be'. Thirty years later, a possessed woman from Worcestershire had 'something arising big in her throat'. In some cases, like those of Alice Samuel and the patients of Richard Napier, it was also claimed that these swellings could move around the body. In 1599 the godly exorcist John Darrell insisted that this symptom was displayed by William Somers, who was 'seen to have a certain variable swelling or lump . . . swiftly running up and down between the flesh and skin'. The appearance of swellings was often accompanied by bodily contortions. Thomas Darling, another of Darrell's subjects, bowed his body so violently that his stomach was raised above his head, and the possessed victims of Edmund Hartley in Lancashire were tormented with many 'strange and sore fits'. A chapbook from 1641 reported that a possessed woman from Durham 'was shaken with such force that the bed and the chamber did shake and move', causing her family to hold 'her down violently in her bed'. In numerous other cases, victims of possession appeared to be thrown against walls or down onto the floor. [7]

As well as their physical symptoms, the behaviour of demoniacs was highly stereotyped. They almost always communicated or received visions in a state of trance or 'bewitchment', in which many of their normal faculties were suspended. In 1621 the daughter of Edward Fairfax 'sunk down in a deadly trance' before witnessing a parade of bizarre apparitions. She described what she had seen only when she 'came to herself'. Similarly, a chapbook account of the possession of Anne Styles of Salisbury in 1653 described her as 'lying in trances' for most of the ordeal. In several cases, this enchanted state allowed the possessing spirit to take control of its host. Again, the conventions surrounding this process were strikingly consistent. When the Devil spoke through its human vessel, its voice was characterised by its difference from the victim's normal tones, and often described as uncommonly deep or shrill. The voice of the Devil in Edward Dinham in 1621 was 'deadly and hollow', while the spirit possessing Joyce Dovey in 1647 had 'a bigger and grosser tone than her ordinary speech'. In cases of child possession, the voice was usually larger and more adult than that possessed by its host. The alien nature of the speech was sometimes emphasised by claims that it issued from unusual places in the body, or occurred without the subject moving their lips. [8]

The actions attributed to possessing spirits also conformed to certain familiar types. When a demon spoke or acted through the body of its host, it normally expressed a repugnance of religion and a delight in blasphemy. This was often directed at particular forms of pious behaviour, such as churchgoing or prayer, or religious texts like the Bible. A fairly typical account of the irreverent conduct of a possessed child was presented in *The Most Strange and Admirable Discoverie of the Three Witches of Warboys* (1593), which recounted the behaviour of Elizabeth Throckmorton:

> She was very quiet and well until motion was made of prayers, all which time it seemed as though it would have rent her in pieces, with such screeching and outcries and vehement sneezing as that it terrified the whole company; but prayers being ended she was quieted, but still in her fit. Then Master Pickering, and others that were acquainted with the manner of it, said that if any should read the Bible or any other godly book before her, it would rage as before so long as they read; but because it was a thing very strange and therefore hardly believed, one did take a Bible and read the first chapter of Saint John, the first verse. At the hearing whereof she was as one besides her mind; when he that read held his peace she was quiet.

In this instance, it seems that the actions of the possessed girl and those around her had settled into a familiar pattern, with both sides feeding off the responses of the other. The reading of the verse from St John's gospel, which had been used as a protection against evil spirits since the Middle Ages, also suggests that they were drawing on popular traditions about the Devil. A similar pattern was evident in the behaviour of William Somers and the observers of his possession, who repeatedly read him the Lord's Prayer, which he interrupted at the line 'Lead us not into temptation'. In 1621 Edward Dinham was thrown into a fit of convulsions and blasphemy when he was handed a prayer book. Likewise, Joyce Dovey cast a Bible into a fire in 1647, though witnesses claimed that it was miraculously preserved. [9]

These illustrations suggest that the drama of possession depended on the interplay between demoniacs and those around them, with both sides exploiting an established repertoire of beliefs and actions. This was exemplified by the 'dumb show' performed by William Somers in 1597, in which the possessed man appeared to mime a catalogue of sins in front of the audience for his exorcism. The idea that demons mimicked human vices was a commonplace in late medieval religion: it was expressed in depictions of Hell and printed guides to the art of dying, which presented the deathbed as a stage for devils acting out the seven deadly sins. The persistence of this idea was acknowledged in 1641 by the pastor Richard Carpenter, who noted that 'many teach that the devils in Hell shall mock the troubled imagination of the damned person with the counterfeit imitation of his sins'. It was in the context of these beliefs that Somers' extraordinary performance made sense to his audience, who perceived his gestures as representations of various criminal and ungodly acts. As his exorcist later recalled, the precise interpretation of these gestures was determined by the crowd as a whole: 'no one man especially, but many confusedly did interpret the dumb show'. A similar process of interpretation was probably at work in those cases in which demoniacs appeared to speak in foreign languages. It was widely assumed that the ability to speak in a foreign tongue, unknown to the afflicted person, was a sign of possession. This belief sometimes caused observers to interpret the utterances of demoniacs as imperfect pronunciations of foreign words. In 1621, for example, those present at the possession of Edward Dinham believed they heard the spirit inside him cry out the Latin word 'laudes', or 'praise', though the context of Dinham's speech suggests that he actually said 'ladies'. In this case, it appears that the reaction of the witnesses was at least as important as the behaviour of the possessed man in confirming the symptoms of his condition. [10]

Just as the symptoms of possession conformed to certain recognised types, the cause of the affliction was understood in conventional terms. In most cases, the victim attributed their sufferings to another person, who had bewitched them or sent demons into their body. Sometimes, as in the case of the Fairfax children, this information was obtained through visions induced by the bewitchment itself; in other instances it was apparently revealed by the possessing spirits. The subjects treated by John Darrell in the late sixteenth century usually described meetings with sinister strangers that preceded their afflictions. Thomas Darling had encountered an aged woman in a wood, who cursed him before he succumbed to the first of his fits. He later identified Alice Gooderidge, who was subsequently tried for witchcraft. Likewise, William Somers was accosted at a coal pit by 'an old woman (as he thought), who asked where he dwelt, and wither he was going'. She demanded money and forced him to eat a piece of bread, which apparently conveyed a demon into his body. In the case of the Throckmorton and Fairfax children, the possessed were tormented with visions of the witches responsible for their sufferings, together with the familiar spirits they employed. Once a suspect was identified, meetings between them and their alleged victim usually agitated the symptoms of bewitchment, sometimes inducing spasms or hallucinations. The strong connection between witches and their victims was underlined in those cases, such as Alice Samuel and the Throckmorton children, in which the symptoms of possession were only relieved once the supposed perpetrator had been punished. [11]

The stereotypical nature of possession was shown most clearly in cases of fraud. It appears that those individuals who confessed to faking bewitchment were exploiting a well known set of behaviours. In several cases, their deceptions were only uncovered after they had convinced large numbers that their afflictions were genuine. Sometimes, as with Thomas Darling and William Somers, allegations of fraud were strongly contested even after the demoniacs had apparently admitted to fabrication. This does not mean that the men and women who believed in these 'possessions' were unusually credulous: they were simply accepting the symptoms of a condition that was widely accepted as real, and which went unchallenged in other instances. An early example of counterfeit possession occurred in London in 1574, when two young girls, Rachel Pinder and Agnes Briggs, confessed to Archbishop Parker that they had simulated the condition. Pinder's performance as a demoniac involved a faithful imitation of the major symptoms. When the Devil spoke through her body, her 'lips moved with no such moving as could pronounce the words uttered, the eyelids moved, but not open, she had great swelling in her throat, and about the jaws, and the voice was somewhat bigger than the child's voice'. Likewise, Briggs 'disfigured herself with diverse strange countenances, feigning diverse strange voices and noises'. Both girls attributed their affliction to a witch, Joan Thornton, though they were unable to provide her address. Fifty years later, Katherine Malpas from West Ham admitted the fabrication of identical symptoms. Among other signs of her affliction, she had a 'rising up in her stomach to the bigness of a half penny loaf', and she cast aside bibles and prayer books when they were handed to her. Before she admitted her deception, she accused two of her neighbours of sending spirits into her body. The main interest in these cases is not that they prove the existence of fraudulent possessions, but that the false demoniacs knew exactly what was expected for their conditions to be accepted. They were deliberately acting out a socially sanctioned role which, in other cases, was probably performed sincerely by the victims of 'genuine' possession. [12]

The Social Context of Possession

According to the indictment against them, the family of the fake demoniac Katherine Malpas had instigated her fraud for financial gain: they had hoped to attract charity from people moved by her pretended distress. In most other cases of possession, however, the behaviour of the alleged victims is much harder to explain. The undoubted existence of fraud, and the observation that possession involved the acting out of socially constructed roles, does not mean that all demoniacs can be dismissed as counterfeits. As Clarke Garrett has argued in the context of divine inspiration, 'to say that the possessed are performing culturally determined roles is not to say that they are faking – at least not often. There are too may accounts from too many cultures which insist that the *experience* of divine possession is real, overwhelming, and unforgettable for those who undergo it'. It appears that the best way to explain the actions of early modern demoniacs is to explore the social functions of the performance in which they were engaged. In some instances, the drama of possession probably offered an explanation for physical symptoms which might, in different contexts, have been diagnosed in medical terms. For victims of the 'falling sickness', or epilepsy, the notion of possession offered one option for understanding and controlling a condition that was notoriously hard to treat. In 1691, Richard Baxter recorded the case of Nathan Crab, a possessed youth from Exeter, who was apparently diagnosed with the falling sickness for over a year before anyone suspected that his illness might have a supernatural origin. As well as explaining physical ailments, the idea of possession offered a framework for interpreting certain types of mental disturbance. Roy Porter has suggested that the diagnosis of possession in early modern Europe allowed some individuals, including those who suffered the symptoms of conditions later understood as forms of 'neurosis' or 'schizophrenia', to make sense of their experiences and obtain support from religious authorities, who fulfilled a role similar to the psychiatric profession in the nineteenth and twentieth centuries. In some cases, like that of the German demoniac Christoph Haitzmann, their treatment at the hands of the exorcists produced 'cures' at least as successful as those achieved by later psychiatric techniques. [13]

As well as providing a context for the understanding and treatment of illness, the roleplay involved in possession conferred authority on its supposed victims. As the main players in a public drama, they were provided with an attentive audience, which often included leading figures from the local clergy and magistracy. Their words were treated with uncommon respect, and those spoken at the behest of possessing spirits were also expressed with impunity. For these reasons, the experience of possession provided an occasion for relatively disempowered individuals to address their social betters from a position of lofty, if precarious authority. This may help to explain why women and young people featured prominently among the victims. The two London girls who feigned possession in 1574 were able briefly to reverse conventional hierarchies of gender, age and social rank. Speaking through the voice of Satan, they asserted their great power and demanded gifts from their elders and social superiors; they compelled the adults around them to listen seriously to their tales of witchcraft, complete with bizarre details about the antics of familiar spirits. At one stage, they commanded the attention of some of the city's most respected ministers, including the celebrated martyrologist and preacher John Foxe, whom Rachel Pinder threatened to 'tear in pieces'. A similar role reversal was effected during the possession of the Throckmorton children in 1592. In this case, which was not generally regarded as a fraud, the entranced children abused and commanded the adults in the household and successfully accused a local woman and her daughter of causing their affliction. They subjected the women to a series of interrogations, in which they addressed them with 'hard words' and gestures quite inappropriate for their age. [14]

By providing an outlet for 'satanic' behaviour, the experience of possession allowed its victims to articulate thoughts and desires that were otherwise socially unacceptable. Indeed, the expression of these sentiments was not only safe, but actually reinforced their forbidden nature, since they were attributed to spirits that were utterly opposed to true religion and morality. Thus demoniacs could 'speak the unspeakable'. As Jim Shape has noted, the words ascribed to possessing spirits contained surprisingly few intimations of sexual desire, though certain communications described elliptically as 'immodest' or 'indecent' might have contained sexual elements. This was possibly the case with William Somers, whose speech was 'many times filthy and unclean, [and] very unfit to be named', and whose gestures included a simulation of 'whoredom'. In a small number of cases, it appears that possessed individuals also took the opportunity to express economic grievances: Somers, for instance, referred repeatedly to 'the insatiable desire of gain, or raising the price of corn in corn men'. Far more common, however, were blasphemous or irreligious statements. Demoniacs commonly expressed contempt for Christian texts and doctrines, and asserted the overwhelming power of Satan. When the Devil took possession of a man in Berwick in 1645, he declared that his hold on his victim's soul was so great that he could never be saved by Christ; he mocked the attempts of the godly exorcist, Robert Balsom, to lead prayers for the man's salvation, and promised that 'I will never give over blaspheming so long as thou stayest in the room'. Occasionally, possessed individuals expressed heterodox or sceptical religious opinions. In 1573, for example, Alexander Nynde declared that Satan was a 'disciple' of God. More boldly, William Somers asserted that 'there is no God' in 1597, and three years later a possessed maid from Hockham in Norfolk announced that 'God is a good man and I can do as much as he'. It is true, of course, that by uttering such words demoniacs confirmed their role in the social drama: Satan was a great liar and blasphemer, after all. But it is equally plausible that the 'voice of Satan' provided possessed men and women with an outlet for religious anxieties and doubts. These possibilities were not exclusive. Similarly, exorcisms may well have offered a public opportunity to overcome religious anxieties and affirm the saving power of God. [15]

POSSESSION AND THE PROTESTANT DEVIL

Opinion within the English church was divided on the reality of demonic possession and the practice of exorcism. This was hardly surprising given the Protestant emphasis on a spiritualized Devil, which contrasted with the fleshly understanding of Satan expressed in contemporary accounts of possession. Strikingly however, support for the casting out of demons was strongest among the 'hotter sort of Protestants' – those men and women towards the 'puritan' end of the religious spectrum – while opposition was associated with more conservative elements within the church. This pattern was indicated in 1574, when the fake possession of Rachel Pinder and Agnes Briggs led to the mockery of those 'zealous' churchmen who had been deceived by the children's antics. The printed account of the case singled out those members of the London clergy who 'had the matter in handling, being, as they professed themselves, godly men, plentifully adorned with faith, and sent of God to disturb the Devil'. More dramatically, the puritan minister John Darrell was arraigned before Archbishop Whitgift's court in 1599 for his involvement in a series of allegedly fraudulent exorcisms. Following Darrell's downfall, the church hierarchy placed new restrictions on the practice of dispossession, which obliged clergy to obtain licences before attempting 'by fasting and prayer to cast out any devil'. Despite this, some pastors continued the practice in the decades before the civil war, and it became common in the 1640s and 1650s. Thus a section of devout Protestant opinion endorsed the reality of demonic possession and exorcism, despite its association with a graphically physical view of the Devil. [16]

This apparent paradox was illustrated in the career of John Darrell. Darrell achieved fame – or notoriety – through a series of spectacular dispossessions in the 1590s. In 1596 he was called to the aid of Thomas Darling, 'the boy of Burton', who was possessed by an unclean spirit sent by a local witch. A year later he drove out the devils possessing seven young girls in Cleworth in Lancashire. Then in 1597 he confronted the demon possessing William Somers in Nottingham, ousting the creature after a prolonged struggle in which the victim blasphemed, gnashed his teeth and bellowed like a 'horse or boar'. Archbishop Whitgift ended his ministry in the following year. The published account of the case of Thomas Darling was suppressed and the printer imprisoned, and the exorcist himself was accused of fraud. The principal witness against him was William Somers, who alleged that his possession had been an elaborate deception devised by the pastor. Darrell was 'condemned for a counterfeit' and removed from his living. He was briefly imprisoned, but appears to have been free two years later. The case provoked a pamphlet war between Darrell and those behind his trial. On the bishops' side, John Deacon and John Walker published lengthy treatises against the exorcist, while much pithier attacks on his alleged fabrications were penned by Samuel Harsnett, the future bishop of Norwich. In 1603 Harsnett described how easy it was for young people – especially those suffering from 'natural' diseases such as epilepsy – to feign the symptoms of possession in order to accuse their neighbours of witchcraft:

The exorcism of William Somers in 1598, from the 1641 edition of John Darrell's *True Relation of the Grevious Handling of William Sommers of Nottingham, Being Possessed with a Devill.*

If any of you have . . . an idle girl of the wheel, or a young drab . . . and hath not fat enough for her porridge, nor her father and mother butter enough for their bread, and she have a little help of . . . epilepsy, or cramp, to teach her to roll her eyes, gnash her teeth, startle with her body, hold her arms and hands stiff, make antic faces, grin, mow and mop like an ape, tumble like a hedgehog, and can mutter out two or three words of gibberish, as *obus bobus*; and then if old Mother Nobs hath called her by chance 'idle young housewife', or bid the Devil scratch her, then no doubt but Mother Nobs is the witch, the young girl is owl-blasted, and possessed.

In response to this onslaught, the beleaguered exorcist published new accounts of the possession cases in which he had been involved, stressing the physical symptoms of those afflicted by 'unclean spirits'. These symptoms, he maintained, were so remarkable that they could not have been produced by fraud or natural illness. In the case of William Somers, for instance, swellings had appeared in the boy's body that were so large that they snapped off the buttons of his clothes, and these travelled up and down his limbs during his ordeal. [7]

Why did Darrell and later Protestant exorcists embrace such a grossly physical view of Satan? Two main factors can be adduced, and these are considered in detail in the rest of this chapter. First, the beliefs and experiences related to the state of possession can be viewed as natural extensions of the godly style of religion, with its intense focus on the need to confront Satan in one's body and mind. In many ways, the godly attitudes towards the Devil described in the first half of this book predisposed those who accepted them to take possession seriously, and encouraged psychological experiences which could be easily perceived as its symptoms. Second, the practice of exorcism presented zealous pastors with an opportunity to assert their authority, to consolidate the community of 'God's people', and to educate the public at large. The incentives to exploit this opportunity were considerable, despite the theological ambiguity that it also entailed.

Temptation and possession

For Robert Burton, the pioneering English psychologist, demonic possession was one of many forms of 'religious melancholy' inspired by the 'thundering ministers' of the early seventeenth century. Burton suggested that over-zealous Protestantism encouraged a morbid obsession with sin and damnation, which could lead to visions of Hell and imaginary encounters with the Devil himself. The doctor's position was hardly surprising: he developed his theories at a time when his prospective patron, James I, was determined to rein in the excesses of 'over-hot' ministers in the English church, and his claim that religious fanaticism was a source of mental illness was broadly consistent with crown policy. Nonetheless, Burton's suggestion that possession experiences were linked to Protestant zeal was probably correct. The most obvious connection was the belief, advanced by godly pastors like Robert Bolton, that Satan could implant impure thoughts directly into the minds of normally pious men and women. Such satanic cognitions were reported by earnest Protestants throughout the seventeenth century. In Burton's view, this belief was a delusion akin to the idea of possession itself: he noted that some sufferers of religious melancholy believed that the Devil 'is within them, as they think, and there speaks and talks as to such as are possessed'. Following Burton's lead, it seems reasonable to view the 'demonic' thoughts that assailed godly Protestants as a kind of possession experience. This was certainly how some of their recipients described them: Hannah Allen referred

to satanic 'injections into my mind', while Bunyan claimed that the
Devil's ideas were 'cast into' him. [18]

As chapter three argued, the idea that the Devil could intervene
directly in a person's mind was one manifestation of the wider belief
that Satan was an indwelling spirit of temptation and deceit. Such
direct interventions were normally unnecessary, since human nature
was already inclined to serve the Devil. The struggle to overcome
one's own sinful desires represented a daily conflict with the spiritual
enemy. As John Woolton noted in 1576, God's children were engaged
in 'a grievous and daily battle which is never ended before the day
of death, for . . . the Devil rusheth upon us with great vehemency,
and undermineth us with a thousand temptations'. In this sense, the
practice of religion was a kind of ongoing personal exorcism. This
idea was reflected in the Book of Common Prayer, which abolished
the Catholic rite of exorcism in the service of baptism: instead, the
reformed ritual simply required the godparents to renounce Satan
on the child's behalf, until the infant 'come of age and take it upon
himself'. According to John Milton in 1641, the act of baptismal
exorcism was an example of the 'frippery and ostentation' that characterised the Roman church, and had been swept away by the 'bright
and blissful Reformation'. In practice, the commitment of devout
Protestants to renounce Satan throughout their adult lives placed
them in a role similar to that of an exorcist. Indeed, the methods
they used to overcome their personal temptations, such as prayer,
fasting and meditation on the scriptures, were often identical to
those described in accounts of godly dispossessions. [19]

The similarity between possession and exorcism and the more
conventional pattern of Protestant piety was particularly striking in the
case of Hannah Allen. Allen never believed she was possessed, but the
experiences she recorded in her journal in the early 1660s frequently
recalled those of demoniacs. In April 1664 she was so assailed by temptations that she felt a 'woeful confusion and combating in my soul';
on another occasion, she told her aunt that 'I am just as if two were
fighting within me, but I trust the Devil will never be able to overcome me'. From her childhood, she suffered from 'horrible' thoughts,
which seemed to be 'cast in' her mind against her will. These included
the urge to hate God and to blaspheme against Him. These symptoms, which echoed the experiences of the victims of possession such
as Edward Dinham and the Throckmorton children, were taken by
Allen as signs of her constant struggle to overcome the Devil, and this

interpretation was reflected in the title of her autobiography, *Satan, His Methods and Malice Baffled*. She managed to 'baffle' the Devil through a daily round of prayer and Bible-reading, diligently assisted by members of her family and a number of godly pastors. In sum, Allen's whole religious life resembled a series of exorcisms, though the incursions the Devil made against her were never so great that he succeeded in completely taking over her body.[20]

In some cases of fully-fledged possession, the similarities between the phenomenon and the conventions of godly religion were equally marked. In 1596, the demoniac Thomas Darling sought relief from his condition by reading the Bible and offering prayers to God, which were joined by the crowd witnessing his affliction. He also embarked on lengthy dialogues with the demon possessing his body, in which he appeared to draw strength from the scriptural account of Christ's temptation by Satan. At the climax of one such exchange, he rebuked the Devil by asserting that 'I care not for all that thou canst do unto me: in the Lord is my trust, who will deliver me when his good pleasure is'. One of the spectators at Darling's possession, Jesse Bee, later described these spiritual 'combats' as *exemplars* of the power of faith and scripture to overcome the fiend, and noted their salutary effect on those who saw them. Darling's own religious zeal was expressed during his dispossession, when he voiced his desire to become a preacher if he survived the ordeal. His subsequent career confirmed his religious sympathies. In 1603 he was sentenced to lose his ears for libeling John Howson, the aggressively anti-puritan vice-chancellor of Oxford University. [21]

The similarity between possession and the everyday struggle of the godly against Satan was also evident in the two accounts of successful exorcisms in Samuel Clarke's *Generall Martyrologie* (1651). In the first, which involved a 'godly man' from Berwick around 1646, the possession was directly preceded by a period of mental 'affliction', in which he was 'much weakened and worn out by the violence of temptation'. Once it was established that he was possessed, the dialogue that ensued between the unclean spirit and the exorcist, Robert Balsom, covered topics familiar from godly literature and sermons. At one point the Devil announced that his victim was so consumed with sin that he could never be saved, allowing Balsom to offer the standard reply that 'the blood of Jesus Christ cleanseth us from all sin'. The whole confrontation recalled John Gerard's guide to the Protestant deathbed, *The Conquest of Temptations* (1621), and Thomas Becon's sixteenth-century book *The Christian Knight*, an imaginary dialogue between a godly man and Satan, which was intended to fortify its readers in their daily struggle against temptation. Clarke's second account followed a similar pattern. The exchanges between the Devil and the exorcist, Richard Rothwell, echoed the language and sentiments often expressed in godly meditations and prayers. Tellingly, Rothwell likened the plight of the possessed man to his own struggles to overcome the tempter. Speaking directly to the possessing spirit, he declared that 'thou hast oft beguiled me, [but] I hope God will in time give me wisdom to discern, and power to withstand thy delusions; and he it is that hath delivered me out of thy hands, and will I doubt not also deliver this poor man'. In both cases, the spirits inside the demoniacs' bodies resembled the 'Devil in the mind' described by godly autobiographers. They interrupted prayers and disturbed attempts to read the Bible, they raised objections to points of Protestant doctrine, and they blasphemed against God. The main difference was that godly Christians normally internalised their struggle with Satan. The demoniacs described in Clarke's book succumbed completely to the Devil's power, so that their exorcists played the role of the Christian conscience struggling to overcome him. [22]

As well as providing a religious context in which individuals could make sense of demonic possession, godly religion created social circumstances in which the affliction was likely to occur. This came about in two ways. First, the community of godly 'professors' was generally receptive to the idea of possession itself, a factor that was important since the condition depended largely on the behaviour of those around its victims. It is likely that networks of devout Protestants, who shared an intense awareness of the Devil's presence in the world, provided an ideal audience for potential demoniacs. In some cases, it seems that the initial diagnosis of possession came from a minister. When Robert Balsom was called to treat the man 'afflicted with temptation' in Berwick, he tried first to counsel him with comforting words from the scriptures. This approach appeared to work, but the man fell back into mental anguish within a couple of days. The pastor returned, and again tried to comfort the man with the promise of God's free grace to all faithful Christians. When this failed to relieve his distress, Balsom tried a different tack:

> Perceiving that no words of comfort would fasten on him, he whispered to him in his ear to this purpose: 'I doubt there is something

within, that you should do well to discover.' Whereupon immediately
the man's tongue swelled out of his mouth, insomuch that he was not
able to speak. Master Balsom continued speaking to him, till at length,
to the astonishment of those in the room, being many, and some of
them persons of quality, a shrill voice was heard, as from out of his throat
(having not any use of his tongue) to this purpose: 'What dost thou
talking to him of promises, and free grace? He is mine.' Master Balsom,
apprehending it to be the voice of the Devil, replied: 'No Satan, thou
dost not know any man to be thine while there is life in him.'

In this dramatic instance, it appears that the minister's suggestion that
the man might be possessed was the catalyst for the definitive symptoms of the condition. As soon as these symptoms appeared, Balsom
confirmed the diagnosis by acknowledging the Devil's presence in the
victim's body. Similarly, Joyce Tovey only displayed the signs of possession in 1647 after she had been examined by a pastor, who 'strongly
imagined' that her fits were caused by the Devil. Once the condition was identified, members of the godly community provided a
supportive audience for the drama of possession. During the affliction
of Alexander Nynde in 1573, a crowd of 'twenty persons and more fell
down and said the Lord's prayer' to assist in his exorcism. Some thirty
years later, the possession of a young boy from Northwich in Cheshire
attracted pastors and layfolk from across the region, who participated
in a series of fasts and prayers for the boy's deliverance. It is reasonable
to assume that such gatherings, which were typical at Protestant exorcisms throughout the period, provided a social environment in which
the phenomenon of possession was likely to flourish. [23]

The second way in which zealous Protestantism created a social
context conducive to possession was very different. In recent years,
historians such as Anthony Fletcher and Lyndal Roper have drawn
attention to the impact of reformed religion on family life. They
have argued that many Protestant households adopted new standards
of religious discipline during the sixteenth century, with fathers
assuming some of the responsibilities for spiritual instruction previously undertaken by priests. Devout parents were obliged to provide
an appropriate regime of theological and moral instruction for their
children and servants. The conduct books of the seventeenth century
suggest that these regimes were often repressive: Richard Baxter was
typical in warning the heads of households to keep their charges
from 'cards, dice and stage plays, play books and love books, and

foolish wanton tales and ballads'. In the context of these restrictions, the drama of possession could provide a drastic but socially acceptable outlet for youthful rebellion. Jim Sharpe has suggested that this helps to explain the possession experiences of adolescents in godly households, such as the Starkeys and the Throckmortons in the 1590s, which were characterised by a violent rejection of the religious values of the adults around them. In a slightly different context, the antics of possessed youths like Thomas Darling, William Somers and Thomas Harrison of Northwich can be viewed as rebellions against the spiritual values promoted by their communities. If this interpretation is correct, the practice of reformed religion created some of the psychological pressures that gave rise to possession experiences, while the godly community itself provided a supportive context in which these experiences could be acted out. [24]

Possession, religious ecstasy and the deathbed

The links between possession and Protestantism can be illustrated further by a brief discussion of two related phenomena: the behaviour of godly Christians on their deathbeds, and the experience of religious ecstasy or 'inspiration'. In both situations, devout men and women displayed symptoms similar to those manifested by demoniacs, but their actions were understood differently by those around them. They were acting out socially sanctioned alternatives to possession, with a different set of rules and expectations governing their performances. During their deathbed struggles with Satan, godly Protestants often entered a trance-like state, and spoke 'idle' and incoherent words in the manner of demoniacs. Once the conflict began, however, they assumed for themselves the role of the exorcist. Like godly dispossessions, their actions were witnessed by gatherings of sympathetic observers, who identified with the symbolic struggle and offered prayers to support them. These audiences also played a crucial role in the interpretation of events, ensuring that they were placed within the framework of conventional ideas about a 'good death'. The witnesses at Katherine Brettergh's bedside, for instance, noticed that she was 'once or twice troubled with vain speeches', but downplayed their significance because they 'saw that these things proceeded of weakness, emptiness of her head, and want of sleep'. Such observations suggest that the actions of dying Protestants, like those of demoniacs, were interpreted selectively, according to a repertoire of conventional assumptions. The parallels between the two conditions are revealing, and indicate that they served similar roles within the godly community: they both dramatised the conflict between Christians and the Devil, and offered a public demonstration of the triumph of Christ. [25]

Other spiritual phenomena described by godly Protestants were also reminiscent of possession. In 1653 John Rogers recalled a remarkable 'judgment of God' from his youth, which he likened explicitly to a possession experience:

> About 1637 ... at Messing in Essex, I was playing with children (my fittest companions then) ... [when] I threw out vain words, and crying 'O Lord!' (which we were not suffered to do), my heart was suddenly smitten upon it, and I was suddenly set a running as if I had been possessed (by I know not what power or spirit), not having any strength to stay myself ... until I was headlong carried through a little gateway, where (as plainly to my thinking and in my appearance as ever I saw anything by the sunshine) there was set a naked sword, glistering with a fearful edge ... I ghastly screeched, and yet had not the least power to stay or stop my precipitant course.

Rogers claimed that he passed through the spectral blade and thought himself to be dead; but when he recovered his wits, he found that the sword had vanished and he was completely unhurt. He interpreted the episode as a warning from God against his breach of the third commandment, but acknowledged its affinities to the experiences of demoniacs. By admitting that he knew 'not what power or spirit' had taken over his body, he even left open the possibility that Satan, rather than the Holy Spirit, had been the immediate cause of his affliction. [26]

While Rogers' enchantment could be explained as a divine judgment, other experiences that resembled possession were more problematic. This was the case with the state of 'rapture', or spiritual ecstasy, in which a person's body was apparently overwhelmed by the Holy Ghost. As the previous chapter argued, godly pastors were sceptical about extreme manifestations of this phenomenon; but nonetheless, the rapturous inrush of divine grace was recorded quite frequently by devout Protestants. Thomas Darling received spiritual ecstasies as well as demonic temptations during his possession in 1596. During a period of illness in Newcastle in the 1630s, Jane Turner felt herself to be 'in a continual converse and exchanging love with

God, as it were lodging and living in the bosom of Christ'. In the decade that followed, ecstatic experiences of this kind were common among the members of religious sects, and later emerged as one of the defining features of the Quaker movement. The practice was controversial, and provoked allegations from critics that those who claimed to be 'inspired' were either charlatans or unwitting demoniacs. Richard Baxter, for instance, declared that Quakers were 'enthusiastics that Satan hath notoriously deluded by pretended angelical revelation'. Despite their polemical motives, critics like Baxter were probably correct to identify a connection between demonic possession and 'inspiration'. The symptoms of the two conditions were similar, with inspired men and women experiencing involuntary spasms, seeing visions, and sometimes speaking in unfamiliar voices or foreign languages. Thus the prophetess Sarah Wright 'spoke as with a new tongue' in 1647; and John Robbins, the leader of a small group of 'shakers' in 1651, proved the genuineness of his ecstasies by speaking in Hebrew, Latin and Greek. In a small number of cases, the words that inspired individuals ascribed to the Holy Ghost resembled the utterances of demoniacs. Most notoriously, Abiezer Coppe was moved by the Spirit to blaspheme, declaring in 1649 that 'what goes for cursing and swearing' in those blessed by God 'is more glorious than praying and preaching in others'. He later suggested that his mystical experiences caused him to be 'infected' with a 'plague of swearing'. The parallels between religious ecstasy and possession meant that the two conditions could be confused. In an arresting episode from Kendal in 1647, a Quaker convert, John Gilpin, was moved by the Spirit to 'a great rapture of joy'. He and his companions initially accepted this experience as genuine, but began to suspect that its source was diabolical rather than divine. After much uncertainty, Gilpin eventually concluded that he was the victim of possession, and attempted to exorcise the Devil from his own body. [27]

As this incident suggests, the diagnosis of religious ecstasy was largely a matter of interpretation, and individuals susceptible to the condition could be perceived as victims of possession in different circumstances. It seems reasonable to assume that the willingness of godly pastors to accept the existence of demoniacs, and their reluctance to acknowledge extreme cases of divine inspiration, normally encouraged such individuals to act out the drama of possession in the period before the civil war. Subsequently, the proliferation of religious sects in the 1640s created new opportunities for men and women to experience spiritual raptures, despite persistent allegations that they were really possessed by Satan. Throughout the reign of Elizabeth and the early Stuarts, Protestant divines had good reason to favour the diagnosis of possession over that of inspiration: individuals touched by the Holy Ghost could command a spiritual authority to rival their own, whereas demoniacs were viewed as victims of the Devil's malice, whose deliverance depended on their ministry. Broadly speaking, the professional concerns of the godly clergy inclined them to dismiss the phenomenon of inspiration while promoting its demonic alternative. Similar interests encouraged some pastors to take up the practice of exorcism, an activity that is considered below.

The politics of exorcism

The performance of a dispossession was viewed by many contemporaries as a form of religious education, akin to a particularly dramatic and instructive sermon. Like a sermon, a successful exorcism advertised the authority of the minister who performed it, and afforded an opportunity to instruct those present in the essentials of reformed Christianity. Unlike many sermons, it was also likely to attract a large and attentive audience. The appeal of such demonstrations to godly pastors is best understood in the wider context of the English Reformation. The introduction of Protestantism encouraged the emergence of the parish clergy as a professional class, whose university training increased both their social status and financial expectations. Paradoxically, the same process undermined their institutional position, since reformed doctrines stripped the church of the magical power of the mass, the control of holy relics, and the authority to assist the souls of the dead. As a result, many ministers came to identify themselves primarily as leaders of the Christian community, whose authority derived mainly from their knowledge of the Bible and fidelity to Christ. The performance of exorcisms was ideally suited to this role: it provided a vivid demonstration of their leadership among God's people, and confirmed the idea that the true church was a gathering of believers rather than a physical institution. These points have been noted by Stephen Greenblatt, who has observed that English exorcists made it clear that their practices 'did not depend upon a state-sponsored ecclesiastical hierarchy'. Exorcists such as John Darrell stressed that their work depended more on their personal faith and knowledge of scripture than the institutional power of the church. As Darrell averred in 1597, his ability to cast out demons derived entirely from his faith in Christ, and did not imply that he possessed any 'special or greater gift . . . than the rest of my brethren'. For such men, dispossessions provided a perfect means of validating their authority and confirming their reputation as faithful servants of God. [28]

This process was neatly illustrated by the lengthy dialogues that often took place between Protestant exorcists and the Devil. In 1593, George Gifford warned Christians not 'to talk and question' with Satan when he spoke through a possessed person, suggesting that they should only 'entreat the Lord to show mercy and to expel him'. This advice was consistent with reformed theology, but it appears to have been frequently ignored. The advantages of disputing with the fiend were demonstrated in Richard Rothwell's exorcism of the possessed man in Nottingham. The dialogue between Rothwell and the Devil, speaking through his victim's body, took the form of a learned debate in which the pastor was able to overcome Satan through a combination of biblical expertise and personal faith. The Devil 'quoted many scriptures out of the Old and New Testament, both in Hebrew and Greek, caviled and played the critic, and backed his allegations with sayings out of the [church] fathers'. Happily, the exorcist 'was mightily enabled by God to detect the Devil's sophistry', and so confounded the fiend that he forced him to surrender the man's body. At the end of the struggle, Satan candidly admitted that his cause was lost: 'What [chance] stand I talking with thee? All men know thou art Bold Rothwell, and fearest no body, nor carest for words. Therefore I will talk to thee no more'. Gower observed that this incident secured the reputation of his friend, who was subsequently known as 'he the Devil called Bold Rothwell'. [29]

As well as establishing the credentials of ministers, cases of possession offered them opportunities to fulfill their role as religious teachers. Public exorcisms were a powerful weapon in the battle against popery. First, they allowed pastors to rebut the popish lies that the Devil expounded through the mouths of demoniacs. In 1573, for instance, the demon possessing Alexander Nynde announced that it was good for Christians to offer prayers to St Mary, only to have these idolatrous words condemned by a godly exorcist. The falsehood of the spirit's claim was eventually proved when it was forced to flee the man's body. Secondly, successful exorcisms could be an effective tool in the campaign to win converts from Rome, especially in regions with large recusant communities. Thus John Darrell claimed in 1599 that some Catholics in Lancashire had promised to 'forsake the church of Rome' if his dispossessions were genuine, since the ability to cast out demons was a sign of the 'true church of Christ'. Accordingly, he condemned those members of the ecclesiastical hierarchy who objected to his activities as 'secret friends of Rome'. In this respect, Protestant exorcisms appear to have played a similar role to the deathbed struggles with Satan experienced by godly individuals like Katherine Brettergh, which were used to validate their beliefs against the claims of the Catholic church. [30]

The use of exorcisms to attack popery was combined with efforts to promote the 'reformation of manners', the attempt to impose new standards of religious and moral behaviour on the laity. The words and actions attributed to people gripped by evil spirits sometimes read like a list of the sins most trenchantly denounced by godly ministers. Thus Darrell gave the following account of the actions of William Somers in 1597:

> This evening he acted many sins by signs and gestures, most lively representing and shadowing them out unto us, as namely: brawling, quarrelling, fighting, swearing, robbing by the highways, picking and cutting of purses, burglary, whoredom, pride both in men and women, hypocrisy, sluggishness in hearing the Word, drunkenness, gluttony, also dancing with the toys thereto belonging, the manner of antic dances, the games of dicing and carding, the abuse of the viole, and other instruments.

It is hard to ignore the propaganda contained in this extraordinary performance, though one can only guess at the impact it made on its audience and the readers of Darrell's account. A similar catalogue of misdemeanours was recorded in the speeches of a possessed boy in the Cheshire town of Northwich, whose exorcism was witnessed by the puritan divine, Thomas Pierson, in 1603. According to Jacqueline Eales, the boy's words 'constituted a bizarre parody of the specific spiritual values that Pierson and his colleagues were trying to inculcate in the town', and afforded them a dramatic opportunity to press home their case for a reformation of manners. [31]

Cases of possession also helped to cement the links between puritan clergy and sympathetic layfolk. Darrell's exorcisms in the 1590s were usually witnessed and assisted by like-minded Protestants in the places he visited. Similarly, Pierson described a large gathering of ministers and layfolk for the exorcism in Northwich. The dispossession took place over several days, and provided the occasion for a series of fasts and sermons. According to Stanley Gower, Richard Rothwell's confrontation with the Devil in Nottingham was witnessed by a 'company' of fellow Christians. Subsequently, the man who had been possessed was the subject of prayers 'every Sabbath and lecture day in many places'. A similar example of the mutual support of godly Protestants occurred in 1634, when Anthony Lapthorne, the pastor of Tretire in Herefordshire, 'invited many foreigners of other parishes' to assist in the exorcism of members of his flock. Such events helped to maintain the networks of godly 'professors' that constituted an informal church structure in many regions.[32]

It was probably these factors, combined with the propensity of devout Protestants to succumb to the affliction, that caused zealous pastors to take the idea of possession seriously. Equally, the campaign by the church hierarchy to discredit and restrict the activity of godly exorcists can be viewed as part of a wider effort to rein in the excesses of 'over hot' ministers, which threatened the authority of the institutional church. With this in mind, it is hardly surprising that Samuel Harsnett, the most vociferous and determined of John Darrell's detractors in the 1590s, went on to become an aggressively anti-puritan bishop of Norwich. During the reign of Charles I, the practice of dispossession was one of many aspects of the puritan ministry that was challenged in the ecclesiastical courts. Anthony Lapthorne, for one, was prosecuted in the High Commission for attempting to cast out demons, along with his refusal to make the sign of the cross in baptism and administer the Eucharist 'according to the prescript form appointed in the Book of Common Prayer'. Similarly, Richard Rothwell and Robert Balsom combined their work as exorcists with opposition to the ecclesiastical policies pursued by Archbishop Laud, and both were troubled by the courts during the 1630s. For both the supporters and opponents of exorcism, it appears that the practice was intimately connected with wider issues of religious affiliation within the English church, and attempts to suppress it were perceived as an attack on the godly ministry as a whole.[33]

By accepting the reality of demonic possession, and taking the lead in its identification and treatment, godly ministers tacitly endorsed many traditional beliefs about the Devil. Their appropriation of popular ideas about unclean spirits, along with the grossly physical view of the Devil that this entailed, led to an unlikely but enduring fusion of reformed religion with older practices and beliefs. This process involved considerable theological ambiguity: indeed, a more consistent application of Protestant doctrine might have led godly men and women to adopt the sceptical opinions promoted by Samuel Harsnett. It appears, however, that the concept of possession was attuned to the practical needs of many godly pastors and their flocks. A similar process of assimilation can be detected in the attitudes of some Protestants towards witchcraft, which is the subject of the following chapter.

WITCHCRAFT

While the English Reformation amplified the power of the Devil and removed many traditional protections against him, it did not unleash a campaign against satanic witches. Indeed, the English experience of witch persecution has long been recognised as comparatively mild. The country was largely spared the kind of mass trials that decimated some regions of the Holy Roman Empire during the late sixteenth and early seventeenth centuries. More tellingly, witch trials in the kingdom of Scotland were more widespread and lethal than in England. When the difference in population is taken into account, accused witches in Scotland were twelve times more likely to be executed than their English neighbours. [1]

The relatively lenient treatment of English witches resulted partly from the judicial system. This was characterized by the authority of the higher courts in cases of witchcraft and the existence of fairly strict legal safeguards on the treatment of suspects. Allegations of murder by *maleficium* – or destructive magic – were first heard by Justices of the Peace, who were required to pass on the strongest cases to the court of assize. At this stage the Grand Jury assessed the validity of the charges, and passed on what they deemed to be 'true bills' of indictment to a full trial under a crown-appointed judge. In those cases where a guilty verdict was reached, appeals could still be made to commute the sentence of death. Thus the process tended to move the case away from the community in which it originally arose and provided legal checks that protected the accused. A relatively low level of executions resulted: the surviving records of the Home Circuit of the assize courts indicate that less than a quarter of accused witches were hanged. [2]

These legal restraints were combined with the ideological reservations of many English Protestants. Here ideas about the Devil were important. It was once widely believed that demonic elements

The Devil preaches to his followers, from *Newes From Scotland* (1591).

were largely absent from English witchcraft: the pioneering studies of Keith Thomas and Alan Macfarlane in the early 1970s established an image of English witch trials centred on the fear of harmful magic in village communities, and largely untouched by continental notions such as the demonic pact that formally bound the witch to the Devil's service. This view has been vigorously challenged, however. Recent scholarship has drawn attention to the familiar spirits or 'imps' – often with distinctly demonic qualities – that featured prominently in English allegations of *maleficium*. The satanic aspects of English witch beliefs were particularly marked in the East Anglian trials of 1645-7, which have been the subject of major recent studies by James Sharpe and Malcolm Gaskill. As Sharpe has pointed out, the records of these trials 'constitute the largest single body of evidence concerning English witchcraft we possess, and it would be unhelpful to dismiss their superficially unusual features as untypical'. In fact, some of the main themes that emerged in the East Anglian persecutions were found in popular accounts of English witchcraft throughout the sixteenth and seventeenth centuries. These include the idea of the demonic pact and the Devil's mark on the witch's body – though these ideas were embedded within a folkloric view of the Devil that was often at variance with Protestant demonology. [3]

It was this tension between the Protestant understanding of Satan and the view of the Devil in popular witch beliefs that made many godly ministers and layfolk wary of witch trials. Their conception of Satan as the 'prince of this world' made it impossible for him to be subjugated to the bidding of witches. If he chose to masquerade as a witch's imp, he was clearly practising a deception intended to spread malice and falsehood. Equally, the doctrine of divine providence encouraged the acceptance of misfortune as part of God's loving plan, rather than the work of witches. These arguments were advanced with great clarity and vigour by the Essex minister George Gifford in his two treatises on witchcraft in 1587 and 1593, and remained influential throughout the seventeenth century. This way of thinking left open the possibility that witches could be punished for their association with the Devil, which constituted a crime against God rather than a crime against their neighbours: thus Protestant demonologists were far more concerned with the supposed pact between witches and Satan than they were with acts of *maleficium*. They were also aware of the Devil's desire, as the 'father of lies', to exploit allegations for his own purposes. Such thinking promoted scepticism about witchcraft accusations, though this was sometimes overridden when the interests of Protestant spirituality appeared to converge with popular fears of diabolical magic. The circumstance in which this occurred will be considered below. But first it is necessary to focus on the demonic elements that were mingled in popular conceptions of the crime. [4]

THE DEVIL IN POPULAR WITCH BELIEFS

James Sharpe has suggested that 'the key to popular conceptions of the connection between the witch and the Devil lay not so much in popular views of witchcraft as in the popular image of the Devil'. This view is confirmed by comparing the portrayal of Satan in witchcraft cases with his depiction in popular literature. When the Devil or his minions were described in witchcraft depositions, their appearance and behaviour often recalled folk tales and ballads. For example, they commonly assumed the form of an animal, like the cat named 'Satan' that performed magic for Agnes Waterhouse in 1565, or the two black frogs who demanded the soul of Joan Cunny in 1589. In later accounts, the Devil took the guise of a black man or a handsome youth wearing striking clothes or possessing some notable physical characteristic. When he appeared in this form, he occasionally revealed his true nature by exposing a cloven hoof. These characteristics were combined neatly in the confession of Margaret Wyard, one of the women examined by Matthew Hopkins in 1645, who encountered Satan as 'a handsome young gentleman with yellow hair and black clothes', whom she observed to possess 'a cloven foot'. Typically, the fiend would deceive the witch with illusory promises of success or wealth. In 1645, for example, Anne Barker described how 'there came to her a little dun dog, and said to her, 'if you cleave to me thou shalt want nothing', and told her she should find money under a step in the hall garden, but she found none'. This account resembled much older tales of the Devil falsely promising to reveal buried treasure, and cheap publications like *A New Ballad Shewing the Great Misery Sustained by a Poore Man in Essex*, which was circulating in the region in the 1620s. Similar parallels were apparent in cases of collective witchcraft. In 1621, for example, Edward Fairfax described a feast attended by witches and the Devil at Timble Gill in the Yorkshire dales. This scene resembled *A Strange Banquet*, an early seventeenth-century ballad depicting a satanic feast 'at the peak in Derbyshire'. [5]

In cases like this, it is difficult to tell if statements about witchcraft were borrowed from folk tales about the Devil or *vice versa*. Most probably, they both originated in widely held beliefs that were only partially influenced by reformed theology. These beliefs were also apparent in another common feature of English witchcraft. This was the tendency to associate the Devil exclusively with unneighbourly or anti-social behaviour. For Protestant demonologists such as William Perkins and George Gifford, all magical practices involved an implicit pact with Satan. Moreover, such activities were just one aspect of his dominion over the minds of 'superstitious' people, who clung to the idolatrous belief that they could gain assistance in life through the use of charms, potions or magical words. In contrast, the great majority of those who gave evidence in witch trials appear to have distinguished between good and harmful magic, and only connected the Devil with the latter. The depositions from one of the earliest witchcraft cases in England, handled by the archdeacon's court in Essex in 1563, show that the accused was originally identified by a village magician, or 'cunning man', who diagnosed a man's lameness as a form of bewitchment. The work of Thomas,

A witch feeds her familiar spirits, from *A Rehearsall Both Straung and True of Hainous and Horrible Actes* (1579).

Macfarlane and Sharpe has provided copious evidence that the most common defence against suspected witchcraft was counter-magic, designed to undo harmful spells or reflect the witch's magic back on the person responsible. In 1621, Edward Fairfax admitted that he was tempted to resort to such devices when his daughters fell victim to bewitchment. He observed that counter-magical practices like 'the sewing of certain words in set forms, the heating of iron tongs [and] the scratching of the witch' were practiced widely in his community, but resolved to leave such practices 'to them that put confidence in them, and to the Devil who devised them'. [6]

Familiar spirits and the Devil

The tension between Protestant theology and popular witch beliefs was illustrated further by the appearance of wicked spirits, or 'familiars', in a large number of English trials. The historical origin of these creatures is obscure, but their behaviour was remarkably consistent throughout the Elizabethan and Stuart period. Usually taking the form of small animals – typically mice, cats or frogs – they performed tasks for their masters in return for small meals of blood. In the earliest accounts, like that provided by the Dorset cunning man John Walsh in 1566, this was offered as a single drop from the finger, which 'the spirit did take away on his paw'. Later depositions had 'familiars' sucking blood from 'teats' on their owner's body, usually located near

A witch with familiar spirit, from *A Rehearsall Both Straung and True of Hainous and Horrible Actes* (1579).

the genitals. The importance of these creatures in English witchcraft is indicated by the efforts made to counteract their malign influence. As George Gifford noted in 1593, the practice of 'scratching' witches to draw blood from their faces was believed to rob their 'spirits' of power; and household protections such as witch bottles and shoes buried in buildings were apparently designed to trap these noxious creatures. The concept of the witch's 'teat' was a variation on the continental idea of the Devil's mark, which was used to identify suspected witches; and it was employed in a similar way in English cases, with midwives employed from the 1570s to examine the bodies of accused women for suspicious growths. The presence of 'familiars' in English witch-craft cannot, however, be attributed to the influence of continental demonology, as these creatures appeared less frequently in European sources. Still less can it be traced to the work of those English theolo-gians who wrote on the subject. Indeed, reports of witches' imps were problematic for many demonologists, as they departed in their appear-ance and behaviour from the reformed understanding of the Devil: it is unlikely that they would have featured in published accounts of the crime unless they appeared in the original allegations. They were also described at length by writers profoundly critical of popular witch beliefs, such as Gifford and Reginald Scot. All this suggests that the belief in these creatures was rooted in popular traditions that probably pre-dated the Reformation. [7]

The distinction between imps and the Devil was often blurred in witchcraft depositions and printed accounts of trials. In some instances, creatures identified as witches' spirits behaved in ways clearly reminiscent of Satan. In 1565, for example, the spirit serving Agnes Waterhouse appeared to her daughter as 'a great dog' and demanded that 'thou shalt give me your body and soul'. Not only did the creature assume a form closely associated in folk belief with the Devil, but it also took the name 'Satan'. At Chelmsford in 1589, familiar spirits offered riches to their human accomplices in return for their souls. Similar behaviour was reported from Lincoln in 1619, when Philippa Flower made the following confession:

> She . . . saith that she hath a spirit sucking on her in the form of a white rat, which keepeth her left breast and hath so done for three or four years; and concerning the agreement betwixt her spirit and herself, she confesseth and saith that when it came first unto her she gave her soul to it and it promised to do her good and cause Thomas Simpson to love her, if she would suffer it to suck her, which she agreed unto.

In an earlier confession from Windsor, Elizabeth Stile claimed to have kept a rat, 'being in very deed a wicked spirit', which she fed from blood drawn from the right side of her body. She admitted 'that she gave her right side to the Devil'. A pamphlet from 1612 conflated the continental idea of the Devil's mark on the witch's body with the teat 'where the spirits suck'. More strikingly, Thomas Potts' account of the Pendle witches in the same year described the Devil sucking blood from the bodies of his disciples, and sometimes transforming himself into an animal to do so. In 1645 the confessions of the East Anglian witches examined by Matthew Hopkins and his associates tended to collapse the distinction between Satan and familiar spirits. When the two were distinguished, it was made clear that the Devil was the master of the witches' 'imps'. Occasionally, the fiend even warned his human confederates to 'send them away' to prevent their discovery by searchers. [8]

It is tempting to attribute the ambiguous relationship between 'familiars' and the Devil to the influence of those educated men who involved themselves in witch trials and the writing of pamphlets. In some cases, learned notions of the Devil might have been imposed on the evidence of ordinary people, who did not themselves perceive 'familiars' in demonic terms. There is a suggestion of this in the 1612 pamphlet, *The Witches of Northampton*, where references to the Devil were made in interpretative passages composed by the narrator. The account of the three spirits possessed by Arthur Bill, for instance, noted that their master gave them 'three special names', but 'the Devil himself sure was godfather of them all'. Elsewhere in the tract, words were ascribed to the Devil which the suspects apparently attributed to their 'imps'. Similarly, it is reasonable to assume that Matthew Hopkins' preconceptions about the Devil's role in witchcraft coloured the testimony of those accused in the East Anglian trials. But this process cannot fully explain the satanic dimension of many witches' 'familiars'. In numerous cases, the encounter between the witch and the Devil 'or wicked spirit' was embedded in a folkloric context that apparently owed little to the assumptions of the interrogators. As Lyndal Roper has suggested, the narratives of many confessions involved a kind of unequal collusion between the suspect and their questioner, with the accused drawing on their own experiences, beliefs and fantasies. Moreover, the conflation of the Devil with other spirits was by no means confined to popular culture. Protestant exorcists such as John Darrell and Richard Rothwell used the words 'demon', 'spirit' and 'Satan' as if they were interchangeable, and frequently addressed individual demons as if they were the fiend himself. In Stanley Gower's account of Rothwell's dispossession of John Fox, for example, the invading spirit was first introduced as an individual demon but later addressed as the Devil and the 'father of lies'. [9]

In all probability, the distinction between Satan, 'imps', demons and familiar spirits was much less important to the witnesses and accused in witch trials than they were to contemporary theologians or modern historians. The victims of witchcraft were more concerned with the harm these creatures caused, and the means available to prevent it, than speculations about their origin or nature. Nonetheless, the similarities between these beings and popular representations of the Devil suggest a connection between the two, though the boundaries were often vague. In *The Discoverie of Witchcraft* (1584), Reginald Scot noted the tendency of 'common people' to attribute the power of witches to the Devil, and George Gifford's *Dialogue Concerning Witches and Witchcraftes* (1593) indicated that popular views on witches, familiar spirits and the Devil were often intertwined. The tendency to conflate 'familiars' with Satan was also apparent in entertainments based on witchcraft. William Rowley's *The Witch of Edmonton*, which was first performed in 1621, presented the Devil as a black dog which performed harmful deeds against its mistress' enemies. Similarly, tales about Mother Shipton in the 1660s attributed to Satan the kind of behaviour normally associated with 'familiars'. In *The Life and Death of Mother Shipton* (1667), for instance, the Devil appeared to Shipton's mother and 'plucked her by the groin, and there immediately grew a kind of teat, which he instantly sucked, telling her that must be his constant custom morning and evening'. [10]

This material suggests there was a broad continuum in popular belief between familiar spirits and the Devil. This impression is confirmed by cases of demonic 'obsession' and possession. In the former instances, individuals were tormented by evil spirits, and in the latter they were physically invaded by demons. In both cases, the sufferings of the victim were usually attributed to witchcraft, and the attacking spirit itself was often believed to be a witch's imp. But once a case of possession was diagnosed, it was relatively easy for the spirit to become identified with the Devil himself, especially if the services of an exorcist were engaged. This process of transformation is so revealing, and its documentation so vivid, that it merits an extended examination.

Witchcraft, obsession and possession

In 1593 a striking case of demonic obsession was recorded in Huntingtonshire. Lying in her bed at night, the wife of Sir Henry Cromwell of Ramsey was suddenly awoken and 'very strangely tormented by a cat (as she imagined) ... which offered to pluck off all the skin and flesh from her arms and body'. A few years later, a similar experience was described by Joan Jorden of Stradbroke in Suffolk, who was terrorized by an evil spirit which visited her repeatedly at night. On one occasion the creature, which also assumed the shape of a cat, 'kissed her three or four times, and slavered on her, and (lying on her breast), he pressed her so sore that she could not speak'. When it returned on other evenings, it 'held her hands that she could not stir, and restrained her voice that she could not answer'. The patients of the Buckinghamshire physician Richard Napier described similar visitations in the 1620s and 1630s. In some instances, these experiences were so prolonged and severe that his patients went for weeks without sleeping. The torments of these men and women recalled the 'night terrors' endured by godly Protestants, and were probably caused by the same sleep disorder – known as 'the mare' – which involves paralysis, lucid dreaming and surges of fear. But unlike the experiences described in chapter three, they were not perceived by their victims as trials of faith. Instead, they were understood as signs of witchcraft, and the creatures responsible were believed to be familiar spirits. [11]

Such attacks were often linked to demonic possession. Lady Cromwell received her nocturnal tormenter on the evening she returned from Warboys to visit the possessed children of the Throckmoton family. Among other symptoms, the children claimed to be menaced by devilish apparitions in the form of animals. The spirit which assailed Joan Jorden at night later possessed her body, giving her such violent convulsions that it took 'six strong men' to hold her down. The patients treated by Napier sometimes believed they were possessed, like the man in 1634 who felt an evil spirit enter his body as he lay in bed on Whitsun eve. It was common in such cases for an individual witch to be accused of sending the 'imp'. In each of the possession cases involving John Darrell in the 1590s, his patients named a person whom they believed was responsible for their suffering. When Thomas Darling was visited by the alleged witch Elizabeth Wright in 1596, he screamed and suffered a violent seizure, which only subsided when she left the room. Likewise, the victims of Edmund Hartley in Lancashire fell down speechless when he came near them. The connection between witchcraft and possession was so strong that fake demoniacs, who subsequently admitted their fraud, included allegations of *maleficium* in their performances. Thus George Purie, 'the boy of Bilson' in Staffordshire, accused a woman of sending a spirit into his body. When he was brought to the assizes to confront her, he pretended to be affected in her presence with 'strange pranks', until his imposture was exposed by the Bishop of Lichfield. In this, and other cases of feigned possession, it seems that the allegation of witchcraft was not intended primarily to accuse an innocent person, but to confirm the genuineness of the victim's alleged condition. The involvement of witches, it appears, was one of the widely recognised signs of the affliction. [12]

The role of familiar spirits in possession sheds light on one of the more puzzling and unpleasant aspects of the phenomenon. This was the moving lumps on the bodies of victims, which were reported throughout the Elizabethan and early Stuart period. For many of those suffering from the condition, it appears that these bodies were perceived as 'wicked spirits' or imps inside them. The ability of 'familiars' to enter human bodies was described crudely in the case from Stradbroke in 1599. Joan Jorden attested that the familiar spirit of Olive Barthram had killed one of her neighbours by getting inside him and tearing 'his heart in pieces'. When the creature subsequently possessed her own body, numerous witnesses claimed to observe a lump moving inside her. In this particular case, the imp was held responsible for a wide variety of intensely physical experiences, ranging from nocturnal visitations to bodily possession and the killing of a person 'from inside'. Similarly, it appears that Thomas Darling was tormented by a witch's familiar before the creature took possession of his body; and when he was finally exorcised, bystanders claimed that a small creature like a mouse scurried out of his mouth. In 1634 Edward Bonavent, a servant from Reading, suffered shaking fits and the sensation that a mouse was running up and down inside his body. He accused one of his neighbours, Edith Walles, of afflicting him with the spirit. A year later, the physician Richard Napier noted that one of his patients, Jane Slade, 'feels something stir in her body with a rising up and down, her face is much swelled and [she is] pained in her teeth, and fears that Joan Bray and her son Harry have bewitched her'. That these swellings were believed to be the physical signs of familiar spirits inside their victims was consistent with the fact that other sufferers of bewitchment, who did not endure the same symptoms, tended to see familiar spirits *outside* their bodies. This was the case with the Throckmorton children in the 1590s and the daughters of Edward Fairfax in 1621. [13]

The belief that 'familiars' could take residence inside a human body was also confirmed by a number of witchcraft confessions. In 1593 Alice Samuel told Robert Throckmorton that her own imps had 'gotten into my belly'. Elizabeth Clarke, the first woman accused of witchcraft in the Chelmsford trials of 1645, informed one of her examiners that her familiar could go 'into his throat, and then there would be a feast of toads' in his stomach. Another confession from the same proceedings affirmed that witches' imps could control a person's behaviour from within. After a servant from St Osyth had fallen into a 'shaking fit', in which he sang 'perfect tunes' and emitted the sounds of various animals, Joyce Boanes admitted that the boy was possessed by three familiar spirits. She claimed that her own 'imp made the servant to bark like a dog, the imp of Rose Hallybread enforced him to sing sundry tunes in the great extremity of pains, the imp of ... Susan Cock compelled him to crow like a cock, and the imp of Margaret Landish made him groan in such an extraordinary manner'. [14]

In the majority of cases, the victims of familiar-possession displayed other classic symptoms associated with demoniacs, including trances, fits, speaking in strange voices, and revulsion from holy objects and prayers. It was easy to interpret these manifestations as the work of the Devil, and the distinction between Satan and the familiar spirit could become blurred. The full range of symptoms was described in an incident from Hockham in Norfolk in 1600. In this instance, the affliction ended when the victim, Joan Harvey, scratched the alleged witch, and no dispossession was required. Thus the surviving account of her bewitchment described the experience of spirit-possession without the intervention of an exorcist:

> In her fits, when she seemed dead and senseless, she spoke very strangely, in the name of an ill spirit, nothing but as an ill spirit, and complained of Mother Francis the witch, telling how many imps she had, and what were their names, and why she vexed this wench, and how many she vexed in the town, and what were their names; and speaking against their prayers, their sending for learned preachers, their giving of her physic; sometimes storming at God and good men, and sometimes blaspheming God, and saying God is a good man, I can do as much as he, I care not for Jesus, etc. Some things were uttered, unknown before to the maid, in a strange and snappish voice, and sometimes to the tune of the witch and in her phrases and terms. And [she said these things] when the maid's mouth was wide open and gaping, and her lips not stirring, nor her tongue, and sometimes when her tongue was seen doubled in her mouth, and pulled into her throat or pinned up to the roof of her mouth, she being as dead and senseless.

For Joan and those who witnessed her ordeal, it appears that the possession experience was centred on the influence of the witch and her familiar. It was not the Devil, but one of these 'ill spirits' which spoke through her body, and she later took on the voice of the witch herself. But this did not mean that the creature possessing her had no satanic affiliations. It blasphemed against God and raged at prayers and preachers; and another passage described how the girl spat violently when she heard the name of Jesus. Such behaviour was typical of the fiend, and suggests that Joan and the witnesses believed the possessing spirit to be at least partly diabolical. Given this, it is easy to see how the Devil himself might have emerged as the spirit responsible for her torments had one of the 'learned preachers'

consulted on the case decided to conduct an exorcism. The willingness of people to conflate familiar spirits with the Devil helps
to explain how other cases of witch-related possession in the 1590s,
such as the Throckmorton children, Thomas Darling, the Starkey
family in Lancashire and William Somers in Nottingham, were transformed into fully-fledged demonstrations of Satan's power. [15]

The blurred distinction between familiar spirits and the Devil
allowed a distinctly unreformed view of Satan to emerge in many
cases of witchcraft. Above all, the Devil described in witchcraft
allegations was emphatically physical. He could take the form of a
small animal that was impeded by physical barriers; he entered and
left his victim's bodies through the mouth or other orifices, and
moved inside them like a parasite. All this was far removed from
the doctrines of William Perkins and other Protestant divines. This
contrast becomes even more acute when one examines popular
forms of protection against witches and familiar spirits.

Witch-bottles and other protections

Archaeology provides some of the most impressive evidence of the
widespread use of protections against evil spirits in Tudor and Stuart
England. The discovery of objects, particularly shoes and bottles,
concealed in the hearths and foundations of buildings sheds light on
popular perceptions of the Devil and familiar-spirits, and the most
appropriate means to combat them. The Concealed Shoes Index at
Northampton Central Museum holds records of over a thousand
items from the British Isles. Given the vagaries of preservation and
reporting, these figures probably represent only a small sample of the
total number of objects hidden in this way. There certainly appears
to have been a considerable market for such artefacts. Large numbers
of specially designed bottles, or 'bellarmines', were imported from
Germany during the sixteenth and seventeenth centuries, and the
trade was apparently still buoyant in 1626, when the potters Thomas
Rous and Abraham Cullen obtained a patent for making similar
objects in England. [16]

What were these objects for? By their very nature, it is impossible
to be certain of their original purpose, and it is quite likely that they
had more than one function. But the location of the artefacts suggests
that they were believed to deter evil spirits that wished to invade the
home. Shoes were most commonly concealed in chimneys or beside

doorways, which provided openings through which hostile entities might pass. Just under half the surviving 'bellarmines' were found in chimneys or under hearthstones, and another ten per cent were found near the entrances of buildings. While these objects have also been recovered from wall cavities and gardens, it appears that their principal use was to defend thresholds. In 1646 the Huntingtonshire minister John Gaule was probably referring to such vessels when he described 'the putting of such and such things under the threshold' in a list of common superstitions practised against witchcraft. The capacity of 'ill spirits' to come down chimneys was recorded in witchcraft depositions. In 1599, for instance, the imp that menaced and possessed Joan Jorden first scuttled down the chimney in the form of a cat, and preceded its subsequent visits by banging and 'scraping on the walls'. When his household was being tormented by familiar spirits in 1663, John Mompesson discharged his pistol at an object moving in the fire-place. Subsequently, he 'found several drops of blood on the hearth'. The role of concealed shoes and bottles as 'spirit traps' is also supported by the nature of the artefacts. According to tradition, the thirteenth-century divine John Schorn had conjured the Devil into a boot, and this legend might have encouraged a belief that boots and shoes could capture evil spirits. More detailed evidence is provided by the appearance and contents of 'bellarmines'. These were normally adorned with a crude representation of a human face, or 'mask', and often contained organic material, particularly hair, urine and bones. Pieces of fabric cut into the shape of a heart were also found in four surviving bottles. Such features suggest that the vessels were intended as 'decoy' bodies, designed to deceive malevolent spirits into attacking them instead of their human targets. This interpretation is consistent with the other most common material found in the bottles: pins and nails, which were probably intended to harm the invading spirit. Again, this hypothesis is supported by documentary evidence. In 1574 the spirit possessing Alice Norrington, a servant from Westwell in Kent, informed her exorcists that it had previously been trapped in a bottle, and was released by its present owner to torment and possess her enemies. [17]

The use of 'bellarmines' and shoes to trap evil spirits reinforces the impression that folkloric perceptions of the Devil and his minions were widespread in England, despite the efforts of reformers to promote alternative views. Presumably, the location and function of 'witch bottles' reflected the belief that demons were restrained by physical barriers. Such attitudes probably influenced beliefs about

Illustration from *The Apprehension and Confession of Three Notorious Witches... at Chelmsforde* (1589).

Satan, since the distinction between the Devil and familiar spirits was unclear. The creature that possessed Alice Norrington, for example, announced that he was 'Satan' and claimed to have a servant called 'Little Devil'. But he also admitted that for twenty years he had been trapped in a bottle belonging to an old woman. Such testimonies suggest that the Reformation made only a limited impression on the image of the Devil in popular witch beliefs: instead of a powerful, pervasive force for spiritual evil, he was often a limited and essentially physical creature who could assume various guises but preferred to appear as a small animal. He busied himself mainly by harming the health and property of innocent Christians, who could defend themselves with magical objects like bottles and shoes. [18]

WITCHCRAFT AND PROTESTANTISM

There was perhaps no stronger illustration of the divergence between popular witch beliefs and Protestant attitudes towards the Devil than the work of William Perkins, the most celebrated English theologian to write on the subject. For Perkins, the prevalence of witchcraft was a sign of Satan's dominion over 'earthly' people, who resorted instinctively to superstitious practices in order to fulfil their needs. The practitioners of magic made an 'implicit' compact with the Devil, even if they intended to do no harm. Thus even so-called 'white witches', who used magic to heal or protect their neighbours, were in reality 'the Devil's prophets'. Perkins spelt out this position in *The Calling of the Ministry* (1605), which contrasted godly preachers to 'cunning' men and women:

Consider the difference between these two: the wizard and charmer
has his fellowship with the Devil, the preacher with God; the charmer
has his calling from the Devil, the preacher has his from God. The
charmer's charm is the Devil's watchword – when he charms, the
Devil does the feat; but the preacher's doctrine is God's watchword
– when he truly applies it, God himself ratifies and confirms it. So
we should fear to have anything to do with the Devil in this way, [by]
seeking guidance from those who are his slaves.

As this passage suggests, Perkins' definition of witchcraft was much
wider than anything found in folk traditions, and was integrated
into a general theory of the nature of true religion. He viewed
Catholicism as little more than a highly organised form of witchcraft,
since its claim to authority rested on the use of charms. John Gaule
echoed this sentiment in his *Select Cases of Conscience Touching Witches
and Witchcrafts* (1646), which noted that the 'prestigious miracles
and superstitious rites' of the Roman church were 'little better than
kinds of witchcrafts'. More broadly, Protestant authors compared the
effects of Catholicism to enchantment throughout the Tudor and
Stuart period. In the 1550s, John Olde accused the Roman church
of 'bewitching the people'; and the preface to a catechism in 1586
claimed that the Catholic shrine at Walsingham had 'enchanted the
minds of kings and princes'. The view that all forms of superstition were tantamount to witchcraft was reflected in the casual use
of the word by Protestant writers in the seventeenth century. Thus
John Reynolds lamented the power of 'the bewitching world, the
alluring flesh and the enticing Devil' in 1635, and the author of a
book of meditations in 1639 decried 'the witcheries and vanities of
this world'. [19]

That these opinions were not confined to the abstract world of
theology is suggested by the remarkable notebook of Richard
Newdigate, a godly lawyer from Nuneaton. In 1631 he attended a
sermon by Josiah Packwood, the pastor of Fillongley in Warwickshire,
in which the minister denounced members of his flock for seeking
help from 'cunning men'. In the eyes of the pastor, such actions
constituted witchcraft. Newdigate recorded the preacher's advice
on how to reprove 'those that seek to witches for remedies'. This
included the most common arguments that such people used,
together with the appropriate response:

Objection: We seek not to the Devil but to God for help.

Solution: God will not have the Devil to be his agent. Should not a people [seek help] from the Lord?

Objection: We go to those that are good men, and we never hear hurt of them.

Answer: The Devil is full of subtlety and simulation. His end is to enlarge his kingdom by curing diseases.

Newdigate went on to list the main arguments against the practice of 'healing' magic. These included the observation that all magicians 'deal with the Devil and his instruments', and the assertion that diseases were 'God's signs', which could be cured only by His hand. His notes indicate the gulf between Protestant demonology and the views of the majority, and show the willingness of some clergy and parishioners to challenge widely held beliefs. The appropriate Protestant response to curative magic was later described by Christopher Love in *The Christians Directory* (1658). Love told the story of a man who feared that his son had been bewitched, and 'was advised by some to go to a witch to have his son helped and unbewitched again'. The man refused because 'he had rather the witch should have his son than the Devil'. [20]

The belief that Satan was responsible for all forms of superstition, from the 'white' magic practised in Josiah Packwood's parish to the abomination of the Roman mass, made Protestants sceptical of reports of witches' 'imps'. After all, such creatures were likely to distract people from the ubiquitous nature of the Devil's power. George Gifford stated the case plainly in his *Discourse of the Subtill Practises of Devilles* (1587). If demons did appear as witches' helpers, he suggested, this was merely a plot by 'the wily and wicked serpent to bring men to believe that he is not nigh them'. Here Satan's strategy was one of misdirection: he distracted people from his dominion in their minds by making them 'suppose he is not abroad unless he be fetched up by conjurers'. Gifford went on to illustrate the absurdity of Satan assuming the guise of a witch's spirit:

He goeth about like a roaring lion, seeking whom he may devour, as Saint Peter saith. Shall we be so sottish to believe that he lieth at the witch's house? He is a mighty tyrant. If God do suffer him that he, being a spirit, do take upon him the shape of some little vermin, as [a] cat or weasel, it is but to deceive. He lieth and sleepeth in warm wool.

The witch doth give him milk, or a chicken, and he doth eat. These are vain illusions. What needeth he [of] such things? He resteth not. He eateth not. He sleepeth not.

Gifford returned to this theme in *A Dialogue Concerning Witches and Witchcraftes* (1593), which lambasted the idea that the Devil – disguised as a witch's imp – needed to shelter in places like the trunks of trees. 'Do you think Satan lodgeth in a hollow tree?' he asked. 'Is he become so lazy and idle? Hath he left off being a roaring lion?' If he chose to present himself in this impoverished way, it was simply to conceal his 'mightiness and effectual working ... in the dark hearts of men'. [21]

Such objections led some Protestants to view familiar spirits as simply figments of the superstitious mind. To Reginald Scot, the activities of 'white spirits and black spirits, grey spirits and red spirits, devil toad and devil lamb, devil's cat and devil's dam' were quite inconsistent with 'the word of God and true philosophy'. For most thinkers, however, the existence of wicked spirits was confirmed by the evidence of scripture and a wealth of contemporary reports. According to John Malin, another preacher recorded in Newdigate's notebook, there were whole 'orders of evil angels' at large in the world. Most pastors followed Gifford in accepting the possibility that demons could disguise themselves as witches' spirits, but rejected the beliefs of the 'common sort' surrounding them. These included the assumption that satanic power was constrained by physical barriers, or could be repelled by magical objects or words. In *The Whole Armour of God* (1616), William Gouge condemned the perilous folly of 'conjurers, sorcerers and such like, who imagine the Devil may be driven away by charms'. On the contrary, such beliefs only confirmed his dominion over their minds. [22]

Given all this, it is clear that the Protestant understanding of the Devil tended to challenge and undermine popular witch beliefs. Godly writers such as George Gifford and Thomas Ady promoted a sceptical demonology that discouraged allegations of *maleficium*. It would be wrong to assume, however, that the gulf between Protestant doctrine and folkloric ideas about witches' imps was unbridgeable. Indeed, some Protestants came tacitly to endorse the understanding of witchcraft that was accepted by the ungodly majority. This improbable alliance sometimes lifted the barriers that prevented major witch trials in England, and contributed significantly to the witch-hunt in the eastern counties in 1645. The rest of this chapter seeks to explain how this strange and occasionally lethal synthesis came about.

'The work of God by the ministry of the Devil'

While Protestant ideas about the Devil departed markedly from traditional witch beliefs, they did not exclude entirely the possibility of bringing witches to trial. Crucially, several passages of scripture condemned trafficking with unclean spirits, including the injunction in Leviticus 20:27 that a man or woman 'that hath a familiar spirit' should be put to death. Thus there were religious grounds for denouncing those who attempted to enter demonic pacts, even if such pacts were based on a false understanding of Satan's power. Moreover, the view that the Devil was involved in *all* magical practices permitted a much wider definition of witchcraft than most ordinary people accepted. In the *Discourse on the Damned Art of Witchcraft* (1608), William Perkins presented this view with unflinching clarity. He defined a witch as 'a magician who either by open or secret league, wittingly and willingly, consenteth to use the aid and assistance of the Devil in the working of wonders'. This interpretation meant that those who were genuinely ignorant of Satan's involvement in magic could not be condemned as witches. Nonetheless, anyone who understood that God had forbidden the use of 'charms and enchantment' but persisted in using them had entered an implicit or 'secret league' with Satan. Perkins argued that apparently 'good' magicians, 'who only heal and cure the hurts inflicted upon men and cattle by bad witches', were more deadly than those who practised *maleficium*. This was because they encouraged people to break God's law and thereby extended the Devil's kingdom. When such people could not be excused by their ignorance of scripture, they were to be punished by death. [23]

The consistent application of this view of witchcraft would have condemned a wide range of magical practices, including many that were commonly regarded as harmless. While the English statutes against witchcraft fell short of condemning all forms of 'white' magic, they advanced a fairly broad interpretation of the crime – though the death penalty was reserved for murder by sorcery and, from 1604, the conjuration of evil spirits. The activities covered by the offence were spelt out in the first Elizabethan statute of 1563:

If any person or persons . . . take upon him or them, by witchcraft, enchantment, charm or sorcery, to tell or declare in what place any treasure of gold or silver should or might be found or had in the earth or other secret places, or where goods or things lost or stolen should be found or become, or shall use or practise any sorcery, enchantment, charm or witchcraft, to the intent to provoke any person to unlawful love . . . [they shall] suffer imprisonment for the space of one whole year.

Men and women were occasionally reported for 'witchcraft' of this kind. This was the fate of seven people from Berkswell near Coventry in 1636. After using magical techniques to 'find out the thief which had stolen a waistcoat of Elizabeth Lane', they were reported to the Bishop of Lichfield for making an 'implicit compact with the Devil'. Such prosecutions were rare, however. Only seven such cases were referred to the consistory court at Lichfield between 1614 and 1639. The suppression of 'white' magic was impeded by the fact that it was normally dealt with by ecclesiastical tribunals, whose punishments were more limited than those available to the secular courts. Moreover, all prosecutions depended on the co-operation of local populations, who were far more concerned with malicious sorcery than apparently trivial acts of magic. [24]

This situation placed godly ministers in a rather ambiguous position. For most of them, the attack on witchcraft was part of a much wider 'reformation of manners' by which they sought to reform popular behaviour and instil the principles of true religion. The practice of magic was only one instance of popular behaviour inspired by Satan. In some cases, pastors openly denounced impious or superstitious parishioners as servants of the Devil. Thus Francis Abbot, the vicar of Poslingford in Suffolk, was reported to the High Commission in 1634 for telling a woman 'she had served the Devil three-score years'. When he was accused of nonconformity by one of his churchwardens, he claimed that Satan was the man's 'black grandfather'. Similarly, the suppression of idolatrous entertainments was sometimes linked explicitly with the struggle against the Devil, as when Thomas Hall announced in 1662 that the only beneficiaries of May games were Satan and Catholic 'locusts from Hell'. But it was difficult for godly clergy to involve themselves in witchcraft cases without appearing to endorse the view that only bad magic was the work of the Devil. Moreover, their active support for the prosecution of witches could bring them into contact with folkloric beliefs about the practice, which were often as dangerous as the crime itself. But a section of the godly community was prepared to take these risks, as the benefits of witch persecution appeared to outweigh the problems it entailed. First, the rooting out of witches could offer an admirable demonstration of the power of the ministry. Thus John Darrell proclaimed in 1599 that the people of Nottingham became zealous hearers of the Word during his stay in their town, when he was responsible for the apprehension of thirteen witches. Secondly, witchcraft was intimately linked to demon-possession, and for reasons discussed in the previous chapter this phenomenon was a subject of special interest to many Protestant divines. [25]

The potential alignment between the godly ministry and traditional fears of *maleficium* was illustrated in several witchcraft pamphlets published after 1590. As Marion Gibson has shown, these texts often sought to present narratives of witchcraft that vindicated the actions of those involved. As witchcraft was an invisible crime, known only to its perpetrators and victims, this process frequently involved the presentation of 'proofs' against the alleged witch; and the authors of pamphlets were sometimes willing to buttress their case by reporting evidence obtained from traditional methods of detecting *maleficium* as well as formal confessions. Printed narratives also provided an opportunity to weld different understandings of the crime into more-or-less coherent accounts. *The Most Strange and Admirable Discoverie of the Three Witches of Warboys* (1593) is a good illustration. The pamphlet described the trial and execution of John and Alice Samuel, and their daughter Agnes, for bewitching the children of the Throckmorton family of Warboys in Cambridgeshire and causing the death of their relative, Lady Cromwell. The observations of various participants in the story were woven into the pamphlet; and these contributions reflected contrasting approaches to the problems posed by the children's affliction. Henry Pickering, one of their uncles and a student at Cambridge, stressed the religious dimensions of the crime and noted the suspects' supposed compact with Satan. This view was apparently endorsed by Francis Dorrington, the rector of Warboys. In contrast, Gilbert Pickering, another of the children's uncles, sought proofs of witchcraft through the traditional methods of scratching the suspects and bringing them into contact with their alleged victims in order to observe the effect that this had on them. Lady Cromwell herself resorted to counter-magical remedies against the alleged witches. The pamphlet combined these various perspectives to build a comprehensive indictment against them. It concluded with the grim proof that Alice Samuel possessed a 'teat' that she used to suckle her imps. This was discovered by the gaoler after her death:

> After the execution was ended, and these three persons were thoroughly dead, the gaoler . . . stripped off their clothes, and being naked, he found upon the body of the old woman Alice Samuel a little lump of flesh, in manner sticking out as if it had been a teat, to the length of half an inch . . . Not willing to conceal so strange a matter, and decently covering the privy place a little above where it grew, they made open show thereof unto diverse [people] that stood by. After this, the gaoler's wife took the same teat in her hand, and seeming to strain it, there issued out at the first as if it had been beesenings (to use the gaoler's word), which is a mixture of yellow milk and water. At the second time there came out a similitude of clear milk; and in the end very blood itself. For the truth of this matter, it is not to be doubted of any: for it is not only the gaoler's report unto all that require of him, but there are forty others also . . . that are ready to confirm the same upon their own sight.

As the account makes clear, this repulsive display was intended to confirm the old woman's guilt; and its inclusion in the pamphlet was presumably meant to underline the credibility of the narrative. At the same time, it drew unmistakably on the kind of traditional beliefs about witchcraft that were rebuked by George Gifford in the same year. Thus the pamphlet combined elements of folklore and demonology in a narrative that supported the Throckmorton family, and mixed aspects of reformed religion into the *melange*. [26]

Such texts in themselves helped to align Protestantism with traditional witch beliefs. They also provide clues to explain the involvement of Protestant clergy in witch persecutions. Thus *The Most Strange and Admirable Discoverie* describes how Francis Dorrington employed the investigation of the Samuel family in his ministry at Warboys. After Alice Samuel confessed to giving her soul to the Devil and sending imps to torment the Throckmorton children, Dorrington delivered a sermon in the presence of the accused woman. As he 'declared in the open assembly all the matter of [her] late confession', Samuel 'did nothing but weep and lament, and many times was so very loud with sundry passions that she caused all the church to look on her'. It is not hard to imagine how this spectacle confirmed the pastor's authority, and amplified the message of his sermon on the need for true repentance. Similar demonstrations were recorded in other witchcraft pamphlets, and their powerful effects were not lost on the opponents of witch trials. Thus Samuel Harsnett, the chaplain to the Bishop of London, complained in 1599 that the puritan exorcist John Darrell exploited the lurid appeal of witchcraft and possession. Harsnett observed that Darrell's activities caused pulpits to ring 'of nothing but devils and witches'. [27]

In return for these opportunities, godly pastors and their lay supporters sometimes tacitly endorsed folkloric ideas about the Devil. Francis Dorrington initially objected to the 'superstitious' practice of scratching witches to remove the power of their evil spirits, but he eventually agreed to attend the scratching of Alice Samuel's daughter, Agnes, by one of her alleged victims. He even addressed a sermon to the unfortunate girl after her ordeal, in which he declared that God would not allow her to be visited with such punishments if she did not have at least 'some knowledge of the wicked practices to which her mother had confessed'. A few years later, the dispossession of Thomas Darling of Burton-on-Trent was preceded by similar attempts at counter-magic. Despite his puritan sympathies, Darling scratched the woman he accused of bewitching him. She was also examined by a cunning man. In 1597 John Darrell endorsed the practice of testing alleged witches by asking them to recite the Lord's Prayer. It was widely believed that they were unable to utter the line 'Forgive us our trespasses' – though testing for witchcraft on this basis came dangerously close to 'tempting God' to pass judgment, and sat uneasily with the Protestant rejection of the magical power of words. In the company of other godly ministers, Darrell tested the 'wise man' Edmund Hartley in this way to affirm that he had sent demons into the children and servants of the Starkey household of Cleworth in Lancashire. The pastor also tolerated popular ideas about possession by witches' 'familiars'. His pamphlet on the case of William Somers implied that the youth ingested the spirit on a piece of bread, which he was forced to eat by a witch. In another text, he claimed that the swelling on Somers' body moved backwards and forwards in response to people around him. It even played tricks on 'some popish persons' by pretending to be afraid of a cross, and allowing them to chase it with that object 'from head to foot'. As he came under mounting pressure from the church hierarchy to defend his activities, Darrell relied increasingly on such physical evidence. In the process, he also appeared to authenticate much of the folklore surrounding demonic possession and witchcraft. [28]

The accommodation between godly religion and popular beliefs about witchcraft did not end with Darrell's career. Several of the clergy involved in the dispossession of Thomas Darling and the Starkey children, such as John Brinsley and John Ireton, went on to become prominent figures in the Jacobean church. In 1612 a relative of the Starkey children, Roger Nowell, initiated a series of witch prosecutions in the north of England. The depiction of the Devil in these cases owed much to folklore, despite the strong tradition of godly religion in Nowell's family. According to the confession of Elizabeth Southernes, one of the ten witches hanged at Pendle in Lancashire, she was walking in a forest when she met 'a spirit or devil in the shape of a boy, the one half of his coat black and the other half brown, who bade . . . her that if she would give him her soul, she should have anything that she would request'. She offered her soul to the boy for the space of six years. When this time had elapsed, the spirit returned 'in the likeness of a brown dog', which sucked blood from her left arm. Subsequently, it taught her magical techniques to harm her neighbours, and threatened her with physical violence when she refused to obey its commands. [29]

Further evidence of the willingness of Protestants to accept traditional witch beliefs was provided by the Fairfax family of Fuyston in Yorkshire. When Sir Edward's daughter, Helen, believed herself to be bewitched by a group of local women in 1621, he rejected as superstitious the magical remedies recommended by his friends. Nonetheless, he allowed one of the accused to be tested with the Lord's Prayer, and affirmed that she was unable to recite the crucial line. He also defended the widespread belief, rejected by the great majority of demonologists, that witches could transform themselves into animals. 'The changing of witches into hares, cats, and the like shapes, is so common', he argued, only 'the stupidly incredulous' could deny it. Fairfax's account of his daughter's afflictions combined traditional beliefs about the Devil with insights from Protestant theology. When the fiend appeared to her in a vision, he assumed a guise familiar from folk tales and ballads: 'she saw a black dog by her bedside, and after a little sleep, she had an apparition of one like a young gentleman, very brave, and [with] a hat with a gold band'. Interestingly, Helen (or her father) placed these encounters within the providential work of God. She announced to an apparition of one of the witches responsible for her torments that 'our God is the God of Heaven, even Jesus Christ our saviour, whom we serve, and your god is the Devil of Hell, and he can do nothing but what our God doth suffer him'. [30]

The godly minister Richard Bernard developed a more careful and nuanced marriage of reformed theology and popular beliefs. Around 1612 Bernard participated in a spectacular exorcism in Nottingham, though this did not involve any allegations of *maleficium*. He subsequently took an interest in allegations of witchcraft near his parish of Batcombe in Somerset, and went on to publish *A Guide to Grand-Jury Men* (1627), a treatise on the nature and detection of the crime. Bernard followed William Perkins in defining witchcraft in religious terms. The pact between the witch and the Devil was the essence of the crime, regardless of the various satanic deceptions that this involved. 'To convict any one of witchcraft', Bernard wrote, 'is to prove a league made with the Devil. In this act only standeth the very reality of a witch.' The *Guide* urged caution and discrimination in the detection of witchcraft, and went to considerable lengths to distinguish between godly and superstitious methods of doing so; it also criticised some of the proceedings followed in earlier cases, including the witches of Warboys. In his list of 'evidences' required for a safe conviction, however, Bernard appropriated folkloric ideas about witches' imps. Thus his first indication of guilt was the discovery of a 'witch's mark' on the body of the accused: this, he noted, was 'sometimes like a little teat' and could be formed by the Devil's 'sucking'. The second sign involved the suspect's conversation with wicked spirits: 'when she or he hath been heard to call upon their spirits, or to speak to them, or to talk of them to any, enticing them to receive such "familiars"'. As his third indication, Bernard pointed to 'the witches' deeds, as when any have seen them with their spirits, or seen [them] to feed some creatures secretly'. Bernard's interest in such evidence reflected his emphasis on the association between the witch and the Devil. But in seeking to confirm this association he relied on traditional beliefs about witches' spirits. These were, after all, proved by experience and 'innumerable instances'. [31]

In each of these examples, Protestants tried sincerely to reconcile their faith with traditional ideas about witchcraft. Thus John Darrell placed his activities in the context of divine providence, observing that demonic possession and witchcraft were 'the work of God by the ministry of the Devil'. Thomas Fairfax agonised over the appropriate response to his daughter's affliction, and only accepted those popular ideas about witches that he believed to be supported by strong evidence. Richard Bernard tried meticulously to accommodate traditional proofs of witchcraft within the framework of reformed theology, and rejected popular beliefs when he felt this was impossible. Nonetheless, it is clear that such men were prepared to appropriate ideas and practices from folklore. As Malcolm Gaskill has observed, 'official and traditional attitudes clashed and converged to produce a plurality of beliefs' about witchcraft. This process may well have been encouraged by spectacular cases involving Protestant ministers, since these attracted large audiences beyond the normal constituency of godly 'professors'. Large crowds gathered to witness the dispossession of Thomas Darling and William Somers, and the pamphlet describing the Throckmorton case claimed that 'five hundred men' visited the afflicted girls during the trial of Alice Samuel. It is unlikely that these people understood the events they witnessed in the same way as the godly individuals who endorsed them. By accommodating popular beliefs about witches' 'imps', and tacitly affirming the view that witchcraft involved obvious wrong-doers rather than practitioners of all forms of magic, some Protestants forged an alliance with traditional ideas about the Devil. The lethal potential of this alliance was realised in the eastern counties in 1645.[32]

The East Anglian witch-hunt

During the winter of 1644-45, a minor gentleman named Matthew Hopkins became alarmed at the activity of a group of witches in his home town of Manningtree in Essex. According to his own account, published two years later, a gathering of 'that horrible sect of witches' was convening at night in an area beside his house. He heard them conversing with their 'imps' and offering 'solemn sacrifices to the Devil'. On one occasion the witches mentioned the name of Elizabeth Clarke, an elderly, one-legged widow, whom Hopkins subsequently reported to the authorities. Clarke was 'thereupon apprehended and searched by women who had for many years known the Devil's marks, and found to have three teats about her, which honest women have not'. She was then subjected to the process of 'watching', whereby she was kept awake at night in the hope that her 'imps' would visit her.

In March 1645 Clarke made a full confession, and similar proceedings began against her supposed associates. Following a string of similar testimonies, thirty-six witches were eventually tried at the Essex assizes in July. By this time the accusations had crossed the border into Suffolk, where at least 117 alleged witches were examined or tried before the end of the year. Hopkins and his associate, John Stearne, played an active role in many of these accusations, which spilled over into Huntingdonshire, Cambridgeshire, Northamptonshire, Bedfordshire and Norfolk in 1646. In total, nearly 250 witches were investigated in the eastern counties between 1645 and 1647, and approximately one hundred were hanged. [33]

The East Anglian persecution was the most serious witch-hunt in English history, and bears comparison with the mass trials in Scotland and mainland Europe. It was made possible by a lethal confluence of factors. The civil war disrupted the judicial processes that normally controlled the prosecution of witches, and placed limits on the admissibility of evidence against them. As Nathan Johnstone has noted, the war also heightened awareness of the Devil's activity throughout English society: its depredations 'were the Devil's hallmarks, a sign that he now walked the earth unfettered'. At a local level, the intervention of Hopkins and Stearne helped to galvanise fears of *maleficium* in village communities. The events in the eastern counties were also encouraged by the blending of Protestant demonology and popular witch beliefs, a process that had occurred sporadically and with less devastating consequences in the reigns of Elizabeth and James. [34]

Historians have been divided on the role of Protestantism in the witch-hunt. Alan Macfarlane observed that the godly were split over Hopkins' actions, and claimed that the witchfinder himself 'cannot be shown to have been a puritan, or particularly interested in religion at all'. More recently, Malcolm Gaskill has painted a different picture. According to Gaskill, Hopkins saw himself as 'a warrior of reformation, bearing the sword of law in one hand, the shield of his election in the other'. This disparity is possible because Hopkins left few recorded comments on his religious beliefs. The views of his associates are easier to discern, however. His principal collaborator, John Stearne, appears to have been an ardent proponent of the reformed faith. In a treatise of 1648, Stearne described the campaign against witchcraft as a form of spiritual combat akin to the struggle with popery. He likened himself to a godly soldier, going 'well armed against these rulers of darkness, devils and evil spirits, furnished with the heavenly furniture and spiritual weapons of which the apostle speaketh ... and being thus qualified and armed to trust in God only, who will keep thee under the shadow of his wings'. When Hopkins and Stearne visited Bury St Edmunds in 1645, a commission was appointed for the trial of witches. Among its members was Samuel Fairclough, a puritan pastor who had been prosecuted for nonconformity by John Darrell's old adversary, Samuel Harsnett, during the 1620s. Another commissioner was the godly divine, Edmund Calumy. Calumy's role in the prosecutions was later applauded by the godly preacher and polemicist Richard Baxter. Baxter himself had no doubt that the 'sad confessions' of the witches were genuine, having spoken 'with many understanding, pious and credible persons that lived in the county, and some that went to them in the prisons'. The involvement of such people does not mean that Hopkins enjoyed the unanimous backing of the Protestant community: indeed, his principal opponent was the puritan pastor, John Gaule. But the activity of Stearne, Fairclough and Calumy in 1645 does show that he commanded support among a section of the godly. [35]

The endorsement of these men is striking given the nature of the allegations in 1645. They were based on an image of the Devil drawn substantially from folklore. Most of the confessions maintained a formal distinction between the Devil and witches' 'imps', but their description of these creatures was frequently demonic. Anne Usher encountered an 'imp' in the guise of a polecat, which skipped onto her lap and 'said if she would deny Christ [and] God he would bring her wittles'. Conversely, the admissions of other witches had the Devil behaving like an 'imp'. According to Elizabeth Greene, he appeared as a man at her bedside 'and nipped her by the neck', and then drew 'three drops of blood of her arm'. He paid a similar visit on Elizabeth Hobart, who confessed that he came 'like a black boy and drew blood against her will at her back'. Some of the confessions from Chelmsford in April 1645 collapsed the distinction completely. This was exemplified by the statement of Helen Clark:

> This informant confesseth that about six weeks since, the Devil appeared to her in her house, in the likeness of a white dog, and that she calleth that familiar Elimanzer; and that this examinant hath often fed him with milk-pottage; and that the said familiar spake to this examinant audibly, and bade her deny Christ, and she should never want, which she did then assent unto.

Another of the accused, Rebecca West, described the appearance of Satan at a gathering of witches:

> Forthwith the Devil appeared to them in the shape of a dog; afterwards in the shape of two kittens, then in the shape of two dogs; and the said familiars did do homage to . . . Elizabeth Clarke, and skipped up into her lap, and kissed her, and then kissed all that were in the room . . . Rebecca told this informant that she promised to keep all their secrets, and moreover, they all told her that she must never confess anything, although the rope were about her neck and she ready to be hanged: and that after she had consented to all these things, the Devil came into her lap and kissed her, and promised to do for her what she could desire.

The merging of Satan with the witches' 'imps' in these confessions faced Hopkins and his supporters with some obvious problems. Was it credible for the 'prince of this world' to appear as a white dog and feed on milk-pottage? Did he really take the form of a small animal to suck blood from his human confederates? Hopkins acknowledged these difficulties in *The Discovery of Witches* (1647), which identified queries 'which have been and are likely to be objected' to his activities. One query stated the problem succinctly: 'How can it possibly be that the Devil, being a spirit, and wanting no nutriment or sustenance, should desire to suck any blood? And indeed, as he is a spirit, he cannot draw [on] any such excrescences [as teats on witches' bodies], having neither flesh nor bone'. Hopkins' response affirmed his own belief that Satan was present in the bodies of the 'imps'. He argued that the Devil 'doth really enter into the body [of a] real, corporeal, substantial creature, and forceth that creature (he working in it) to his desired ends, and useth the organs of that body to speak withal, [and] to make his compact up with the witches, be the creature [a] cat, rat or mouse'. [36]

As well as conflating Satan with the witches' 'imps', the Hopkins trials assimilated a plethora of traditional witch beliefs. The confession of Ellen Driver, for instance, combined folklore and personal fantasy. She claimed that 'the Devil appeared to her like a man, and that she was married to him in one . . . parish, and that he lived with her three years, and that she had two children by him in that time, which were changelings'. One night 'in bed with him, she felt of his feet and they were cloven'. John Stearne confirmed the popular belief that witches could transform themselves into animals.

He told the tale of a witch who received an injury while in the shape of a dog, and then displayed the same wound when restored to her human body. The prosecutions also appeared to endorse the practice of counter-magic against witchcraft, which was mentioned in a number of the Chelmsford depositions in 1645. The evidence from Hopkins against the original suspect, Elizabeth Clarke, was supported by testimony from another Manningtree resident, John Rivet. After his wife had been 'taken sick and lame, with such violent fits that . . . [he] conceived her sickness was something more than natural', Rivet went to 'a cunning woman, the wife of one Hovye at Hadleigh in Suffolk', who told him that Clarke had bewitched her. Another witness in the proceedings scratched an alleged witch in order to relieve her stomach pains, which she believed the suspect had caused. She claimed that her 'extraordinary pains left her' as soon as she made the accused woman bleed. [37]

In accepting such testimonies, the supporters of the East Anglian trials compromised the Protestant understanding of witchcraft that had developed in the sixteenth and early seventeenth centuries. Indeed, they were almost obliged to do so by the logic of their position. The eradication of witches depended on reports from local communities against notorious suspects; and such reports were invariably coloured by long-standing beliefs about *maleficium* and its detection. Thus John Gaule, a godly critic of Hopkin's activities, noted that incautious witchfinding was a 'great occasion to augment the vulgar people's superstitions'. Most fundamentally, Hopkins and his assistants were alerted only to the practice of *harmful* magic. This ignored the insight of Protestant demonologists that ostensibly benign magic was as culpable before God – and potentially more deadly to its earthly devotees – than the destructive acts normally attributed to witches. Again, Gaule emphasised this point. He asserted that allegedly 'white' witches posed a more potent threat to the community than those who practised *maleficium*: 'For as Satan, being a fiend of darkness, is then worst when he transforms himself into an angel of light, so likewise are his ministers.' By relying on popular reports of harmful magic, Hopkins and Stearne not only ignored such people: they actually gave them credence by endorsing magical techniques to identify witches. When such methods were used, those responsible committed witchcraft themselves. As Gaule noted bitterly, the Devil encouraged this practice 'to nourish others in their superstitions'. [38]

The Devil and witches, from Joseph Glanvill's
Saducismus Triumphatus (1689).

Hopkins and Stearne consolidated these problems by presenting
witchcraft as a collective enterprise. The belief that witches joined
together to practice magic had surfaced in the Lancashire trials of
1612, and was mentioned in Thomas Fairfax's account of his family's
afflictions in 1621; but it was generally absent from English prosecutions before the civil war. By publicising the idea of a 'horrible sect
of witches', the Hopkins trials endorsed the view that the menace
of witchcraft was confined to the performance of evil magic, and
implied that this practice was contained within a diabolical cult.
The source of Hopkins' idea of a witch cult remains unclear, though
James Sharpe has suggested that it had some roots in popular culture.
It seems certain that many other aspects of the 1645 trials originated
in folk belief and 'superstition'; and this was the main reason why
some godly Protestants such as John Gaule, and later Thomas Ady,
condemned the proceedings. Like George Gifford before them,
they perceived the danger of embracing 'damnable' opinions in the
attempt to rid the world of evil. This was indeed a satanic bargain. [39]

THE CHANGING FACE OF SATAN

The Protestant Devil was preeminently a spirit of temptation and lies; he was an intimate enemy who built his kingdom in the 'dark hearts of men', but who could operate only within the limits of divine providence. This image was rich in possibilities. In times when believers were acutely aware of their own sins and the spiritual failings of their community, or felt assailed by powerful enemies, Satan's presence could seem dreadful and pervasive; but signs of divine favour could also remind the faithful that his hold on the world was ultimately frail. Correspondingly, the Devil loomed large in times of conflict. As the master of falsehood, he could be detected in a diversity of opinions: indeed, any belief perceived to be wicked or untrue was potentially his work. The reformed view of Satan was also adaptable to various cultural forms. Thus the invisible tempter of godly autobiographies could appear as a handsome stranger in ballads and chapbooks describing witchcraft or murder. Like a black mirror, the Devil reflected his viewers' assumptions. This quality made him an enduring figure in English culture, and helps to explain his development in the centuries after the Reformation. This chapter will offer a brief sketch of Satan's career in this period and survey some of the guises in which he appeared.

THE DEVIL IN WAR AND PEACE

In one of the most lurid images of the English Civil War, the title page of the royalist pamphlet *The Devil Turn'd Roundhead* (1642) depicted Satan giving birth to a 'crop-headed' supporter of the king's rebellious parliament. In the accompanying text, the fiend assumed the guise of a fanatical puritan who professed to 'hate all good manners, all orders, orthodox divinity, rule and government in the commonwealth and church'. This vicious tract provoked a parliamentarian rejoinder. *A Short, Compendious and True Description of the Round-heads and the Long-heads* (1642) exposed the king's supporters as 'the seed and spawn of the Devil', distinguished by their 'gross and palpable ignorance and blindness in spiritual and heavenly things', their addiction to prostitution, and their 'hatred against the appearance of any goodness'. The invocation of Satan in these works was typical of the propaganda created by both sides during the war. At the level of high politics, godly preachers urged the parliament to redouble its efforts against the satanic enemy, who was readily identified with the opponents of a 'thorough reformation' of the English church. As Robert Baillie informed the House of Commons in February 1643, 'the great and chief leader of all who oppose the reformers of a church or state is the Devil'. In a less elevated context, each side in the conflict routinely demonised the other in cheaply produced newsbooks, pamphlets and ballads. [1]

One effect of the war was to accelerate the process of integration between Protestant ideas of Satan and traditional beliefs. The propaganda needs of both sides encouraged them to exploit popular images of the Devil. On the parliamentarian side, it was rumoured that the royalist commander, Prince Rupert, had entered a pact with the fiend, and his favourite dog was a demonic familiar. These rumours were exploited in ballads like the *Dialogue Between the Devil & Prince Rupert* (1645). Other tracts depicted Satan as an avenging figure who punished the transgressions of royalist troops, often in a crudely physical fashion. In publications like *A Wonderfull and Strange Miracle, or God's Just Vengeance Against the Cavaliers* (1642), the blasphemy and drunkeness of the king's soldiers singled them out as targets for satanic retribution. Such tracts reinforced the popular wisdom that only the outwardly wicked were punished by the fiend. Later attacks on sectarian groups like Baptists and Quakers integrated folkloric tales about Satan with the Protestant theme that he was the 'father of lies'. In *A Sad Caveat to all Quakers* (1657), a Quaker apprentice from Worcester was beguiled by the tempter, who appeared to him as Jesus:

> It seems that the prince of darkness had appeared to him in the shape
> of some godly personage, and this credulous young man was apt to

> believe that it was Christ . . . [He said] that Christ had taken him by
> the hand, and that he had appointed him to come to him again, and
> that he must go unto him.

The unfortunate youth vanished soon afterwards, and his body was
found in the river. The spiritual message of this tragedy was pressed
home by one of the town's pastors, who preached on the temptations of Satan 'and how near of kin is spiritual pride to Hell'. Such
tales reinforced the idea that the Devil was the animating 'spirit of
falsehood' behind separatist groups in the 1650s, a theme developed
at length in the writings of godly Protestants such as Jane Turner and
Richard Baxter. [2]

Among royalist sympathisers, the assimilation of popular beliefs
about Satan was evident in tales that the leaders of the republic established in 1649 were tormented by demons for their crimes against
the king. In some versions, the Devil appeared almost as a supernatural ally of earthly supporters of the monarchy. For instance, *The
Just Devil of Woodstock* (1660) chronicled the 'apparitions, the frights
and punishments' inflicted by a vengeful fiend on the despoilers of
royal estates. It claimed that the surveyors of Woodstock park were
disturbed by 'dreadful noises' and apparitions, which showed that 'the
Devil himself dislikes their doings'. The tract also announced that the
Lord Protector was so terrified by demonic visitations that he kept
'nightly guards in and about his bed-chamber, and yet so oft [had] to
change his lodgings'. Such reports echoed earlier broadsheet ballads
and Protestant texts, such as *Strange Newes From Antwerpe* (1612),
which presented Satan as a just destroyer of the enemies of true religion and good government. [3]

Satan's withdrawal

If the tumultuous years between 1642 and 1660 were the zenith of
Satan's political career, the period after the Restoration marked the
beginning of his slow retirement from some areas of public life. As
has often been noted, belief in witchcraft diminished among intel-
lectuals in the last quarter of the seventeenth century. This was
accompanied by an increased scepticism about the physical manifestations of Satan's power, which provoked clerical authors like
Joseph Glanvill and Richard Baxter to compile lengthy empirical
treatises on the reality of the fiend, together with other residents of

the invisible 'world of spirits'. While Baxter regarded physical 'proofs' of Satan's existence as less compelling than theological arguments, he hoped they would leave sceptics 'that readeth them either convinced or utterly without excuse'. Despite such efforts, however, educated opinion was increasingly divided on the question of the Devil's power in the world. In 1677 the physicist Robert Boyle lamented that supernatural agencies of all kinds were derided by 'too many that would pass for wits'. A few years later, Henry Hallywell noted that belief in the Devil was an invitation to mockery. This movement in opinion was part of a much wider trend in intellectual circles, influenced by developments in science, the establishment of new standards of empirical evidence, and a general distaste for the perceived excesses of religious 'enthusiasm'. It is beyond the scope of this book to discuss these developments in detail, but it is reasonable to assume that each of them contributed to scepticism about the pervasive influence of Satan. [4]

The reduction of religious conflict in the later seventeenth century may also have played a role in promoting new attitudes. Under Elizabeth and the early Stuarts, the perception of devout Protestants that they were a threatened minority – surrounded by hostile 'world-lings' at home and military enemies abroad – encouraged them to emphasise the Devil's great power. By the last quarter of the century, confessional warfare had subsided in Europe and conflict within the established church was rather less intense. As James Sharpe has noted, it would be misleading to state that religious intolerance declined sharply after the Restoration. Nonetheless, he argues that a changed 'mental environment' did emerge, in which 'consensus was valued, where the dangers of religious heterodoxy had been demonstrated by recent experience, and where theological debate interacted constantly with the strain of maintaining a new political equilibrium'. This new environment did not necessarily entail a decline in Protestant commitment. Rather, it encouraged some thinkers to develop the potential that had always existed within Protestant doctrines to diminish Satan's power by emphasising the supreme authority of God. In the early seventeenth century, some divines had argued that Christians should not dwell excessively on the Devil's power. As Richard Greenham advised a devout lady in 1618, such speculations were pointless 'since all is done and governed by divine providence for your good'. But such a relaxed approach had only limited appeal in an atmosphere of religious conflict and political instability. Arguably, such attitudes were more likely to flourish in the more settled circumstances of the later seventeenth century. [5]

The emergence of less pessimistic ideas about the Devil did not mean that the Protestant theology of Satan faded away. There was considerable diversity of opinion within the late Stuart church, and the legacy of William Perkins remained vital among a section of the clergy. Even Archbishop John Tillotson, a celebrated proponent of the pragmatic view that religion should 'tend to the public welfare of mankind and the peace and happiness of human societies', appears to have endorsed a Calvinist interpretation of the demonic predisposition of human nature: he affirmed that 'the lusts and passions of men do sully and darken their minds, even by a natural influence', and 'the foundation of Hell is laid in the evil disposition of men's minds'. Equally, popular traditions about the Devil continued to develop and flourish, often garnished with anti-Catholic sentiments. There is good reason to assume that the assimilation of popular beliefs and Protestant doctrines continued after the period covered by this book, since the factors that caused this to happen remained in place. First, the strict application of the Protestant view of Satan was counter-intuitive: it required individuals to accept that their natural inclinations were demonic, and all people without true faith were unwitting slaves of Satan. This idea was hard to communicate in popular media such as pictures, stories and songs. Secondly, ministers on the evangelical wing of the church were frequently tempted to exploit traditional beliefs about the Devil, either to enhance their reputations by casting out demons or to promote their own religious agenda. It appears that similar dynamics operated long after the seventeenth century. With this in mind, the final section will offer a brief glimpse at the later career of the Protestant Devil. [6]

SATAN IN THE EIGHTEENTH AND NINETEENTH CENTURIES

Writing in the 1680s, John Aubrey lamented the willingness of 'vulgar' people to believe in tales of fairies, apparitions and demons. These stories, he asserted, were commonly passed down from 'old women' to their children, 'who can hardly be of any other opinion, so powerful a thing is custom joined with ignorance'. Aubrey's insistence on the tenacity of such beliefs was echoed by other antiquarians in the early eighteenth century. In 1725 Henry Bourne, a curate from Newcastle, noted that many folk 'in country places' claimed to have seen fairies and spirits, 'and some have even seen the Devil himself, with a cloven foot'. The work of historians such as Owen Davies and James Obelkivich suggests that folkloric ideas about Satan remained firmly entrenched in much of the country throughout the eighteenth and nineteenth centuries. These ideas stressed the existence of Satan as a physical being rather than a spiritual tempter. An account from the late eighteenth century, for example, recorded the fiend's appearance in a farmhouse in north Yorkshire. In the startling form of a 'pig all a-fire', he smashed china on the kitchen floor. More commonly, Satan appeared as a well-dressed man. It was in this disguise, according to the nineteenth-century folklorist, John Penny, that he accosted a Lincolnshire man as he walked home penniless from a night's drinking. When the man stooped to pick up a half crown from the road, he was approached by a stranger who offered him riches if he agreed to become his servant. The Devil fled when the man replied that he was a servant of God. In other cases, clergymen dressed in black were mistaken by villagers for the evil one, coming to drag them to Hell. As Obelkivich notes, such beliefs owed very little to official religious teachings. In contrast to academic theology, the Devil 'in popular religion was a person, not a principle; he was a familiar, with nicknames, whom one met face to face'. [7]

As in the seventeenth century, some evangelical clergy were willing to endorse folkloric beliefs about the Devil. From the 1740s onwards, Methodist pastors in particular were prepared to condone popular ideas about witchcraft, possession and exorcism, despite scepticism and disapproval from the church hierarchy. In part, this reflected John Wesley's well-publicised belief in the reality of witchcraft. Throughout his career, Wesley took a keen interest in cases of alleged possession and maintained a detailed correspondence on the subject. The willingness of Methodist pastors to act as exorcists also reflected their desire to establish their credentials as true servants of Christ. This desire was, perhaps, especially strong because of the movement's semi-independent relationship with the Church of England, and its reliance on a powerful preaching ministry. One of the most dramatic Methodist exorcisms took place in Bristol in 1788. The demoniac, George Lucas, claimed to be possessed by seven demons, and believed that only the faithful prayers of seven ministers could drive them out. After an unsuccessful plea to the local Anglican clergy, the dispossession was performed by Joseph Easterbrooke, the vicar of Temple, together with six Wesleyan pastors. While the Devil in George Lucas 'bid them defiance, cursing and vowing dreadful vengeance on all present', the company valiantly prayed, sang hymns, and commanded him to quit the man's body. Their efforts were rewarded when the fiend left his victim with a dreadful howl. While this case attracted considerable publicity, Wesley's journal and the 'spiritual experiences' published in his *Arminian* magazine suggest that similar cases occurred periodically throughout the eighteenth century, and were particularly associated with the Methodist ministry. Such incidents were siezed on by the movement's enemies in the established church, who cited them as evidence of its irrationality and dangerous 'enthusiasm'. [8]

Some Methodist preachers were prepared to embrace other popular ideas about Satan. In an early example from Bristol in 1739, a thunderstorm during a Methodist meeting caused one striken member of the congregation to yell that the 'fearful thunder is raised by the Devil; in this storm he will bear me to Hell'. According to John Cennick, the Wesleyan preacher who witnessed the tempest, Satan had indeed raised the storm to frustrate the work of the Holy Spirit. The willingness of Methodist clergy to endorse such ideas was particularly marked in rural areas. During the 1820s, Primitive Methodist preachers in Cheshire and Lincolnshire were convinced of the power of witches, and accepted that the process of religious conversion could involve physical encounters with Satan. As R. W. Ambler has noted, 'God and Christ were remote or talismanic figures' to many Lincolnshire Methodists, but Satan was a 'very real' presence in the world. In their struggle to save souls, local preachers often 'met and overcame what they saw as personal manifestations of the Devil, using language and imagery which were meaningful for their converts'. These experiences were assimilated readily into accounts of local 'revivals', like the one recorded at the Holbeach branch of the Primitive Methodists in 1851:

> The consciences of the guilty have been grappled with; a free, full and present salvation has been urged; and though we have had some dreadful conflicts with the powers of darkness, the hosts of Israel have been more than victorious. Satan's right to the souls of those whom he has long held as his slaves has been courageously disputed by the servants of the living God; and the grand adversary has, in many cases, been defeated. Jesus has come to our help; the prey has been taken

from the mighty; and upwards of sixty souls have professed to obtain
the blessing of sin forgiven, and united with the church of Christ.

In this instance, it appears that Protestant demonism was overlaid on
folk traditions, while evangelical clergy continued to endorse older
beliefs about witchcraft, evil spirits and the Devil. [9]

Despite its formal split with the established church in the 1790s,
and its subsequent division into a constellation of smaller denomina-
tions, the Methodist movement remained within the mainstream of
English Protestantism. Outside the orbit of conventional Protestant
theology, other groups developed their own, more idiosyncratic
views about the Devil. A spectacular example was provided by the
Southcottian movement of the early nineteenth century, founded
by the west country prophetess, Joanna Southcott. Throughout
her career as a religious leader, Southcott fought a series of ferocious battles with Satan. In *A Dispute Between the Woman and the
Powers of Darkness* (1802), she recorded a week-long combat with
the enemy, whom she eventually overcame through the power of
the Holy Ghost. Like Methodist exorcists, she presented her victory
as a vindication of her faith; but she went on to proclaim that she
enjoyed a special status as the mouthpiece of the Lord. Her work
also incorporated traditional ideas about women and the Devil, and
echoed seventeenth-century chapbooks about the power of the
female tongue to lash the fiend. At the end of their struggle, Satan
proclaimed that 'God hath done something to chose a bitch of a
woman that will down-argue the Devil, and scarce give him room
to speak . . . It is better to dispute with a thousand men than with
one woman'. In a further twist, he offered to surrender his earthly
kingdom if he was defeated in a 'fair election'. This proposal neatly
complemented the Southcottian practice of 'sealing', whereby the
movement's supporters signed a petition demanding the defeat of
Satan and the beginning of Christ's kingdom on earth. [10]

Joanna Southcott's exotic mixture of Protestantism, personal
inspiration and folk beliefs was mirrored by another early nineteenth-century figure, the 'infidel' London preacher Robert
Wedderburn. Like Southcott, Wedderburn espoused a millenarian
version of evangelical Christianity, but he combined this with radical
anti-clericalism and an agenda for political reform. His writings also
included elements of religious scepticism, though Iain McCalman
has argued that he remained 'a radical Christian with millenarian

leanings' throughout his career, while many of his followers 'believed in a mixture of folk magic and Christian supernaturalism'. In 1828 Wedderburn produced a remarkable, semi-satirical tract expounding 'the holy liturgy, or divine service, upon the principles of pure Christian diabolism'. This presented Satan, or 'the God of this world', as a powerful but flawed divinity, deserving both the fear and respect of ordinary mortals. Despite his malevolent qualities, he would one day be converted to goodness, and this conversion was 'the necessary preliminary to the consumation of all earthly things'. It appears that to Wedderburn the Devil was a more immediate figure than the remote and omnipotent God of conventional Protestant doctrine, and this view probably reflected the beliefs of the plebian radicals who attended his meetings. [11]

The careers of Southcott and Wedderburn suggest that ordinary men and women could appropriate the message of evangelical Christianity in creative and unpredictable ways. They also indicate the continuing potential for Protestant teachings to become entwined with folk beliefs. Both the prophetess and the London preacher came from lowly social backgrounds, and they both gathered a following among the poorest sections of English society. Both were initially attracted to Methodism, and incorporated some of its teachings in their idiosyncratic world-views. The combination of the evangelical movement, with its willingness to co-opt folklore to the cause of godly religion, and the readiness of ordinary people to select and reject elements of reformed Christianity according to their own tastes, meant that popular conceptions of the Devil were constantly mixed together with Protestant ideas. This process had already begun in the sixteenth century, and was one of the many ambiguous legacies of the English Reformation.

APPENDIX:
SELECTED SOURCES

The Devil's influence was felt in almost every aspect of English culture in the sixteenth and seventeenth centuries. Beyond the confines of academic theology, the fiend pursued a lively career in the theatre and cheap literature, and played a prominent role in politics and contemporary anxieties about witchcraft. This makes it virtually impossible to present a representative sample of contemporary writing about him. The following texts have been chosen because they illustrate some of the major themes developed in this book. In particular, they show the failure of English reformers to impose a thoroughly Protestant view of Satan on the 'common sort' of Christians, despite the anti-Catholic sentiments expressed in texts such as *God's Judgment Upon Hereticks* (1729). They also indicate the willingness of some godly men and women to accept traditional ideas about the Devil, especially in cases of witchcraft and demonic possession.

THE DEVIL THRASHED

This comic ballad, first printed around 1625, contains many elements that were common in pre-Reformation depictions of the Devil. The fiend appears as a physical creature with bodily weaknesses, and the whole story is presented as an entertainment. As was common in such tales, Satan is defeated by a determined woman, but her behaviour is linked to a typically feminine vice: in this case the practice of 'scolding' or abusing her husband. The depiction of the fiend in the form of an animal was common in the seventeenth century. The image of a woman riding a devil-horse also echoed contemporary witchcraft pamphlets, which described witches travelling in this way. Thomas Potts' *The Arraignement and Triall of Jennet Preston* (1612) and *The Wonderfull Discoverie of Witches in the Countie of Lancaster* (1613) described a familiar spirit 'like unto a white foal, with a black spot on the forehead'. After a gathering of witches at Malkin Tower in Lancashire, the witches departed 'on horseback like unto foals, some of one colour, some of another'. [1]

A Pleasant New Ballad you Here may Behold, How the Devil Though Subtle, was Gulled by a Scold (c. 1625)

A woman well in years
Liv'd with a husband kind,
Who had a great desire
To live content in mind.
But t'was a thing impossible
To compass his desire,
For night and day with scolding
She did her husband tire . . .

Had he bid her go homely,
Why then she would go brave.
Had he called her good wife,
She called him rogue and slave.
Bade he, wife go to church,
And take the finest pew,
She'd go unto an alehouse,
And drink, lie down and spew.

The Devil being merry,
With laughing at this mirth,
Would needs from Hell come trotting
To fetch her from the earth.
And coming like a horse,
To tell this man his mind,
Saying, 'Sit her but astride my back,
I'll hurry her through the wind'.

'Kind Devil', quoth the man,
If thou a little will wait,

I'll bid her do that thing,
Shall make her back thee straight . . .

Content the Devil cry'd,
Then to his wife goes he,
'Good wife, go lead that horse,
So black and fair you see'.
'Go lead, sir knave?', quoth she,
'and wherefore not go ride?'
She took the Devil by the reins,
And up she goes astride.

The Devil neighed loud,
And threw his heels i'th air,
'Kick in the Devil's name' quoth she,
'A shrew doth never fear'.
Away to Hell he went,
With this most wicked scold,
But she did curb him with the bit,
And would not loose her hold . . .

The Devil shewed her all
The pains within that place,
And told her that they were
Ordain'd for scolds so base . . .

Then did she draw her knife,
And give his ear a slit.
The Devil never felt
The like from mortal yet.
So fearing further danger,
He to his heels did take,
And faster than he came,
He post haste home did make.

'Here take her', quoth the Devil,
'To keep her here be bold,
For Hell will not be troubled
With such an earthly scold'.

TWO JUDGMENT TALES

These simple and unpleasant stories indicate the problems involved in communicating the Protestant message that all people were 'slaves of Satan' unless they were saved by Christ. It was much easier to depict the Devil punishing individuals who were guilty of particular crimes. In the first tale, published shortly after the outbreak of the civil war, a woman is carried away by demons after breaking a pledge to her sweetheart. This theme recurred in contemporary stories such as *A Good Warning for all Maidens* and *A Most Straunge and True Discoverie of the Wonderfull Judgement of God* (1600), which depicted satanic retribution on 'inconstant' women. In this instance, the text indicates that the woman's fate is sanctioned by divine providence; but by focusing on a blatant act of betrayal it also implies that only outwardly bad people will be punished in this way. The second tale, published in 1729, conveys a similar message. It tells the story of Mr Wollstain, who was 'carried away by the Devil from the house of Mr Stout, a barber in Abchurch Lane, on Wednesday the 9th day of April, 1729'. The story illustrates the persistence of grossly physical depictions of the Devil, who left his victim 'on a dunghill near Shoreditch, with his bowels fallen out', and the view that only obvious malefactors attracted Satan's attention. As the victim was a notorious papist, the story also demonstrates the fusion of anti-popery with traditional ideas about the Devil.

Strange and Miraculous News From Coventry (1642)

In Coventry, within twelve miles of Warwick, one Richard Boad, being in league with a maid, a mercer's daughter dwelling by the cross, her name Anne Kirke, a contract [was] passed between them. He being in this troublesome time bent to the wars, came to her to take her leave, and to remember her former vows and promises. She vowed and protested she would never marry any man but him if he survived this battle . . . This she on her knees did swear in private to him only, and desired him to take that for a real satisfaction and called God to witness: That if she ever made a promise to any other in his absence, or thought of marriage, unless with him, that the same day she was married that the Devil might fetch her, and have no pity nor compassion but take her away, when she proved false in thought or deed.

They thus parted with many protestations and weeping tears, he to fight for the king and parliament, she to remain at Coventry, his trusty and true joy, and all his delight. The battle at Keynton being done, and he not hurt, he got leave of his captain on a Sunday morning, being then at Warwick, to ride to Coventry to see this false perjured maid. When he thither came, inquiring at the end of the city of this maid, his only joy and most delight, answer was made, 'She was this day married'...

The young soldier, being grieved, lay down on a bed, and sent one to know when they were at their dancing...The time being come, thither he went, unknown to any, the chamber being full with music and virgins dancing to the joy of the nuptials. The bride passing by, he took her by the hand and said, 'Oh thou false fair one, hast thou broke thy vow?' She then replied, 'A rash vow is either broke or kept. Where is your witness?'

Just at that instant, two gentlemen being alighted at the door, all in black, came up into the room. And [they] desired, being there wedding mirth and dancing, that one of them might have a dance with the bride. She gladly entertained it in the dance. The other [gentleman] standing by, fell in at last, [and] they took her up and away they carried her. They in the room ran after; but no news could they hear of the false perjured bride. They ran into the fields, there being still a noise in the air. At last, the two gentlemen in black came to them, with the bride's garments, and said, 'Take these again, we have power over her, but no power over her clothes'. Then her sweetheart the soldier related to them the whole passage of her perjury.

God's Judgment Upon Hereticks (1729)

> For Wollstain now, that papist dog,
> His sins full ripe were grown,
> For not believing God or Devil,
> And worshipping of stone...

> For lo! A form of monstrous size,
> Black face and hideous mein,
> With horrid shape, and glaring eyes,
> The like was never seen.

'Thou wicked wretch', the Devil said,
That thought'st my name a bubble;
Blazing to Hell I'll carry thee,
And save the priests the trouble …

Next morn near Shoreditch, in a jakes,
His head quite turned behind,
His eyes sunk in, his tongue swell'd out,
Just so they did him find.

A GODLY EXORCISM

This arresting account is taken from the biography of Richard Rothwell, the 'apostle of the North', in the collection of godly lives appended to Samuel Clarke's *A Generall Martyrologie* (1651). Clarke attributed the biography to the minister Stanley Gower. As well as providing a colourful narrative of a Protestant exorcism, the text indicates the relationship between demonic possession and the wider struggle between godly individuals and the Devil. The first part of the extract describes how Rothwell himself suffered a possession-like experience. He later related this to the affliction of John Fox, whom he exorcised around 1612. The dialogue between Rothwell and the Devil dramatised the struggle between godly Protestants and the tempter. Nathan Johnstone has noted how this and similar confrontations allowed ministers to debate issues of theology with the Devil, and also echoed accounts of satanic falsehoods presented in devotional literature. After his dispossession, Fox kept a record of the temptations he continued to receive from Satan, and invited godly ministers to help him to overcome them. Gower's story also includes some elements that were common in popular representations of the Devil. The fiend's attempt to prevent Rothwell from crossing a bridge, for example, resembles similar incidents described in contemporary witchcraft pamphlets; and his attempt to deceive the exorcist by playing word games echoes traditional accounts of the Devil as a trickster.

Stanley Gower, **The Life of Master Richard Rothwell**
(1651)

Two things (amongst many others) I think worthy [of] inserting into his life. The one is a strange sickness and recovery he had once at Bernard's Castle. His sickness was a *vertigo capitis*. He would have forty fits at least in an hour, and every one of them accompanied with mischievous temptations, which when the fit was over, he dictated, and I writ down. These held him about three weeks, in which time he had the advice of learned physicians from London, York, Newcastle, Durham, and other places. They all jumped in their judgments, imputing it to [too] much study, fasting, and inward trouble of spirit; their prescriptions wrought kindly, but removed not his disease.

He desired divers Christians to pray for him on a day prefixed, and promised to join with them as well as he could, with some others that should be with him, assuring them that he was confident that disease would not be removed but by prayer and fasting. The morning of that day, he had a fit [which] continued four hours together upon him, and the Devil set upon him all that while, with most dreadful temptations, telling him he would make him the scorn of religion, and every man should reproach it for his sake, that had before by his means looked towards it, [and] that he should never preach more, but should blaspheme the name of God . . . The Devil told him if he did fast and pray that day, he would torment and hinder him. We met at the time appointed, and Master Rothwell would needs have me to perform the duty, which through God's goodness I did, and the Devil was not permitted to hinder or interrupt him or us, and God heard our prayers, so that he had never a fit after that . . .

The other is a relation which I had from himself, and from divers others to whom the story was known, that are yet alive . . . There was one John Fox living about Nottingham, who had no more learning than enabled him to write and read. This man was possessed with a devil, who would violently throw him down, and take away the use of every member of his body, which was turned as black as pitch in those fits, and then speak with an audible voice in him, which seemed sometimes to be heard out of his belly, sometimes out of his throat, and sometimes out of his mouth, his lips not moving. He lay thus, if I mistake not, [for] some years. Many prayers were put up to God for him, and great resort, especially of godly ministers, [was made] to him, amongst the rest Master Bernard of Batcombe . . . and Master Langley of Truswell, betwixt whom and John Fox, I have seen divers passages in writing, he relating by pen his temptations, and they giving answers when he was stricken dumb.

As Master Rothwell was riding to see him, the Devil told all that were in the house, 'Yonder comes Rothwell: but I will make a fool of him before he goes.' The people looked forth, and saw him coming, about a quarter of a mile from the house. As soon as he entered the room, the Devil said, 'Now Rothwell is come' . . . After a while, he further said:

Devil: *Say nothing* [to] *me of this man, for I tell thee he is damned*, and he added thereto, many fearful blasphemies.

Rothwell: Thou are a liar and the father of lies, nor art thou so well acquainted with the mind of God concerning this man, which makes thee thus to torment him, therefore I believe thee not, I believe he shall be saved by Jesus Christ.

Devil: *He is a murderer, and thou knowest no murderer must enter into Heaven.*

Rothwell: Thou liest again, for David murdered, and is in Heaven; and the Jews with wicked hands crucified the Lord of glory, yet both Christ prayed for them, and Peter exhorts them to repentance, that their sins may be blotted out.

Devil: *But this man hath not, cannot, shall not repent.*

Rothwell: If he had not, thou wouldst not have told him so, but if he have not, I believe God will give him repentance, and thou shalt not be able to hinder it.

Devil: *Thou art a murderer thyself, and yet talkest thus?*

Rothwell: Thou liest again. I have fought the Lord's battles against his known enemies, the idolatrous and bloody papists in Ireland, rebels to the queen my sovereign, by whose authority I bore arms against them, [but] otherwise I have killed no man.

Devil: (Swore and blasphemed) *Thou didst murder one this day as thou camest hither, and there is one behind thee will justify it.*

Rothwell looked over his shoulder, and with that the Devil set up a hideous laughter, that nothing could be heard for a great while, and then said:

Devil: *Look you now, did not I tell you I would make Rothwell a fool? And yet it is true, thou didst murder one this day. For as thou camest over the Bridge* (which he named), *there I would have killed thee, and there thy horse trod upon a fly and killed it.*

Master Rothwell's horse you must know stumbled there. It seems the Devil had power to cause it, but without hurt either to Master Rothwell or his horse.

Rothwell: Thou hast oft beguiled me, I hope God will in time give me wisdom to discern, and power to withstand all thy delusions; and he it is that hath delivered me out of thy hands, and will I doubt not also deliver this poor man.

The Devil blasphemed fearfully, quoted many scriptures out of the Old and New Testament, both in Hebrew and in Greek, caviled and played and critic, and backed his allegations with sayings out of the Fathers and Poets in their own language, which he readily quoted, so that the company trembled to hear such things from one that understood no learning, and that moved neither tongue nor lip. Master Rothwell was mightily enabled by God to detect the Devil's sophistry.

Devil: *What stand I talking with thee? All men know thou art Bold Rothwell, and fearest nobody, nor carest for words. Therefore I will talk to thee no more.* (That name he carried to his grave: they would say, 'that is he the Devil called Bold Rothwell'.)

Rothwell, turning to the people, said, 'Good people, you see the goodness of our God, and his great power. Though the Devil made a fool of me now, through my weakness, God hath made the Devil dumb now. Do you see how he lieth? Therefore let us go to prayer, that God who hath made him dumb, will (I doubt not) drive him out of this poor man' . . . They did so. Mr Rothwell kneeled by the bed on which the poor man lay. The Devil for a quarter of an hour together, or more, made a horrid noise. Nevertheless, Master Rothwell's voice was louder then the Devil's . . .

At length, the Devil lay silent in the man, and after that departed from him. The man fetched divers deep sighs, insomuch as they thought he had been expiring, but his colour returned to him, and the use of all his members, senses, and understanding; and at the next petition [in the prayer], he said, 'Amen', and continued to repeat his 'Amen' to every petition. Prayer was now turned into thanksgiving, and so concluded.

After prayer, John Fox said, 'Good Master Rothwell, leave me not. I shall not live long, for the Devil tells me he will choke me with the first bit of meat that I eat.' Master Rothwell answered, 'Wilt thou believe the Devil that seeks thy destruction, before thou wilt trust in God through Jesus Christ, that seeks thy salvation? Hath not God by his almighty power dispossessed him? Had he had his will, thou had'st been in Hell before now. But he is a liar, and as he is not able to hinder thy soul's life, so neither shall he be able to destroy the life of thy body.' Wherefore get me something ready, saith he, for him, and I will see him eat before I go, and will crave a blessing upon it. When it was brought, 'Eat', saith Master Rothwell, 'and fear not the Devil', shewing him that he might do it in faith of that ordinance by which God appoints meat for means to preserve life . . . With much ado, and in great trembling at last, the man took, and ate it. 'Look', says Master Rothwell, 'you all see the Devil is a liar. The first bit hath not choked him, nor shall the rest'.

Master Rothwell left him, after which he was stricken dumb for three years together. I had a book written with his own hand, of the temptations the Devil haunted him with afterwards, and the answers divers godly and reverend ministers gave to those temptations; but the cavaliers got them and all, my book and writings. Thus the poor man remained tempted, but no longer possessed. At length, by prayer also (which was instantly put up to God for him, every Sabbath and lecture day, in many places), the Lord opened his mouth, and restored his speech to him, one using this petition, 'Lord open thou his mouth that his lips may shew forth thy praise.' He answered in the congregation, 'Amen', and so continued to speak, and spake graciously to his dying day.

THE DEMON OF TEDWORTH

This text describes an infamous case of demonic 'obsession' suffered by the Mompesson family of Tedworth in Wiltshire. In March 1661, John Mompesson reported 'an idle drummer' to the constable of a neighbouring town. Subsequently, his family was tormented by strange knocking sounds and spectral visitations, which were attributed to witchcraft. The drummer was tried at Salisbury assizes in 1663 and sentenced to transportation. The details of the case, which were later written up by Joseph Glanvill, illustrate the conflation of the Devil with a witch's 'imp'. The creature assailing the Mompessons resembled the 'familiar spirits' described in chapter seven: it came down the chimney, visited its victims at night in the form of a small animal, and attacked the bodies of children. At the same time, it was explicitly identified as Satan, and likened to the 'unclean spirits'

The demon of Tedworth, from Joseph Glanvill's
Saducismus Triumphatus (1689).

described in the New Testament. The creature's behaviour, and the repeated attempts by its victims to destroy it with weapons such as pistols and swords, indicate the continuing belief that demons were vulnerable to physical attack. The nocturnal apparitions also recall the symptoms of sleep disorders such as 'the mare'. [3]

Joseph Glanvill, Saducismus Triumphatus *(1689)*

During the time of the knocking, when many were present, a gentleman of the company said, 'Satan, if the drummer set thee to work, give three knocks and no more', which it did very distinctly and stopped. Then the gentleman knocked, to see if it would answer him as it was wont, but it did not. For further trial, he bid it for confirmation, if it were the drummer, to give five knocks and no more that night, which it did, and left the house quiet all the night after. This was done in the presence of Sir Thomas Chamberlain of Oxfordshire, and divers others.

   On Saturday morning, an hour before day, Jan 10 [1663], a drum was heard beat upon the outsides of Mr Mompesson's chamber, from whence it went to the other end of the house, where some gentlemen strangers lay, playing at their door and without, four or several tunes, and so went off into the air . . . One morning, Mr Mompesson, rising early to go [on] a journey, heard a great noise below, where the children lay, and running down with a pistol in his hand, he heard a voice, crying 'A witch, A witch', as they had also heard it once before. Upon his entrance, all was quiet.

Having one night played some little tricks at Mr Mompesson's bedsfeet, it went into another bed, where one of his daughters lay. There it passed from side to side, lifting her up as it passed under. At that time there were three kinds of noises in the bed. They endeavoured to thrust at it with a sword, but it still shifted and carefully avoided the thrust, still getting under the children when they offered at it. The night after, it came panting like a dog out of breath. Upon which, one took a bedstaff to knock, which was caught out of her hand, and thrown away, and company coming up, the room was presently filled with a bloomy smell, and was very hot, though without fire, in a very sharp and severe winter. It continued in the bed panting and scratching an hour and a half, and then went into the next chamber, where it knocked a little, and seemed to rattle a chain. Thus it did for two or three nights together.

After this, the old gentlewoman's Bible was found in the ashes, the paper being downwards. Mr Mompesson took it up, and observed that it lay open at the third chapter of St Mark, where there is mention of the unclean spirits falling down before our saviour, and of his giving power to the twelve [disciples] to cast out devils, and of the scribes' opinion that he cast them out through Beelzebub. The next night they strewed ashes over the chamber, to see what impressions it would leave. In the morning they found in one place the resemblance of a great claw ...

There came one morning a light into the children's chamber, and a voice crying, 'A witch, A witch', for at least a hundred times together. Mr Mompesson at another time (being in the day), seeing some wood move that was in the chimney of a room where he was, as of itself, discharged a pistol into it, after which they found several drops of blood on the hearth, and in divers places of the stairs.

For two or three nights after the discharge of the pistol, there was calm in the house, but then it came again, applying itself to a little child newly taken from nurse, which it so persecuted that it would not let the poor infant rest for two nights together, nor suffer a candle in the room, but carry them away lighted up the chimney, or throw them under the bed. It so scared this child by leaping upon it, that for some hours it could not be recovered out of the fright. So that they were forced again to remove the children out of the house.

The next night after which, something about midnight came up the stairs, and knocked at Mr Mompesson's door, but he lying still, it went up another pair of stairs to his man's chamber, to whom it appeared standing at his bed's foot. The exact shape and proportion he could not discover, but he saith he saw a great body with two red and glaring eyes, which for some time were fixed steadily upon him, and at length disappeared.

Another night, strangers being present, it purr'd in the children's bed like a cat, at which time also the clothes and children were lifted up from the bed, and six men could not keep them down. Hereupon they removed the children, intending to have ripped up the bed. But they were no sooner laid in another, but the second bed was more troubled than the first. It continued thus four hours, and so beat the children's legs against the bed-posts, that they were forced to arise, and sit up all night. After this it would empty chamber-pots into their beds, and strew them with ashes, though they were never so carefully watched. It put a long spiked iron into Mr Mompesson's bed, and into his mother's a naked knife upright ...

About the beginning of April 1663, a gentleman that lay in the house, had all his money turned black in his pockets. And Mr Mompesson, coming one morning into his stable, found the horse he was wont to ride, on the ground, having one of his hinder legs in his mouth, and so fastened there that it was difficult for several men to get it out with a lever. After this, there were some other remarkable things, but my account goes no further. Only Mr Mompesson writ me word, that afterwards the house was several nights beset with seven or eight [apparitions] in the shape of men, who, as soon as a gun was discharged, would shuffle away together into an arbour.

WITCHCRAFT AND POSSESSION

John Darrell's account of the possession and exorcism of William Somers in 1597 illustrates the intertwining of witchcraft, godly religion and traditional beliefs about the Devil. Somers originally claimed that his affliction was caused by witchcraft, and described an encounter with an old woman who introduced a spirit into his body. His symptoms included the mobile swellings that were often associated with possession by familiar spirits. These manifestations were also understood by Somers and those around him to be signs of the Devil.

The dispossession itself was an affirmation of the reformed faith. It was attended by three pastors as well as the exorcist himself, and apparently attracted a large crowd of spectators; and Somers' deliverance demonstrated the power of God's Word to drive out the Devil.

Darrell's success was short lived, however. In 1598 Somers claimed that his possession had been faked and accused the minister of connivance in the fraud. Darrell was summoned to London to be examined by an ecclesiastical commission, provoking a public controversy between the exorcist and his accusers in the church hierarchy. He was tried and convicted in 1599. The case resulted in the publication of alternative versions of the events described below, which shed some light on the demoniac's symptoms. In 1599, for example, Samuel Harsnett challenged Darrell's assertion that the possessed man turned his head so that it faced backwards. Instead, he cited a witness who claimed that Somers had 'turned his face a good way towards his shoulder', but no further. The same witness observed that the effects of poor lighting made the demoniac's behaviour appear more remarkable than it really was. Despite these claims, Darrell and his associates maintained the genuineness of Somers' affliction, and in the process they tacitly endorsed many folkloric ideas about witchcraft and the Devil. [4]

John Darrell, **A True Narration of the Strange and Grevous Vexation by the Devil . . . of William Somers of Nottingham** *(*1600*)*

About the 20th day of March 1596 [William Somers'] master Thomas Porter sent him to Walton in Derbyshire, the now dwelling house of Sir William Bowes, to a sister of his wife's there named Mary Milwood. In his going thither, there met him in Blackwell Moors at a deep coal pit hard by the high way side, an old woman (as he thought) who asked him where he dwelt, and whither he was going, without any more words. Above two mile and half further (he having gone forward [at a] journeying pace without stay), she met him again, and passed by him without any words. The next day, he returning from Walton homewards, she met him at the aforesaid pit, and asked him how he did, saying further, 'I must have a penny from thee.' He answered that he had no money. 'Thou hast', quoth she, 'Mary Milwood gave thee a pence, I will have a penny of it or I will throw thee into this pit, and break thy neck' . . . He gave her three pence which indeed had been given him by the said Mary. After this she put her hand to a bag she had about her, and taking thence a piece of bread with butter spread on it, bad him eat it. He refusing, she threatened him again to throw him into the pit and break his neck if he would not eat it. Whereupon (greatly against his will, and for fear), he did eat it, and in the eating it seemed as sweet as any honey . . . Then a cat (as the boy thought) leapt up into her bosom, the which she embraced, and with her arms clasped it unto her, and thus they parted each from other.

About the beginning of October 1597, the said Somers (being at Nottingham in the house of his master Thomas Porter) did use such strange and idle kind of gestures in laughing, dancing and such like light behaviour, that he was suspected to be mad. Sundry times he refused all kind of meat for a long space together, in so much as he did seem thereby to pine away. Sometimes he shaked as if he had had an ague. There was heard a strange noise or flapping from within his body. He was often seen to gather himself on a round heap under his bed clothes, and being so gathered to bounce up a good height from the bed; also, to beat his head and other parts of his body against the ground and bedstead, in such earnest manner, and so violently, that the beholders did fear that thereby he would have spoiled himself, if they had not by strong hand restrained him, and yet thereby received he no hurt at all. In most of his fits he did swell in his body, and in some of them did so greatly exceed therein, as he seemed to be twice so big as his material body. Oft also was he seen to have a certain variable swelling or lump to a great bigness, swiftly running up and down between the flesh and skin, through all the parts of his body, and many times when that swelling was [seen], these or the like words were heard out of his mouth: 'I will go out at his eyes, or ears, or toes', at which speeches the said swelling, evidently appearing in such parts, did immediately remove and vanish away. This swelling did not only run from eye to eye, from cheek to cheek, and up and down along still in the body, but besides being now in the one leg, presently it would be in the other, and so of the arms in like manners . . .

In sundry of his fits, he did utter so strange and fearful shrieking as cannot be uttered by man's power, and was of such strength as sometimes four or five men, though they had much advantage against him by binding of him to a chair, yet could they not rule him. And in shewing that strength he was not perceived to pant or blow, no more then if he had not strained nor struggled at all. Sometimes he cried extremely, so as tears came from him in great abundance. Presently after, he would laugh aloud and shrill, his mouth being shut closed. And being demanded concerning those accidents, he protested he knew of no such matter, neither felt he any pain. Moreover, he was often times cast into the fire, some bare part of his body also lying in the fire, and yet was not burned; and sometimes [he was] cast violently against the ground, and against the wall or posts of the house, without any hurt of his body, and in many ways seek to destroy himself, by reason whereof they were driven to take away his knife, girdle, garters, etc . . . His speeches were usually vain, delivered in very scoffing manner, and many times filthy and unclean, very unfit once to be named, or blasphemous, swearing most fearfully, using one bloody oath after another, [and] sometimes saying, 'I am God', and sometimes, 'There is no God.'

Being moved to say the Lord's Prayer, when he came to these words, 'Lead us not into temptation', he would say, 'Lead us into temptation'. Diverse fond speeches did he use to interrupt them that prayed for him. Many strange speeches also were uttered by him, not in his own name, but as spoken by an evil spirit possessing him . . . [He said] that his name was Lucy, that he was king, that he was prince of darkness. 'You think I have no power of him, yet I can use his tongue, his teeth, lips, hands, legs, his body and all parts of him.' And as the spirit named each part, he used it . . .

I was importuned on his behalf, first by two letters, after by another from the mayor, and thereupon I went unto him . . . Towards that evening I came being the 5th November, he seemed to be sick, and his sickness greatly to increase upon him, so as they feared he would have died, or had been dead, for he lay an hour with his face and hands black, cold as ice, no breath being perceived to come from him. . . . I did assure him that he was possessed, and had in that body of his a devil, and did so frame the words of my mouth, as might best serve to prepare and stir him up to a spiritual fight against Satan, or resistance of him in faith. This evening he acted many sins by signs and gestures, most lively representing and shadowing them out unto us, namely: brawling, quarrelling, fighting, swearing, robbing by the high ways, picking and cutting of purses, burglary, whoredom, pride both in men and women, hypocrisy, sluggishness in hearing the Word, drunkenness, gluttony, also dancing with the toys thereto belonging, the manner of antic dances, the games of dicing and carding, the abuse of the viole, with other instruments. At the end of sundry of these he laughed exceedingly, divers times clapping his hands on his thighs for joy. And at the end of some of them, as killing and stealing, he shewed how he brought them to the gallows, making a sign thereof. During this time, which continued about an hour, as he was altogether silent, so was he most active, though his eyes were closed . . . In a word, these things were in such lively and orient colours painted out (as I may say) unto us that were present, being to the number of some sixty, that I for my own part, (and I am persuaded the rest of the beholders are of my mind) doe verily think, that is not in the skill and power of man to do the like. Whilst we were recommending him and his grievous estate to the Lord, and entreating his Majesty in his behalf, he uttered these words: 'I must be gone.'

The next day being the Lord's day, I came not to him until about three a clock in the afternoon, (finding company with him), at which time I used some speech, wherein I endeavoured to prepare both him and his master's family, and also his parents . . . unto the holy exercise the day after to be performed. Towards evening, much people reported to the house. Then some words of exhortation were used by myself, for the sanctifying of so many of us, whose spirits God should stir up [to] join in that solemn service and worship of God to be performed on the day following . . . This evening, and all the night long, [Satan] handled him more extremely then before. At this time, among other things, the spirit retorted his tongue into his throat, and this he did often, whereupon many looked with a candle into his mouth, where they could see not tongue nor part of it, only in his throat they beheld the root thereof. He uttered often these words, 'For corn, for corn', with a few more thereunto, noting the insatiable desire of gain, or raising the price of corn in corn men . . . This evening I requested the minister of that congregation, Mr Aldridge, Mr Aldred, and Mr Halem, pastors of two several towns near adjoining unto Nottingham, to join with me on the morrow in the ministration of the Word and prayer, whereunto they condescended . . .

In the morning, many of us were assembled together in the next convenient and seemly room to [the] place of his abode. The boy was brought . . . by six or seven strong men, who had all of them enough ado to bring him, and laid him on a couch in the midst of us . . . All this day he was continually vexed and tormented by Satan, having little rest at all, so as the same for vexation by the spirit, far exceeded any of the days before. His torments in his fits were most grievous and fearful to behold, wherein his body being swelled, was tossed up and down. In these fits his strength was very great, so as being held down with five strong men, he did notwithstanding all their strength, against their wills, rise and stand upright on his feet. He was also continually torn in very fearful manner, and disfigured in his face, wherein sometimes his lips were drawn awry, now to one side, now to the other. Sometimes his face and neck distorted to the right and to the left hand, yea sometimes writhen to his back. Sometimes he thrust out his tongue very far and big, and sometimes turned backwards into his throat, gaping so wide that we might afar off perceive it. Now he gnashed with his teeth, now he foamed like to the horse or boar, dripping down to his breast, notwithstanding there was one purposely standing by with a cloth ever and anon to wipe it away. Not to say anything of his fearful staring with his eyes, and incredible gaping.

This day, notwithstanding he was so held, as is aforesaid, he went about to have choked and so destroyed himself. Speeches he used none, save once in a great voice, 'Corn!' And when I applied that speech of our saviour, all things are possible to him that believeth', he used these words, 'Thou liest'. Divers times he shrieked or cried aloud in a strange and supernatural manner. Sometimes he roared fearfully like a bear and cried like a swine.

Towards the evening, as I was treating of these words, 'Then the spirit cried and rent him sore, and came out, and he was as one dead, insomuch that many said he is dead', the boy was rent sore indeed, cried, and that aloud. Then the people which were present . . . cried out all at once, as it were with one voice unto the Lord, to have mercy upon him. And within a quarter of an hour (they and he still crying aloud), he held down on a bed by five men, and offering as though he would have vomited, was on the sudden violently cast. And his body there was turned so as his face lay downwards to the ground and at the bed's feet, and his back upward with his feet on the bed's head. And thus he lay as if he had been dead for a season. Thus we have heard not only how it went with Somers in the time of his possession and at and little before his dispossession, but also how and by what means I came unto him, and being there carried myself in the present action.

NOTES AND REFERENCES

CHAPTER 1

1. Philip Morgan considers the iconography of the dying room in St Wulfstan's hospital, now the Commandery museum in Worcester, in Peter C. Jupp and Clare Gittings, eds., *Death in England* (Manchester University Press 1999), 128-9.

2. The quotation from Conrad is taken from *Under Western Eyes* (1911). Jeffrey Burton Russell, *Lucifer: The Devil in the Middle Ages* (Cornell University Press: Ithaca and London 1984), 23.

3. In 1587 the Essex minister George Gifford affirmed that all unclean spirits were united under the name of the Devil: 'There be great multitudes of infernal spirits, as the Holy Scriptures do everywhere show, but yet they do so join together in one that they be called the Devil in the singular number.' Gifford, *A Discourse on the Subtill Practises of Devilles* (1587), Dr. The biblical quotation in this paragraph is from Luke 10:18.

4. For the diversity of pictorial representations of Satan, see Luther Link, *The Devil: The Archfiend in Art from the Sixth to the Sixteenth Century* (Harry N. Abrams: New York 1996), especially 183-4.

5. The description of Faust's death is from the *Judgement of God Shewed upon one John Faustus* (c. 1590), *The Euing Collection of English Broadside Ballads* (Glasgow 1971), 277. Reginald Scot, *A Discourse upon Devils and Spirits* (1584), 541.

6. Nathan Johnstone, *The Devil and Demonism in Early Modern England* (Cambridge University Press 2006), 106.

7. Thomas Morton, *Ezekiel's Wheels: A Treatise Concerning Divine Providence* (1653), 209-10.

8. *Stand up for Your Beliefe, or A Combat Betweene Satan Tempting and A Christian Triumphing* (1640).

9. For the emergence of the Devil in the Old Testament see Jeffrey Burton Russell, *The Devil: Perceptions of Evil from Antiquity to Primitive Christianity* (Cornell University Press: Ithaca and London 1977), chapter five. Henry Angstar Kelly presents a revisionist reading in *Satan: A Biography* (Cambridge University Press 2006).

10. A version of this argument remains influential in modern theology. According to Alvin Plantinga, the existence of a good and all powerful God is logically compatible with the existence of natural evil if one assumes that a 'mighty nonhuman spirit' is responsible for natural disasters. Since this spirit could not have been created free without the possibility of its rebellion, God's perfect goodness and omnipotence are preserved. Plantinga uses the Devil as a construct in his argument without asserting that such a spirit necessarily exists. Alvin

Plantinga, *God, Freedom and Evil* (William B. Eerdmans: Michigan 1974), 57-9.

11. Luther's personal engagement with Satan is well documented. For a lively over-
view of the subject, see Heiko Oberman, *Luther: Man Between God and the Devil*
(Yale University Press 1989), especially chapter three. For Luther's theology of
the Devil, see Jeffrey Burton Russell, *Mephistopheles: The Devil in the Modern
World* (Cornell University Press: Ithaca and London 1986), 38, 46, and Bernhard
Lohse, *Martin Luther's Theology: Its Historical and Systematic Development* (T & T
Clark: Edinburgh 1999), 253-6.

12. Richard Bernard, *A Guide to Grand-Jury Men* (1627), 2; Francis Raworth, *Jacobs
Ladder, or the Protectorship of Sion* (1655), 20; Edward Leigh, *A Treatise of Divinity*
(1646), 128; Arthur Dent, *A Sermon of Gods Providence* (1609), 21; John Milton,
Paradise Lost, Book I, lines 216-18.

13. Gilbert Dugdale, *A True Discourse of the Practises of Elizabeth Caldwell* (1604),
Dedication, B2r, D1r-D1v.

14. The historical debate about the doctrine of predestination in Elizabethan and
early Stuart England is outside the range of this book. Nicholas Tyacke has
argued that the doctrine was an essential component of the religious settlement until it was challenged by Charles I, whose innovations in the theology
and practice of the established church eventually provoked a Calvinist 'counter
revolution'. This interpretation has been contested by Peter White, who claims
that Tyacke overestimates the extent of consensus on the doctrine prior to
Charles' accession, and suggests that it was always treated with caution by
the crown. For an excellent collection of essays on the subject see Kenneth
Fincham, ed, *The Early Stuart Church* (Macmillan: London 1993).

15. Frank Luttmer has observed that the doctrine of predestination could populate
the world with unregenerate men and women who served as Satan's agents,
thereby endangering God's children. Frank Luttmer, 'Persecutors, Tempters and
Vassals of the Devil: The Unregenerate in Puritan Practical Divinity', *Journal
of Ecclesiastical History*, 51:1 (2000), 43, 58-9, 62-3. Russell, *Mephistopheles*, 35,
37; Edward Cradocke, *A Shippe of Assured Safetie* (1572), 151; Arthur Dent, *The
Plaine Mans Path-way to Heaven* (1601), 117.

16. John Calvin, *Institutes of the Christian Religion*, reprinted in Alan Kors and
Edward Peters, eds, *Witchcraft in Europe, 1100-1700: A Documentary History*
(University of Pennsylvania Press: Philadelphia 1972), 204.

17. Martin Luther, *Commentary on St Paul's Epistle to the Galatians* (Philadelphia
1875), 590-1.

18. For the international context of witch trials, see Robin Briggs, *Witches and
Neighbours* (2nd ed. HarperCollins: London 1998), and Wolfgang Behringer,
Witches and Witch Hunts (Polity Press: Cambridge 2004). Brian P. Levack pres-
ents an illuminating comparison of English and Scottish witch persecutions
in *Witch-Hunting in Scotland: Law, Politics and Religion* (Routledge: London and
New York 2008).

19. John Foxe, preface to the 1570 edition of *Acts and Monuments*, in E. P.
Trinterud, ed., *Elizabethan Puritanism* (Oxford University Press 1971), 65.

20. The title 'father of lies', which was often attached to Satan in Tudor and Stuart
texts, was adapted from John 8:44: 'He was a murderer from the beginning, and
abode not in the truth, because there is no truth in him. When he speaketh a lie,
he speaketh of his own: for he is a liar, and the father of it.' Johnstone, *The Devil*,
43-9, 288; the quotation from Tyndale is taken from 46.

21. The 1650 edition of *The Christian Sword and Buckler* attributes the text to
'Doctor Sprint'. The pamphlet is partially and erratically paginated.

22. Sprint, *The Christian Sword*.

23. Charles Taylor identifies the construction of the 'buffered self', in which the mind is unpenetrated by supernatural powers, as a characteristic of secular society. Charles Taylor, *A Secular Age* (Harvard University Press: Cambridge, Massachusetts, and London 2007); 32-41; Sprint, *The Christian Sword*; Robert Bolton, *The Saints Selfe-Enriching Examination* (1634), 206-7; Johnstone, *The Devil*, 102.

24. See Johnstone, *The Devil*, 62-6, for the reform of the baptism service. For the reform of the deathbed see Danae Tankard, 'The Reformation of the Deathbed in Mid-Sixteenth-Century England', *Mortality*, 8:3 (2003).

25. Johnstone, *The Devil*, 26; *Merry Drollery Complete* (1670), 17-21, 200-204, 214, 215.

26. Interestingly, the Devil takes possession of the ram rather than simply assuming its shape, leaving behind a stinking 'carcass of mutton' after taking flight. This may reflect the theological view that Satan was incorporeal and therefore relied on the flesh of others. *Merry Drollery*, 109-10.

27. Vavasor Powell, *The Life and Death of Mr Vavasor Powell* (1671), 8; Thomas Beard, *The Theatre of Gods Judgements: Revised and Augmented* (1631), 147, 572.

CHAPTER 2

1. *A L Mery Talys* (1526), 1v-2v.

2. *Ibid*, 2v; R.W. Scribner, *Popular Culture and Popular Movements in Reformation Germany* (Hambledon: London 1987), 88; *The Cloud of Unknowing*, ed. Halcyon Backhouse (Hodder and Stoughton: London 1985), 84.

3. Ronald C Finucane, *Miracles and Pilgrims: Popular Beliefs in Medieval England* (2nd ed. Macmillan: London 1995), 108-9; *Mery Talys*, 6v.

4. This legend was mocked by the Protestant polemicist Stephen Bateman in his *Golden Booke of the Leaden Goddes* (1577), 29-30.

5. Eamon Duffy, *The Stripping of the Altars: Traditional Belief in England, 1400-1580* (Yale University Press: New Haven and London 1992), 216, 268-9, 279-81.

6. The invocation of demons is discussed in Richard Kieckhefer's *European Witch Trials: Their Foundations in Popular and Learned Culture, 1300-1500* (Routledge and Kegan Paul: London 1976) 34-5, 69-71. A detailed description of invocation in sixteenth-century England is contained in *The Examination of John Walsh of Dorsetshire* (1566). Funicane, *Miracles*, 204; Augustus Jessopp, *Random Roaming and Other Papers* (London 1894), 109-12.

7. *Tales and Quicke Answeres, Very Mery and Pleasant to Rede* (c. 1530), C2r, H1r, H3v; *Mery Talys*, 13r.

8. For the depiction of Satan in medieval drama see *English Mystery Plays*, ed Peter Happe (Penguin: London 1975), 393-4, 556-64.

9. Julian of Norwich, *Revelations of Divine Love*, ed. Clifton Walters (Penguin: London 1966), 84, 182, 199. For Margery Kempe see Richard Kieckhefer, *Unquiet Souls: Fourteenth-Century Saints and Their Religious Milieu* (University of Chicago Press 1984), 183-84.

10. Richard Whitford, *A Werke for Housholders* (1530), B3r; Thomas Becon, *The Workes of Thomas Becon* (1564), I, 390v-391v, 423v-424r.

11. Martin Luther, *Commentary on St Paul's Epistle to Galatians* (Philadelphia 1875), 287-90. For Luther's views on the Devil see Heiko Oberman, *Luther: Man Between God and the Devil* (Yale University Press 1989), 102-6. William Chub,

The True Travaile of all Faithfull Christians (1584), 137v; Jeffrey Burton Russell, *Mephistopheles: The Devil in the Modern World* (Cornell University Press: Ithaca and London 1986), 30-33.

12. Whitford, *Werke*, E4v; William Perkins, *The Foundation of the Christian Religion Gathered Into Sixe Principles* (1641 edition), 3, 16; Richard Sibbes, *The Saints Safetie in Evill Times* (1634), 6; John Bradford, *A Godlye Medytacyon Composed by the Faithfull and Constant Servant of God J B* (1559), 27-8; William Gouge, *The Whole Armour of God* (1627 edition), 28.

13. *Short Rules Sent by Maister Richard Greenham to a Gentlewoman Troubled in Minde* (1618); Olde, *Short Description*, 29v; Stephen Bateman, *A Christall Glasse of Christian Reformation* (1569), C1r; John Reynolds, *The Triumphs of Gods Revenge Against the Crying and Execrable Sinne of . . . Murther* (1634), preface.

14. Olde, *Short Description*, 2v; Arthur Dent, *The Plaine Mans Path-way to Heaven* (1601), 10; *The Euing Collection of English Broadside Ballads* (Glasgow 1971), 107.

15. William Perkins, *Lectures Upon the First Three Chapters of the Revelation* (1604), 57-8; *Roxburghe*, III, 165.

16. Bunyan's tale presents a subtle exposition of the Protestant view of grace. Mr Badman lacks true understanding of the sinful condition that he shares with all humankind, and is abandoned by God to live 'in peace and quiet with sin'. Thus the Devil claims him as his own. John Bunyan, *The Life and Death of Mr Badman* (Hesperus: London 2007), 19-20, 60, 173.

17. Perkins, *Lectures*, 187; Perkins, *Foundation*, 3; George Gifford, *A Brief Discourse of Certaine Points of the Religion Which is Among the Common Sort of Christians, Which may be Termed the Countrie Divinity* (1584), 26; Sibbes, *Saints Safetie*, 17-18; Bradford, *Godlye Medytacyon*, 27; Elizabeth Grymeston, *Miscelanea, Meditations, Memoratives* (1604), D2r.

18. On the royalist side see, for example, *The Devil Turn'd Roundhead: or Pluto Become a Brownist* (1642); for a parliamentarian version see Ellis Bradshaw, *A Dialogue Betweene the Devil & Prince Rupert* (1645). Becon, *Worckes*, I, 314r; S. S., *A Briefe Instruction for all Families* (1586), dedication; Richard Carpenter, *Experience, Historie and Divinitie* (1641), 148; Gouge, *Whole Armour*, title page; Martin Seymour-Smith, ed., *The English Sermon, 1550-1650* (Carcanet Press: Cheadle 1976), 279.

19. Olde, *Description*, 30r-30v; Stephen Bateman, *The Golden Booke of the Leaden Goddes* (1577), 30; Richard Kenneth Emmerson, *Antichrist in the Middle Ages: A Study of Medieval Apocalypticism, Art and Literature* (Manchester University Press 1981), 207, 210.

20. Olde, *Short Description*, 7r-7v; *The First Examinacyon of Anne Askewe, Latelye Martyred in Smythfelde . . . With the Elucidacyon of Johan Bale* (1546), 25r; Perkins, *Lectures*, 354; I. H., *The Divell of the Vault, or the Unmasking of Murther* (1606), 22; Lucy Hutchinson, *Memoirs of the Life of Colonel Hutchinson*, ed. N. H. Keeble (Everyman: London 1995), 6, 58-9.

21. Bunyan described the Devil as a spider in *Mr Badman*, 175. He described his own direct encounters with the fiend in *Grace Abounding* (Penguin: London 1987), 55. Samuel Clarke, *A Generall Martyrologie* (1651), title page, 1.

22. Gouge, *Whole Armour*, 11; John Darrell, *The Triall of Maist. Dorrell* (1599), 34; *Strange Newes From Antwerpe* (1612), 6.

23. Numerous pamphlets described divine judgments against those who invoked the Devil's name in jest. See, for example, *Gods Handy-worke in Wonders* (1615) and *A Wonderfull and Strange Miracle, or Gods Just Vengeance Against the Cavaliers* (1642). Perkins, *Foundation*, 3; Gouge, *Whole Armour*, 11.

24. Beezaleel Carter, *A Sermon of Gods Omnipotencie and Providence* (1615), 45.

25. Russell, *Mephistopheles,* 31-2.

26. The genre of deathbed literature is considered in chapter three. *Cloud of Unknowing,* 59-60; Arthur Dent, *Plaine Mans Path-way* (1601), 9, 127-8; Greenham, *Short Rules,* no. 25; Bateman, *Christall Glasse,* M4r.

27. Greenham, *Short Rules,* nos. 21, 26; Grymeston, *Miscelanea,* H1v; Robert Burton, *The Anatomy of Melancholy,* eds. Thomas Faulkener, Nicholas Kiessling and Rhonda Blair (1989-94), III, 414-5.

28. Paul Helm, *The Providence of God* (InterVarsity Press: Illinois 1993), 194.

29. The preface to Gough's translation is reproduced in Leonard J. Triterund, ed. *Elizabethan Puritanism* (Oxford University Press 1971); B. Lowe, 'Religious Wars and the Common Peace: Anglican Anti-war Sentiment in Elizabethan England', *Albion* 28, 415-35; Marten is quoted by Julian Lock in 'How Many Tercios has the Pope? The Spanish war and the Sublimation of Elizabethan Anti-Popery', *History* 81 (1996), 200; Warwick County Record Office, 'MSS of the first Sir Richard Newdigate', 1626, MI/351/5/21, Welford-on-Avon churchwardens' receipt, 1635, DR911/7/1; Coventry City Record Office, corporation minute book, 1555-1640, A14a, 250v. For Protestant opposition to a pro-Spanish foreign policy see the essays by Thomas Cogswell and Peter Lake in Richard Cust and Ann Hughes, eds, *Conflict in Early Stuart England* (Longman: London 1989).

30. Public Record Office (PRO), Kew, Bill of complaint from Stratford corporation to the Star Chamber, 1621, STAC 26/10; Clarke, *Generall Martyrologie,* 391; Vavasor Powell, *The Life and Death of Mr Vavasor Powell* (1671), 9-10; PRO, Star chamber proceedings against William Hall, 1622, STAC8/245/27; William Perkins, *The Art of Prophesying* (Banner of Truth Trust: Edinburgh 1996), 93; Ephraim Huitt, *The Anatomy of Conscience* (1626), 34-5; Sibbes, *Saints Safetie,* 17; Robert Harris, *The Works of Robert Harris* (1654), 254; Samuel Clarke, *The Saints Nose-Gay, or a Posie of 741 Spirituall Flowers* (1642), 146; *Merry Drollery,* II, 50.

31. Christopher Haigh, 'Success and Failure in the English Reformation', *Past and Present,* 173:1 (2001); see also Haigh's *English Reformations* (Clarendon: Oxford 1993), chapter sixteen and conclusion, and Geoffrey Parker, 'Success and Failure During the First Century of the Reformation', *Past and Present* 136 (1992). Gifford, *Countrie Divinity,* title page; Perkins, *Foundation,* epistle to the reader; Margaret Hoby, *The Private Life of an Elizabethan Lady: The Diary of Lady Margaret Hoby,* 1599-1605, ed. Joanna Moody (Sutton: Stroud 1998), 181; John Fielding, 'Opposition to the Personal Rule of Charles I: The Diary of Robert Woodford, 1637-1641', *Historical Journal* 31 (1988), 769-88; Ann Hughes, 'Thomas Dugard and his Circle in the 1630s', *Historical Journal,* 29 (1986), 771-93.

32. Luttmer also suggests that 'Christian warfare was a defining characteristic of the Christian experience' for godly preachers. Frank Luttmer, 'Persecutors, Tempters and Vassals of the Devil: The Unregenerate in Puritan Practical Divinity', *Journal of Ecclesiastical History,* 51:1 (2000), 43, 46; I. H., *The Divell,* 11; Huitt, *Anatomy,* 34-5; Harris, *Works,* 255; Isaac Colfe, *A Comfortable Treatise Concerning the Temptations of Christ* (1592), title page, 5v; Gifford, *Countrie Divinity,* 26.

33. Ephraim Huitt, *The Whole Prophecie of Daniel Explained* (1643), 226; John Milton, *Prose Writings,* ed. K. M. Burton (Dent: London 1958), 6; Colfe, *Comfortable Treatise,* 2v; Elaine Pagels, *The Origin of Satan* (Penguin: London 1995), 180-1.

CHAPTER 3

1. Vavasor Powell, ed., *Spirituall Experiences of Sundry Believers* (1652 edition), 82–3.

2. R. Willis, *Mount Tabor, or Private Exercises of a Penitent Sinner* (1639), 108.

3. Charles Taylor, *A Secular Age* (Harvard University Press: New Haven and London 2007), 3, 173.

4. The awareness of Satan's alliance with sinful human nature meant that the demonization of others could involve various degrees of subtlety. At one extreme, God's enemies could be characterized as monstrous limbs of Antichrist; at another, they could be viewed as sincere but deluded victims of satanic guile. William Gouge, *Of Domesticall Duties* (2nd ed. 1626), 47; William Gouge, *The Whole Armour of God* (1627 edition), 21.

5. Nathan Johnstone, *The Devil and Demonism in Early Modern England* (Cambridge University Press 2006), 26

6. Elizabeth Avery described how Satan appeared to her as a stranger who sought to persuade her that she was damned. She recalled this encounter in John Rogers, *Ohel, or Beth-Shemesh* (1653), 405. Rogers, Ohel, 427; Robert Burton, *The Anatomy of Melancholy*, eds. Thomas Faulkener, Nicholas Kiessling and Rhonda Blair (1989–94), 422; Hannah Allen, *Satan His Methods and Malice Baffled* (1683), 22; Vavasor Powell, *The Life and Death of Mr Vavasor Powell* (1671), 8; John Bunyan, *Grace Abounding* (Penguin: London 1987), 29.

7. John Preston, *The Saints Daily Exercise. A Treatise Unfolding the Whole Duty of Prayer* (1629), 39.

8. Burton, *Anatomy*, 413, 415.

9. Thomas Nashe surveyed these phenomena in *The Terrors of the Night* (1590). His text is available in Thomas Nashe, *The Unfortunate Traveller and Other Works* (Penguin: London 1990). John Bradford, *A Godlye Medytacyon Composed by the Faithfull and Constant Servant of God J B* (1559), 44.

10. Rogers, *Ohel*, 419–20; Powell, *Spirituall Experiences*, 272–3; *The Journal of Richard Norwood*, eds W. F. Craven and Walter Hayward (New York 1945), 26.

11. *Journal of Richard Norwood*, 26; Owen Davies, 'The Nightmare Experience, Sleep Paralysis, and Witchcraft Accusations', *Folklore*, 114 (2003), 199. For a contemporary medical account of the condition, see J. A. Cheyne, et al., 'Hypnagogic and Hypnopompic Hallucinations during Sleep Paralysis: Neurological and Cultural Construction of the Night-Mare', *Consciousness and Cognition*, 8 (1999).

12. Bunyan, *Grace Abounding*, 8; Rogers, *Ohel*, 413; Birmingham Central Reference Library, 'A Briefe Narrative of the Life and Death of Mr Thomas Hall', LF78.1 HAL/467148, 29.

13. William Perkins, *The Foundation of the Christian Religion Gathered Into Sixe Principles* (1641 edition), 16; Robert Bolton, *The Saints Selfe-Enriching Examination* (1634), 206–7; A. W., *The Young Mans Second Warning-Peece* (1643), 4; Bunyan, *Grace Abounding*, 29; Allen, Satan, 3, 5.

14. Perkins, *Foundation*, 16; Bolton, *Saints Selfe-Enriching Examination*, 206.

15. Powell, *Spirituall Experiences*, 173; Jane Turner, *Choice Experiences of the Kind Dealings of God* (1653), 25, 117–8; Allen, *Satan*, 15, 17; Clarke, *A Generall Martyrologie* (1651), 458.

16. William Chub, *The True Travaile of All Faithfull Christians* (1585), 137r; Warwick County Record Office, notebook of Richard Newdigate, 1630, CR136/A14, 284; Bunyan, *Grace Abounding*, 14; Elizabeth Grymeston, *Miscelanea. Meditations. Memoratives* (1604), C4r; Theodore de Welles, 'Sex and Sexual Attitudes in Seventeenth-Century England: The Evidence from Puritan Diaries', in

Renaissance and Reformation 12 (1988), 50-1; John Woolton, *The Christian Manuell, or Of the Life and Maners of True Christians* (1576), 189v; William Perkins, *Lectures Upon the First Three Chapters of the Revelation* (1604), 186-7.

17. Richard Carpenter, *Experience, Historie and Divinitie* (1641), 102; *Stand up to Your Beliefe, or A Combat Betweene Satan Tempting and a Christian Triumphing* (1640); Thomas Becon, *The Worckes of Thomas Becon* (1564), cccxiii r; Willis, *Mount Tabor,,* 208-9; Allen, *Satan,* 16; Powell, *Life,* 12; Richard Baxter, *The Life and Times of Richard Baxter,* ed. Orme, I, 243-4.

18. *The Miracle of Miracles* (1614), preface; Turner, *Choice Experiences,* preface.

19. Gryffith Williams, *The True Church: Shewed to All Men That Desire to be Members of the Same* (1629), 556-7; Rogers, Ohel, 429; Powell, Life, 9, 12; *Powell, Spirituall Experiences,* 34-5, 358.

20. Margaret Hoby, *The Private Life of an Elizabethan Lady: The Diary of Lady Margaret Hoby,* 1599-1605, ed. Joanna Moody (Sutton: Stroud 1998), 10, 54, 105, 136, 143, 168, 180, 181, 182.

21. Hoby, *Diary,* 180-1; WCRO, correspondence of Lady Anne Newdigate, CR136/B310, B314; WCRO, 'MSS of the first Sir Richard Newdigate', MI/351/5/21; William Gouge, *The Whole Armour of God* (1627 edition), 21; Powell, *Life,* 9; Samuel Clarke, *The Saints Nose-gay, or a Posie of 741 Spirituall Flowers* (1642), 146.

22. Perkins is quoted by Ralph Houlbrooke in 'The Puritan Deathbed, 1560-1660', Christopher Durston and Jacqueline Eales, eds., *The Culture of English Puritanism, 1560-1700* (Macmillan: London 1996), 125. John Gerard, *The Conquest of Temptations: or Mans Victory Over Satan,* translated from German by R. Bruch (1615), 111; Clarke, *Generall Martyrologie,* 416, 472; *The Euing Collection of English Broadside Ballads* (Glasgow 1971), 198; *A Brief Discourse of the Christian Life and Death of Mistris Katherin Brettergh* (1606 edition), 12; *Euing,* 198; *A Brief Discourse,* 13; Philip Stubbes, *A Christall Glasse for Christian Women* (1618 edition), C3r.

23. *Brettergh,* 15; Clarke, *Generall Martyrologie,* 416, 472; Stubbes, *Christall Glasse,* C4r.

24. Stubbes, *Christall Glasse,* C3v-C4r; *Brettergh,* 21-2, 37, 38.

25. Bunyan likened Mr Badman's fate to the rich man in Luke, who 'died and was buried; and in Hell he lift up his eyes, being in torments' (Luke 16:22-3). John Bunyan, *The Life and Death of Mr Badman* (Hesperus: London 2007), 55, 174. Edmond Bicknoll, *A Swoord Against Swearyng* (1579), 34v.

CHAPTER 4

1. Gifford returned to this theme in two books about witchcraft, in which he used to the doctrine of providence to correct what he perceived to be common misconceptions about the crime. Edward Cradocke, *A Shippe of Assured Safetie* (1572), 251; George Gifford, *A Catechisme Conteining the Summe of Christian Religion* (1583), A6v-A7r.

2. John Aubrey, *Brief Lives,* ed. Oliver Lawson Dick (Penguin: London 1949), 114-5.

3. For the apparent failure of the Reformation to convert ordinary people, see Christopher Haigh, 'Success and Failure in the English Reformation', *Past and Present,* 173:1(2001); also J. J. Scarisbrick, *The Reformation and the English People* (Clarendon: Oxford 1988) and Christopher Haigh, *English Reformations: Religion, Politics and Society Under the Tudors* (Clarendon: Oxford 1993). The view that Protestantism enjoyed strong popular support is set out in the revised edition of A. G. Dickens, *The English Reformation* (2nd ed. Pennsylvania State University Press: Philadelphia 1990).

4. *The Historie of the Damnable Life and Deserved Death of Doctor John Faustus*, ed. H. Logeman (Amsterdam 1900), 38-9; *Merry Drollery*, I, 103-4; *The Examination and Confession of Certain Wytches at Chelmsford* (1566), in Peter Haining, ed., *The Witchcraft Papers* (Robert Hale: London 1974), 33; *The Disclosing of a Late Counterfeyted Possession by the Devyl in Two Maydens* (1574), 13-4; Abraham Fleming, *A Straunge and Terrible Wunder Wrought Very Late in the Parish Church of Bungay* (1577), 2-3; *The Miracle of Miracles* (1614), 3, 5; Bodleian Library, Oxford, Ashmole MSS, Casebooks of Richard Napier, MS 412, 115r, 141v.

5. Elizabeth Jocelin, *The Mothers Legacie to her Unborne Childe* (1624), 40; *The Examination of John Walsh Before Maister Thomas Williams* (1566), in Barbara Rosen, *Witchcraft in England, 1558-1618* (University of Massachusetts Press: Amherst 1969), 69; C. L'Estrange Ewen, *Witch Hunting and Witch Trials* (Dial Press: New York 1929), 304; *Mother Shiptons Christmas Carrols* (1668), 2; James Obelkevich, *Religion and Rural Society* (Clarendon: Oxford 1978), 276.

6. Around 1635 Richard Napier's nephew made a list of his uncle's patients who had been troubled by apparitions of various kinds. Ashmole, Napier, MS 1790, 108r. Keith Thomas presented his interpretation of popular beliefs in *Religion and the Decline of Magic* (Weidenfeld and Nicolson: London 1971). For responses to this work, see Eamon Duffy, *The Stripping of the Altars* (Yale University Press: New Haven and London 1990) and Jerome Friedman, *Miracles and the Pulp Press in Revolutionary England* (UCL: London 1994). Emma Wilby has identified similarities between the Devil, familiar spirits and fairies in 'The Witch's Familiar and the Fairy in Early Modern England and Scotland', *Folklore*, 111 (2000). Rosen, *Witchcraft*, 69, 377; Joseph Glanvill, *Saducismus Triumphatus* (1689), 325; D. R. Woolf, 'The Common Voice: History, Folklore and Oral Tradition in Early Modern England', *Past and Present*, 120 (1980); *The Euing Collection of English Broadside Ballads* (Glasgow 1971), 108.

7. R. Willis, *Mount Tabor, or Private Exercises of a Penitent Sinner* (1639), 93.

8. The ballad describing the Devil's thwarted attempt to carry a woman to Hell is reproduced in the appendix. *Roxburghe*, II, 370-1; C. L'Estrange Ewen, *Witchcraft and Demonianism* (Heath Cranton: London 1933), 148; *Merry Drollery*, I, 7-11, 103, II, 13, 27; *Euing*, 107; *The Wonder: or the Devil Outwitted* (1736).

9. H. C. Porter, ed., *Puritanism in Tudor England* (1970), 279; Arthur Dent, *The Plaine Mans Path-way to Heaven* (1601), 9-11; *Strange Newes From Warwicke* (1642), 6; *Sad and Dreadful News From Horsley Down* (1684); *The Devil and the Strumpet* (1701), title-page.

10. The ballad recounting the fate of the woman from Coventry is reprinted in the appendix. *Strange Newes From Warwicke*, 7-8; *Euing*, 108-9, 197, 227, 566.

11. Thomas Decker, *Newes From Hell Brought by the Divells Carrier* (1606), preface, B2r; *Roxburghe*, I, 331-6; *Euing*, 569; *Merry Drollery*, II, 26-8.

12. *Merry Drollery*, II, 12-15; *The Strange and Wonderful History of Mother Shipton* (1686), 8-9; *Roxburghe*, II, 368; Thomas Decker and George Wilkins, *Jests to Make You Merie* (1607), 2; *Roxburghe*, II, 368.

13. Ewen, *Witchcraft*, 180; *Roxburghe* I, 224, 228, 396, 400; II, 496; Decker, *Newes*, B4v; Samuel Clarke, *A Mirrour or Looking Glasse Both for Saints and Sinners* (1654 edition), 23.

14. The oldest surviving copy of *The Famous Historie of Fryer Bacon* was published in 1627, but an earlier edition appears to have inspired Robert Greene's play in the 1590s. Amanda Power, 'A Mirror for Every Age: The Reputation of Roger Bacon', *English Historical Review*, 492 (2006); *Historie of the Damnable Life*, 4, 38; Robert Greene, *The Honorable Historie of Frier Bacon and Frier Bongay* (1594), A4v.

15. *The Merry Devil of Edmonton* (1608), ed. William Amos Abrams (Durham, North Carolina 1942), 13-15, 107; *The Life and Death of the Merry Devill of Edmonton* (1631), A4r-Br, Bv.

16. For an extended discussion of the Mother Shipton literature and its implications for popular ideas about the Devil, see Darren Oldridge, 'Mother Shipton and the Devil', in Angela McShane and Garthine Walker, eds., *The Extraordinary and the Everyday in Early Modern England* (Macmillan: London 2010). Richard Head, *The Life and Death of Mother Shipton* (1667), in *Mother Shipton: A Collection of the Earliest Editions of Her Prophecies* (Manchester 1882), 30-2; *Mother Shiptons Christmas Carrols*, 2; Head, *Mother Shipton*, 78; *Mother Shiptons Christmas Carrols*, 3; *Strange and Wonderful History*, 6-8.

17. Richard Head's cheerfully demonic *The Life and Death of Mother Shipton* (1667) went through four new editions between 1684 and 1697. For Thomson's play, see Oldridge, 'Mother Shipton and the Devil'. T.T., *The Life of Mother Shipton, A New Comedy* (1670), 53-4.

18. Stephen Bateman, *A Christall Glasse of Christian Reformation* (1569), J1r.

19. R. W. Scribner, *For the Sake of Simple Folk: Popular Propaganda for the German Reformation* (Clarendon: Oxford 1981); *Popular Culture and Popular Movements in Reformation Germany* (Hambledon: London 1987), chapters three and thirteen; Tessa Watt, *Cheap Print and Popular Piety, 1550-1640* (Cambridge University Press 1991).

20. Bateman, *Christall Glasse*, B1r, D2v, D4r, M4r.

21. William Gouge, *The Whole Armour of God* (1616), title page; *Newes From Hell, Rome, and the Innes of Court* (1642), title page; *The Young Man's Conquest Over the Powers of Darkness* (1683).

22. Clarke, *A Generall Martyrologie* (1651), 388.

23. Thomas, *Religion*, 563; *A Wonderfull and Strange Miracle, or Gods Just Vengeance Against the Cavaliers* (1642), 5; Walter Powell, 'The fearfull end of him who drank a health to the Devill', appended to *A Summons for Swearers* (1645).

24. *Strange Newes From Antwerpe* (1612), 2, 7, 9; *A Relation of a Strange Apparition* (1641), 2; *God's Judgment Upon Hereticks, or The Infidel's Overthrow* (1729), 3, 7. The last of these texts is reproduced in the appendix.

25. *A Most Horrible & Detestable Murder Committed by a Bloudie-Minded Man Upon his Owne Wife* (1595), preface, 1; *The Examination, Confession and Condemnation of Henry Robson* (1598), 1, 6, 7.

26. Gilbert Dugdale, *A True Discourse of the Practises of Elizabeth Caldwell* (1604), dedication, B2r, C1v, C4r, D1r.

27. Peter Lake discusses the first two texts mentioned here in 'Popular Form, Puritan Content? Two Puritan Appropriations of the Murder Pamphlet From Mid-Seventeenth-Century London', in Anthony Fletcher and Peter Roberts, eds. *Religion, Culture and Society in Early Modern Britain* (Cambridge University Press 1994). John Reynolds, *Triumphs of Gods Revenge Against the Crying and Execrable Sinne of Willful and Premeditated Murder* (1635), preface, 371-80.

28. Lawrence Southerne, *Fearefull Newes From Coventry* (1642), title page, 5-6; *Roxburghe*, II, 226-7; Head, *Mother Shipton*, 34.

29. Southerne, *Fearefull Newes*, 4, 6, 8.

30. *Roxburghe*, III, 29, 34, 137, 138.

31. *Roxburghe*, III, 156; *Euing n*, 108-9; *Roxburghe*, I, 370; *Euing*, 107.

32. *Roxburghe*, II, 224-8; Ewen, *Witchcraft*, 192; Ashmole, Napier, MS 404, 181v.

33. For ghosts in the English Reformation, see Peter Marshall, *Beliefs and the Dead in Reformation England* (Oxford University Press 2004), chapter six, and Peter

Marshall, 'Deceptive Appearances: Ghosts and Reformers in Elizabethan and Jacobean England', in Helen Parish and William Naphy, eds., *Religion and Superstition in Reformation Europe* (Manchester University Press 2002). *A Godly Warning for all Maidens, by the Example of Gods Judgement Shewed on one Jermans Wife of Clifton* (c. 1670).

34. Samuel Clarke, *A Mirrour or Looking Glasse, Both for Saints and Sinners* (1646), 65.

35. Richard Kenneth Emmerson, *Antichrist in the Middle Ages* (Manchester University Press 1981), 82-3; Olde, *Short Description* , 4v, 30r; John Gough, *A Godly Book* (1561), reprinted in Leonard J. Triterud, ed., *Elizabethan Puritanism* (Oxford University Press 1971), 32.

36. Emmerson, *Antichrist*, 228; *The Divell of the Vault* (1606), 19, 22; *Miracle Upon Miracle, or A True Relation of the Great Floods Which Happened in Coventry* (1607), 3; *A Disputation Betwixt the Devill and the Pope* (1642), 2; *Newes From Hell, Rome and the Inns of Court* (1642); Ellis Bradshaw, *A Dialogue Between the Devil & Prince Rupert* (1645), 3; John Booker, *The Bloody Almanack: To Which England is Directed to Fore-Know What Shall Come to Passe* (1643), 3, 4; *Six Strange Prophesies Predicting Wonderfull Events* (1642).

37. *Historie of the Damnable Life*, 5, 9-10; *Merry Drollery*, I, 104; *Euing*, 107; Rosen, *Witchcraft*, 64-7; Emmerson, *Antichrist*, 228; *The Tryal and Examination of Mrs Joan Peterson* (1652), 3-5.

38. *Grand Plutoes Remonstrance* (1642), 1-2; *A Disputation*, 3.

39. *Ibid*, 4.

40. *Euing*, 107; *Merry Drollery*, I, 103-4; *Life and Death of the Merry Devill*, B2r-B3v; *The Wonder: or The Devil Outwitted* (1736), 5, 8.

41. Head, *Mother Shipton*, 30-34, 60, 64, 78; Christopher Haigh, *English Reformations* (Clarendon: Oxford), 290; Watt, *Cheap Print*, 126.

CHAPTER 5

1. In an alternative version of the story, Margaret overcame the Devil with a crucifix. Here again her role was more passive than that of male figures such as St George: the symbol of God, rather than her own efforts, achieved her delivery. Some 250 English churches were dedicated to Margaret, and her cult was associated particularly with the cure of the possessed and the protection of women in labour. Her career was described in the medieval collection of saints' lives, *The Golden Legend*.

2. The best general account of women's religious experiences in the period is Patricia Crawford's *Women and Religion in England, 1500-1720* (Routledge: London 1993). Other valuable texts include Anne Laurence, *Women in England, 1500-1760* (Weidenfeld and Nicolson: London 1994) and Diane Willen, 'Godly Women in Early Modern England: Puritanism and Gender', in *Journal of Ecclesiastical History*, 43 (1992).

3. For a discussion of the pamphlets mentioned here, see Jerome Friedman, *Miracles and the Pulp Press During the English Revolution* (UCL: London 1993), 182-3, 195. References to the Whore of Babylon were common in cheap print in early modern England: see, for instance, Stephen Bateman, *A Christall Glasse of Christian Reformation* (1569), D2v, *Six Strange Prophesies Predicting Wonderfull Events* (1642), 5, 7, and *Merry Drollery*, II, 51. Nicholas Breton, *The Good and the Badde, or Descriptions of the Worthies and Unworthies of This Age* (1616), 27-8.

4. Friedman. *Miracles*, 179-80.

5. The accession of Elizabeth spurred Protestant thinkers to find theological justifications for female authority, which often involved reinterpretations of the story

of Eden. See Amanda Shephard, *Gender and Authority in Early Modern England* (1993), chapter two. Richard Carpenter, *Experience, Historie and Divinitie* (1641), 66; William Gouge, *The Whole Armour of God* (1627 edition), 26; William Gouge, *Of Domesticall Duties* (1626 edition), 141, 329.

6. Margaret Hoby, *The Private Life of an Elizabethan Lady: The Diary of Lady Margaret Hoby*, 1599-1605, ed. Joanna Moody (Sutton: Stroud 1998), 54, 75; Jane Turner, *Choice Experiences of the Kind Dealings of God* (1653), 52-3; East Sussex Record Office, Letter from Anna Temple to her daughter, Dunn MSS 51/54; Crawford, *Women and Religion*, chapter eight.

7. Willen, 'Godly Women', 567; Bateman, *Christall Glasse*, H3r; Philip Stubbes, *The Anatomie of Abuses* (1583), F2r, Gv.

8. King James' view was shared by William Perkins, who claimed that 'the woman, being the weaker sex, is sooner entangled by the Devil's illusions with this damnable art than the man'. Bateman, *Christall Glasse*, H3r; James VI of Scotland, *Daemonologie* (1597), 43-4; Alan Macfarlane, *Witchcraft in Tudor and Stuart England* (2nd ed., Routledge: London 1999), 161.

9. Turner, *Choice Experiences*, preface, 53.

10. *A Most Straunge and True Discourse of the Wonderfull Judgement of God* (1600), 2, 3, 10.

11. *God's Handy-Worke in Wonders* (1615), 5, 7; *The Euing Collection of English Broadside Ballads* (Glasgow 1971), 197; Friedman, *Miracles*, 52, 180.

12. Mother Shipton was first identified explicitly as a witch in Richard Head's *Life and Death of Mother Shipton* (1667), reprinted in *Mother Shipton: A Collection of the Earliest Editions of her Prophecies* (Manchester 1882), 78. Jim Sharpe, 'Women, Witchcraft and the Legal Process', in Jenny Kermode and Garthine Walker, eds, *Women, Crime and the Courts in Early Modern England* (UCL: London 1994); Clive Holmes, 'Women, Witnesses and Witches', in *Past and Present*, 140 (1993); *A Most Certain, Strange and True Discovery of a Witch* (1643); Reginald Scot, *The Discovery of Witches* (1581), reprinted in Barbara Rosen, *Witchcraft in England, 1558-1618* (University of Massachusetts Press: Amherst 1969), 174; Archives of the Yorkshire Archaeological Society, 'Presumptions against Witches', DD146/12/2/10.

13. For a helpful survey of work touching on the links between English and continental witchcraft, see Bent Ankarloo and Gustav Henningsen, eds., *Early Modern European Witchcraft: Centres and Peripheries* (Clarendon, Oxford 1993), introduction. See also Barry Reay, *Popular Cultures in England, 1550-1750* (Longman, London 1998), chapter four. *The Examination and Confession of Certain Wyches at Chelmsford* (1565), reprinted in Peter Haining, ed., *The Witchcraft Papers* (Robert Hale: London 1974), 28; *A Rehearall Both Straung and True of Hainous and Horrible Acts* (1579), reprinted in Rosen, 86; *The Apprehension and Confession of Three Notorious Witches* (1589), in Rosen, 184; Haining, *Witchcraft Papers*, 73-4; *Dr Lamb's Darling: or Strange and Terrible News From Salisbury* (1653), 5.

14. Joad Raymond, ed., *Making the News: An Anthology of the Newsbooks of Revolutionary England*, 1641-1660 (Windrush Press: Gloucester 1993), 152, 153-4; *Merry Drollery*, II, 12-15; *The Wonder: or The Devil Outwitted* (1736), 8; *Roxburghe*, 335-6; *The Wonder*, 8; *Roxburghe*, II, 368-71.

15. *The Book of Margery Kempe*, ed. Barry Windeatt (Penguin: London 1985), 41-2.

16. John Bunyan, *Grace Abounding* (Penguin: London 1987), 14.

17. Margaret Cavendish, *Poems and Fancies* (1653), preface; Raymond, *Making the News*, 140-1; C. L'Estrange Ewen, *Witch Hunting and Witch Trials* (Dial Press: New York 1929), 304, 305.

18. Ralph Houlbrooke, 'The Puritan Deathbed, 1560-1660', in Chris Durston and Jacqueline Eales, eds., *The Culture of English Puritanism,* 156-1700 (Macmillan: London 1996), 136; *A Brief Discourse of the Christian Life and Death of Mistris Katherin Brettergh* (1606 edition), 12, 13, 15; Elizabeth Jocelin, *The Mother's Legacie to her Unborne Childe* (1624), 33, 83.

19. Hoby, *Diary,* 54, 60.

20. *Book of Margery Kempe,* 46; *The Young Man's Second Warning -Peece* (1643), 7.

21. Vavasor Powell, ed., *Spirituall Experiences of Sundry Believers* (1652 edition), 167, 168-9, 174-5; Burrill's memoir is included in Rogers, *Ohel or Beth-Shemesh* (1653), 413.

22. Gilbert Dugdale, *A True Discourse of the Practises of Elizabeth Caldwell* (1604), C1v; Hannah Allen, *Satan His Methods and Malice Baffled* (1683), 7-8; Stevie Davies, *Unbridled Spirits: Women of the English Revolution,* 1640-1660 (Women's Press: London 1998), 131.

23. Bodleian Library, Oxford, Ashmole MSS, Casebooks of Richard Napier, MS 404, 289v; MS 412, 150v.

24. Ottavia Niccoli, 'The End of Prophecy', in *Journal of Modern History,* 61 (1989), 677, 680-2; Moshe Sluhovsky, 'A Divine Apparition or Demonic Possession? Female Agency and Church Authority in Demonic Possession in Sixteenth-Century France', in *Sixteenth Century Journal,* XXVII/4 (1996), 1039-55.

25. For the tradition of visionary women in England, see Crawford, *Women and Religion,* chapters four and five.

26. John Hacket, *Scrinia Reserata: A Memorial Offer'd to the Great Deservings of John Williams* (1692), 47-8.

27. Edward Fairfax, *Demonologia,* ed. William Grainge (R. Ackrill: Harrogate 1882), 62-4.

28. Crawford, *Women and Religion,* 107; *A Strange and True Relation of a Young Woman Possest With the Devil* (1647), 1-2.

29. *The Most Strange and Admirable Discoverie of the Three Witches of Warboys* (1593), reprinted in Rosen, *Witchcraft,* 269; Philip Stubbes, *A Christall Glasse for Christian Women* (1618 edition), C3v; Davies, *Unbridled Spirits,* 128-33.

CHAPTER 6

1. *The Most Strange and Admirable Discoverie of the Three Witches of Warboys* (1593), 1r.

2. Stanley Gower's account of the possession in Nottingham is reproduced in the appendix. The possession of Edward Dinham was described in a manuscript by Lord Londesborough, reproduced in Thomas Wright, *Narratives of Sorcery and Magic,* II (Redfield: New York 1851), 139-43. Clarke, *A Generall Martyrologie* (1651), 459; C. L'Estrange Ewen, *Witchcraft and Demonianism* (Heath Cranton: London 1933), 452; Bodleian Library, Oxford, Ashmole MSS, Casebooks of Richard Napier, MS 412r, 152r, 169r.

3. Kathleen H. Sands, *Demon Possession in Elizabethan England* (Praeger 2004), 13; Ewen, Witchcraft, 186; *The Wonderfull Discoverie of the Witchcrafts of Margaret and Phillip Flower* (1619), in Barbara Rosen, ed., *Witchcraft in England, 1558-1618* (University of Massachusetts Press: Amherst 1969), 377; Ewen, Witchcraft, 180; C. L'Estrange Ewen, *Witch Hunting and Witch Trials* (Dial Press: New York 1929), 297.

4. For the construction of witchcraft narratives involving demonic possession, see Marion Gibson, *Reading Witchcraft: Stories of Early English Witches* (Routledge: London and New York 1999), 120-8, 187-90.

5. The possessed man in Nottingham was exorcised by the godly minister, Richard Rothwell, and the puritan John Darrell presided at the dispossession of Thomas Darling and the victims of Edmund Hartley. Darrell subsequently accused those who opposed his practices of popish inclinations. Darrell, *The Triall of Maist. Dorrell* (1599), 66; Lyndal Roper, *Oedipus and the Devil: Witchcraft, Sexuality and Religion in Early Modern Europe* (Routledge: London and New York 1994), 173-4, 177-801.

6. John Hall, *Select Observations on English Bodies* (1679), 142-3.

7. John Darrell published a vivid account of William Somers' possession and exorcism, which is reprinted in the appendix. John Darrell, *A True Narration of the Strange and Grevous Vexation by the Devil of 7 Persons in Lancashire, and William Somers of Nottingham*, 15-6; Darrell, *Triall*, 17; *A Strange and True Relation of a Young Woman Possest With the Devill* (1647), 2; Ewen, *Witchcraft*, 176, 186; *Most Fearfull and Strange Newes From the Bishoppricke of Durham* (1641), 3; Richard Baxter, *The Certainty of the Worlds of Spirits* (1691), 47.

8. Edward Fairfax, *Demonologia*, ed. William Grainge (R. Ackrill: Harrogate 1882), 54; *Dr Lambs Darling*, 6; Wright, *Narratives*, 139; *A Strange and True Relation*, 2.

9. *Most Strange and Admirable Discoverie*, C2r; Darrell, *True Narration*, 16; Wright, *Narratives*, 143; *A Strange and True Relation*, 3.

10. Eamon Duffy, *The Stripping of the Altars: Traditional Religion in England, 1400-1580* (Yale University Press 1992), 317; Richard Carpenter, *Experience, Historie and Divinitie* (1641), 23; Darrell, *Triall*, 50; Wright, *Narratives*, 143.

11. See the appendix for Darrell's narrative of the meeting between Somers and the witch. Fairfax, *Demonologia*; Ewen, *Witchcraft*, 176-81.

12. *The Disclosing of a Late Counterfeyted Possession by the Devyl* (1574), 8, 11; Peter Haining, ed., *The Witchcraft Papers* (Robert Hale: London 1974), 131-2.

13. Clarke Garrett, *Spirit Possession and Popular Religion* (Johns Hopkins University Press: Baltimore and London 1987), 5; Baxter, *Certainty*, 47; Roy Porter, *A Social History of Madness* (Weidenfeld and Nicolson: London 1987), 83-9.

14. *Disclosing*, 2-4; *Most Strange and Admirable Discoverie*, G3r-v.

15. Sharpe, 'Disruption', 206; Darrell, *True Narration*, 16, 18; Clarke, *Generall Martyrologie*, 403; *A Booke Declaringe the Fearfull Vexasion of One Alexander Nynde* (1573), 9; Ewen, *Witchcraft*, 191.

16. *Disclosing*, preface; *Constitutions and Canons Ecclesiastical* (1605), LXXII.

17. Darrell, *True Narration*, 19; Samuel Harsnett, *A Declaration* (1603), 136-7; Darrell, *Triall*, 22, 34-5.

18. Robert Burton, *The Anatomy of Melancholy*, eds. Thomas Faulkener, Nicholas Kiessling and Rhonda Blair (1989-94), III, 414-5, 422-3; Hannah Allen, *Satan His Methods and Malice Baffled* (1683), 3; John Bunyan, *Grace Abounding* (Penguin: London 1987), 29.

19. Baptismal exorcism was abolished in the 1552 prayer book, and this reform was preserved in the 1559 version. John Woolton, *The Christian Manuell* (1576), 179v; John Milton, *Prose Writings*, ed. K. M. Burton (Dent: London 1958), 5-6.

20. Allen, *Satan*, 3, 8, 13-20.

21. *The Most Wonderfull and True Storie of a Certaine Witch Named Alse Gooderige* (1597), 16, 29-30; D. P. Walker, *Unclean Spirits: Possession and Exorcism in France and England in the Late Sixteenth and Early Seventeenth Centuries* (Scolar Press: London 1981), 54-6; Keith Thomas, *Religion and the Decline of Magic* (Weidenfeld & Nicolson: London 1971), 577.

22. The account of the exorcism performed by Richard Rothwell was composed by Stanley Gower. This is reproduced in the appendix. Clarke, *Generall Martyrologie*, 402-3, 458-61.

23. Clarke, *Generall Martyrologie*, 402; *A Strange and True Relation*, 2; *A Booke Declaringe the Fearfull Vexasion*, 5; Jacqueline Eales, 'Thomas Pierson and the Transmission of the Moderate Puritan Tradition', *Midland History*, 20 (1995), 81.

24. Anthony Fletcher, *Gender, Sex and Subordination in England* (Yale University Press 1995); Lyndal Roper, *The Holy Household: Women and Morals in Reformation Augsburg* (Clarendon: Oxford 1990). Extracts from Baxter's *Poor Mans Family Book* (1674) are reproduced in Mary Abbott, *Life Cycles in England 1560-1720* (Routledge, London 1996), 193-5; Sharpe, 'Disruption', 205-9.

25. In 1591, for example, the verbal battle between the dying Katherine Stubbes and the Devil resembled a godly exorcism. When her adversary taunted her that her transgressions were so great that she was destined for Hell, she declared that Christ's 'precious blood [is] a full satisfaction for my sins'. Philip Stubbes, *A Christall Glasse for Christian Women* (1618 edition), C3v; *A Brief Discourse of the Christian Life and Death of Mistris Katherin Brettergh* (1606 edition), 14, 17.

26. John Rogers, *Ohel or Beth-Shemesh* (1653), 423-4.

27. Walker, *Unclean Spirits*, 54-5; Jane Turner, *Choice Experiences of the Kind Dealings of God* (1653), 2; Richard Baxter, *Certainty*, 175; Patricia Crawford, *Women and Religion in England, 1500-1720* (Routledge: London 1993); *The Declaration of John Robins* (1651), ed. Andrew Hopton (Aphoria: London 1992), 22; Abiezer Coppe, *Selected Writings*, ed. Andrew Hopton (1987), 27, 80-1; Samuel Clarke, *A Mirrour or Looking Glasse for Both Saints and Sinners* (1654 edition), 231-8.

28. Stephen Greenblatt, *Shakespearean Negotiations: The Circulation of Social Energy in Renaissance England* (University of California Press: Berkeley 1988), 97; Darrell, *True Relation*, 6.

29. George Gifford, *A Dialogue Concerning Witches and Witchcraft*, reproduced in Haining, *Witchcraft Papers*, 94; Clarke, *Generall Martyrologie*, 458-61.

30. *Booke Declaring the Fearfull Vexasion*, 5-6; Darrell, *Triall*, 66.

31. Darrell, *True Narration*, 18; Eales, 'Thomas Pierson', 81-2.

32. Clarke, *Martyrologie*, p. 461; Proceedings of the High Commission, Calendar of State Papers, Domestic Series, 1634-5, 263.

33. For Harsnett's episcopal career, see E. J. Evans, *Seventeenth-Century Norwich* (Clarendon: Oxford 1979); CSPD. 1634-5, 263.

CHAPTER 7

1. For a *per capita* comparison between witch trials in England and Scotland, see Brian P. Levack, *Witch-Hunting in Scotland: Law, Politics and Religion* (Routledge: London and New York 2008), 1-2.

2. The figures for the Home Circuit are analysed in detail in C. L'Estrange Ewen, *Witch Hunting and Witch Trials* (Dial Press: New York 1929), 98-100, and Alan Macfarlane, *Witchcraft in Tudor and Stuart England* (2nd ed. Routledge: London and New York 1999), chapter three.

3. James Sharpe, *Instruments of Darkness: Witchcraft in England, 1550-1750* (Hamish Hamilton: London 1996), 131; Malcolm Gaskill, *Witchfinders: An English Tragedy* (John Murray: London 2005).

4. For an illuminating discussion of George Gifford's pastoral demonology, see Timothy Scott McGinnis, *George Gifford and the Reformation of the Common Sort* (Truman State University Press: Kirksville, Missouri 2004), chapter five.

5. Sharpe, *Instruments*, 75; Barbara Rosen, *Witchcraft in England, 1558-1618* (University of Massachusetts Press: Amherst 1969), 74, 184; Ewen, *Witch Hunting,*

306, 312; *Roxburghe*, II, 224-7; Edward Fairfax, *Demonologia*, ed. William Grainge (R. Ackrill: Harrogate 1882), 107-8; *The Euing Collection of English Broadside Ballads* (Glasgow 1971), 569.

6. Peter Haining, ed., *The Witchcraft Papers* (Robert Hale: London 1974), 24; Fairfax, *Demonologia*, 88-9. The superstitious connotations of witch scratching were noted in *The Witches of Northampton* (1612).

7. Familiar spirits which took animal form and fed on blood were described in pre-Reformation cases of sorcery. In 1510, for example, John Steward of Knaresborough was accused of keeping bumble bees which he fed with 'a drop of blood of his finger'. George Lyman Kittredge, *Witchcraft in Old and New England* (Harvard University Press: Cambridge, Massachusetts 1929), 179; Rosen, *Witchcraft*, 69; Barry Reay, *Popular Cultures in England, 1550-1750* (Longman: London and New York 1998), 113; Jim Sharpe, 'Women, Witchcraft and the Legal Process', in Garthine Walker and Jenny Kermode, eds, *Women, Crime and the Courts in Early Modern England* (UCL: London 1994), 108-13.

8. Rosen, *Witchcraft*, 77-8, 86, 184, 138, 349, 358-9, 362; Ewen, *Witch Hunting*, 309.

9. Stanley Gower's text, taken from Samuel Clarke's *Generall Martyrologie* (1651), is reproduced in the appendix. For the collaboration between witchcraft suspects and their interrogators in the elaboration of fantasy, see Lyndal Roper, *Oedipus and the Devil: Witchcraft, Sexuality and Religion in Early Modern Europe* (Routledge: London 1994), chapters nine and ten; and Malcolm Gaskill, 'Witchcraft and Power in Early Modern England: The Case of Margaret Moore', in Walker and Kermode, *Women*, 125-45. Rosen, *Witchcraft*, 350-1.

10. Richard Head, *The Life and Death of Mother Shipton* (1667), in *Mother Shipton: A Collection of the Earliest English Editions of Her Prophecies* (Manchester 1882), 32.

11. C. L'Estrange Ewen, *Witchcraft and Demonianism* (Heath Cranton: London 1933), 188; *The Most Strange and Admirable Discoverie of the Three Witches of Warboys* (1593), D4r; Bodleian Library, Ashmole MSS, Casebooks of Richard Napier, MS 412, 121r, 150v.

12. Ewen, *Witchcraft*, 189; Ashmole, Napier, MS 412, 152r; Ewen, *Witchcraft*, 177, 186; Richard Baddily, *The Life of Dr Thomas Morton, Late Bishop of Duresme* (1669), 72-5.

13. Ewen, *Witchcraft*, 176-7, 180, 188-9; Ewen, *Witch Hunting*, 252; Ashmole, Napier, MS 412, 169r.

14. *Most Strange and Admirable Discoverie*, 1r; Haining, *Witchcraft Papers*, 144, 167, 169.

15. Ewen, *Witchcraft*, 191.

16. M.R. Holmes, 'The So-Called Bellarmine Mask in Imported Rhenish Stoneware', *Antiquaries Journal* XXXI (1950), 173-9; John Allan, 'Some Post Mediaeval Documentary Evidence for the Trade in Ceramics', in Peter Davey and Richard Hodges, eds., *Ceramics and Trade: The Production and Distribution of Later Mediaeval Pottery in North-West Europe* (University of Sheffield Press 1983), 37-45.

17. Denise Dixon-Smith, 'Concealed Shoes', *Archaeological Leather Group Newsletter*, 6 (1990); John Gaule, *Select Cases of Conscience Touching Witches and Witchcrafts* (1646), 76; Ewen, *Witchcraft*, 148, 188; Joseph Glanvill, *Saducismus Triumphatus* (1689), 331; Ralph Merrifield, *The Archaeology of Ritual and Magic* (B.T. Batsford: London 1987), 134.

18. Ewen, *Witchcraft*, 148.

19. William Perkins, *The Art of Prophesying* (Banner of Truth Trust: Edinburgh 1996), 111-2; Gaule, *Select Cases*, 17; Olde, *Short Description*, 30v; S.S., *A Briefe Instruction for all Families* (1586), dedication; John Reynolds, *The Triumphs of Gods Revenge* (1635), preface; R. Willis, *Mount Tabor, or Private Exercises of a Penitent Sinner* (1639), 91.

20. Warwick County Record Office, Richard Newdigate's notebook, 1631, CR 136/A7; Christopher Love, *The Christians Directory* (1658), 35.

21. George Gifford, *A Discourse of the Subtill Practises of Devilles by Witches and Sorcerers* (1587), G2v; George Gifford, *A Dialogue Concerning Witches and Witchcraftes* (1593), C2r, Kr.

22. Rosen, *Witchcraft*, 161; WCRO, Newdigate's notebook, 1626, MI /351/5/21, 581; William Gouge, *The Whole Armour of God* (1627 edition), 11.

23. William Perkins, *A Discourse on the Damned Art of Witchcraft* (1608), 167, 170-1, 174.

24. Rosen, *Witchcraft*, 55-6; Lichfield Joint Record Office (LJRO), episcopal visitation, 1636, B/V/1/58, 40r; LJRO, episcopal visitations, 1614, B/V/1/29, 18; 1623, B/V/1/45, 18; 1629, B/V/1/52, 9; 1635, B/V/1/55, 18, 28; 1636, B/V/1/58, 40r, B/V/1/59, 119, B/V/1/61, 16; 1639, B/V/1/66, 17.

25. Calendar of State Papers Domestic, 1634-5, 319-20; Thomas Hall, *Fuebria Florae, The Downfall of May-Games* (1661), 11, 46; John Darrell, *The Triall of Maist. Dorrell* (1599), 76.

26. Philip C. Almond presents a compelling narrative of this case in *The Witches of Warboys* (I. B. Tauris: London and New York 2008). Marion Gibson, *Reading Witchcraft: Stories of English Witchcraft* (Routledge: London 1999), 121-3; *Most Strange and Admirable Discoverie*, D4-D4v, O3v.

27. *Most Strange and Admirable Discoverie*, H2v-H3r; D. P. Walker, *Unclean Spirits: Possession and Exorcism in France and England in the Late Sixteenth and Early Seventeenth Centuries* (Scolar Press: London 1981), 64.

28. For the rejection of word magic by Protestant demonologists, see Stuart Clark, 'The Rational Witchfinder', in Stephen Pumfrey, Paolo Rossi and Maurice Slawinski, eds., *Science, Culture and Popular Belief in Renaissance Europe* (Manchester University Press 1991), 241-5. *Most Strange and Admirable Discoverie*, Nv, N4r-v; Ewen, *Witchcraft*, 176, 178, 186; John Darrell, *A True Narration of the Strange and Grevous Vexation by the Devil of 7 Persons in Lancashire, and William Somers of Nottingham* (1600), 15; Darrell, *Triall*, 34.

29. Knowle was the half-uncle of Nicholas Starkey, whose daughters were dispossessed by John Darrell in 1597. Darrell named John Brinsley and John Ireton as men of 'judgement and credit' who testified to the authenticity of his exorcisms in *A Detection of That Sinnful Shameful Lying and Ridiculous Discours of Samuel Harshnet* (1600), 170. Rosen, *Witchcraft*, 358-60.

30. Fairfax, *Demonologia*, 38, 68, 87-9, 97.

31. The dispossession in Nottingham involving Richard Bernard was described in Samuel Clarke's *Generall Martyrologie*, and is reproduced in the appendix. Keith Thomas has suggested that Bernard also assisted John Darrell in his exorcisms in the 1590s. Richard Bernard, *A Guide to Grand-Jury Men* (1627), 216, 218, 220-21; Clarke, *Generall Martyrologie*, 459; Keith Thomas, *Religion and the Decline of Magic* (Weidenfeld & Nicolson: London 1971), 576.

32. Darrell, *Triall*, 25; Malcolm Gaskill, *Crime and Mentalities in Early Modern England* (Cambridge University Press 2000), 45; *Most Strange and Admirable Discoverie*, N4r.

33. For the probable number of executions in 1645-7, see Sharpe, *Instruments*, 129. Matthew Hopkins, *The Discovery of Witches* (1647), 2.

34. Malcolm Gaskill, 'Witchcraft and Evidence in Early Modern England', *Past and Present*, 198 (2008), 198, 46-7; Nathan Johnstone, *The Devil and Demonism in Early Modern England* (Cambridge University Press 2006), 213.

35. Hopkins indicated his religious sympathies by claiming that the Devil used the Book of Common Prayer to consecrate his marriage to witches. Samuel Clarke

described the career of Samuel Fairclough in *The Lives of Sundry Eminent Persons* (1683), 153–92. Macfarlane, *Witchcraft*, 186; Gaskill, *Witchfinders*, 113, 224; John Stearne, *A Confirmation and Discovery of Witchcraft* (1648), 3; Richard Baxter, *The Certainty of the Worlds of Spirits* (1691), 52–5.

36. Ewen, *Witch Hunting*, 291, 292, 306; Haining, *Witchcraft Papers*, 150, 154; Hopkins, *Discovery* (1647), 4–5.

37. Ewen, *Witch Hunting*, 303–4; Kittredge, *Witchcraft*, 176; Haining, *Witchcraft Papers*, 142, 157.

38. Gaule, *Select Cases*, 31, 76–7, 92.

39. In *A Candle in the Dark* (1655), Thomas Ady rejected the great majority of popular witch beliefs because they were unsupported by scripture. For earlier allegations of collective witchcraft, see Rosen, *Witchcraft*, 367–8, and Fairfax, *Daemonologia*, 107–8. Sharpe, *Instruments*, 75–79.

CHAPTER 8

1. *The Devil Turn'd Round-head: or Pluto Become a Brownist* (1642), 4; *A Short, Compendious and True Description of the Round-heads and the Long-heads* (1642), 6–7; Robert Baillie, *Satan the Leader in Chief of all who Resist the Reparation of Sion* (1643), 33.

2. *A Sad Caveat to all Quakers* (1657), 8–9, 11; Jane Turner, *Choice Experiences of the Kind Dealings of God* (1653), 110–26; Richard Baxter, *The Certainty of the Worlds of Spirits* (1691), 175–6.

3. *The Just Devil of Woodstock* (1660), preface.

4. Richard Baxter, *Certainty*, preface; Keith Thomas, *Religion and the Decline of Magic* (Weidenfeld & Nicolson: London 1971), 693–4.

5. James Sharpe, *Instruments of Darkness: Witchcraft in England, 1550-1750* (Hamish Hamilton: London 1996), 243–4; Richard Greenham, *Short Rules Sent by Maister Richard Greenham to a Gentlewoman Troubled in Minde* (1618).

6. The quotations from Tillotson are taken from C. H. Sisson, ed., *The English Sermon, 1650-1750* (Carcanet: Cheadle 1976), 193–4, 196.

7. D. R. Woolf, 'The Common Voice: History, Folklore and Oral Tradition in Early Modern England', in *Past and Present* 120 (1988), 50; Margaret Spufford, *Small Books and Pleasant Histories* (Cambridge University Press 1981), 5; Mary Williams, *Witches in Old North Yorkshire* (Hutton: Beverley 1987), 7; James Obelkivich, *Religion and Rural Society* (Clarendon: Oxford 1978), 277–8.

8. For Wesley's views on possession and witchcraft, see Henry Rack, *Reasonable Enthusiast: John Wesley and the Rise of Methodism* (Epworth: London), 195–7, 387–8; Owen Davies, *Witchcraft, Magic and Culture, 1736-1951* (Manchester University Press 1999), 19–22.

9. Rack, *Reasonable Enthusiast*, 195; R. W. Ambler, *Ranters, Revivalists and Reformers: Primitive Methodism and Rural Society in South Lincolnshire, 1817-1875* (Hull University Press 1989), 52, 73.

10. For a lively account of Soutcott's struggles with Satan, see Marina Benjamin, *Living at the End of the World* (Picador: London 1998), 125–7.

11. Iain McCalman, *Radical Underworld: Prophets, Revolutionaries and Pornographers in London, 1795-1840* (Clarendon: Oxford 1993), 145, 191; Robert Wedderburn, *The Horrors of Slavery and Other Writings*, ed. Iain MacCalman (Edinburgh University Press 1991), 153–4.

APPENDIX

1. Thomas Potts, *The Wonderfull Discoverie of Witches in the Countie of Lancaster* (1613), G4v.

2. Nathan Johnstone, *The Devil and Demonism in Early Modern England* (Cambridge University Press 2006), 104, 105.

3. For an illuminating discussion of the evolution of the narrative presented here, see Michael Hunter, 'New light on the "Drummer of Tedworth": Conflicting Narratives of Witchcraft in Restoration England', *Historical Research* 78:201 (2005).

4. For Darrell's dispossession of William Somers and his subsequent trial, see Kathleen R. Sands, *Demon-Possession in Elizabethan England* (Praeger: Westport, Connecticut, and London 2004), chapter eleven, and D. P. Walker, *Unclean Spirits: Possession and Exorcism in France and England in the Late Sixteenth and Early Seventeenth Centuries* (Scolar Press: London 1981), chapter four.

SELECT BIBLIOGRAPHY

CONTEMPORARY TEXTS

Ady, Thomas, *A Candle in the Dark* (1655)

Allen, Hannah, *Satan His Methods and Malice Baffled* (1683)

The Apprehension and Confession of Three Notorious Witches (1589)

Aubrey, John, *Brief Lives*, ed. Oliver Lawson Dick (Penguin: London 1949)

Baddily, Richard, *The Life of Dr Thomas Morton, Late Bishop of Duresme* (1669)

Baillie, Robert, *Satan, the Leader in Chief of all who Resist the Reparation of Sion* (1643)

Bale, John, *The First Examinacyon of Anne Askewe, Latelye Martyred in Smythfelde* (1546)

Bateman, Stephen, *A Christall Glasse of Christian Reformation* (1569)

Bateman, Stephen, *The Golden Booke of the Leaden Goddes* (1577)

Baxter, Richard, *The Poor Mans Family Book* (1674)

Baxter, Richard, *The Certainty of the Worlds of Spirits* (1691)

Beard, Thomas *The Theatre of Gods Judgements: Revised and Augmented* (1631)

Becon, Thomas, *The Workes of Thomas Becon* (1564)

Bernard, Richard, *A Guide to Grand-Jury Men* (1627)

Bolton, Robert, *The Saints Selfe-Enriching Examination* (1634)

A Booke Declaringe the Fearfull Vexasion of One Alexander Nynde (1573)

Booker, John, *The Bloody Almanack: To Which England is Directed to Fore-Know What Shall Come to Passe* (1643)

Bradford, John, *A Godlye Medytacyon Composed by the Faithfull and Constant Servant of God J B* (1559)

Bradshaw, Ellis, *A Dialogue Betweene the Devil & Prince Rupert* (1645)

Breton, Nicholas, *The Goode and the Badde, or Descriptions of the Worthies and Unworthies of This Age* (1616)

A Brief Discourse of the Christian Life and Death of Mistris Katherin Brettergh (1606 edition)

A Briefe Instruction for all Families (1586)

Bicknoll, Edmond, *A Swoord Against Swearyng* (1579)

Bunyan, John, *Grace Abounding* (Penguin: London 1987)

Bunyan, *The Life and Death of Mr Badman* (Hesperus: London 2007)

Burton, Robert, *The Anatomy of Melancholy*, eds. Thomas Faulkener, Nicholas Kiessling and Rhonda Blair (1989–94)

Carpenter, Richard, *Experience, Historie and Divinitie* (1641)

Carter, Beezaleel, *A Sermon of Gods Omnipotencie and Providence* (1615)

Cavendish, Margaret, *Poems and Fancies* (1653)

Chub, William, *The True Travaile of all Faithfull Christians* (1584)

Clarke, Samuel, *The Saints Nose-Gay, or a Posie of 741 Spirituall Flowers* (1642)

Clarke, Samuel, *A Generall Martyrologie* (1651)

Clarke, *A Mirrour or Looking Glasse for Both Saints and Sinners* (1654 edition)

Clarke, Samuel, *The Lives of Sundry Eminent Persons* (1683)

The Cloud of Unknowing, ed. Halcyon Backhouse (Hodder and Stoughton: London 1985)

Colfe, Isaac, *A Comfortable Treatise Concerning the Temptations of Christ* (1592)

Coppe, Abiezer, *Selected Writings*, ed. Andrew Hopton (1987)

Cradocke, Edward, *A Shippe of Assured Safetie* (1572)

Darrell, John, *The Triall of Maist. Dorrell* (1599)

Darrell, John, *A Detection of That Sinnful Shameful Lying and Ridiculous Discours of Samuel Harshnet* (1600)

Darrell, John, *A True Narration of the Strange and Grevous Vexation by the Devil of 7 Persons in Lancashire, and William Somers of Nottingham* (1600)

Decker, Thomas, and Wilkins, George, *Jests to Make You Merie* (1607)

Decker, Thomas, *Newes From Hell Brought by the Divells Carrier* (1606)

The Declaration of John Robins (1651), ed. Andrew Hopton (Aphoria: London 1992)

Dent, Arthur, *The Plaine Mans Path-way to Heaven* (1601)

Dent, Arthur, *A Sermon of Gods Providence* (1609)

The Devil and the Strumpet (1701)

The Devil Turn'd Roundhead: or Pluto Become a Brownist (1642)

The Disclosing of a Late Counterfeyted Possession by the Devyl in Two Maydens (1574)

A Disputation Betwixt the Devill and the Pope (1642)

The Divell of the Vault, or the Unmasking of Murther (1606)

Dr Lamb's Darling: or Strange and Terrible News From Salisbury (1653)

Dugdale, Gilbert, *A True Discourse of the Practises of Elizabeth Caldwell* (1604)

The Examination and Confession of Certain Wyches at Chelmsford (1565)

The Examination, Confession and Condemnation of Henry Robson (1598)

The Examination of John Walsh of Dorsetshire (1566)

Fairfax, Edward, *Demonologia*, ed. William Grainge (R. Ackrill: Harrogate 1882)

The Famous Historie of Fryer Bacon Containing the Wonderfull Things That he did in his Life (1627)

Fleming, Abraham, *A Straunge and Terrible Wunder Wrought Very Late in the Parish Church of Bungay* (1577)

Gaule, John, *Select Cases of Conscience Touching Witches and Witchcrafts* (1646)

Gerard, John, *The Conquest of Temptations: or Mans Victory Over Satan*, trans. R. Bruch (1615)

Gifford, George, *A Catechisme Conteining the Summe of Christian Religion* (1583)

Gifford, George, *A Brief Discourse of Certaine Points of the Religion Which is Among the Common Sort of Christians, Which may be Termed the Countrie Divinity* (1584)

Gifford, George, *A Discourse on the Subtill Practises of Devilles by Witches and Sorcerers* (1587)

Gifford, George, *A Dialogue Concerning Witches and Witchcraftes* (1593)

Glanvill, Joseph, *Saducismus Triumphatus* (1689)

Gods Handy-worke in Wonders (1615)

God's Judgment Upon Hereticks, or The Infidel's Overthrow (1729)

A Godly Warning for all Maidens, by the Example of Gods Judgement Shewed on one Jermans Wife of Clifton (c 1670)

Gouge, William, *Of Domesticall Duties* (2nd ed. 1626)

Gouge, William, *The Whole Armour of God* (1627 edition)

Gough, John, *A Godly Book* (1561)

Grand Plutoes Remonstrance (1642)

Greene, Robert, *The Honorable Historie of Frier Bacon and Frier Bongay* (1594)

Greenham, Richard, *Short Rules Sent by Maister Richard Greenham to a Gentlewoman Troubled in Minde* (1618)

Grymeston, Elizabeth, *Miscelanea, Meditations, Memoratives* (1604)

Hacket, John, *Scrinia Reserata: A Memorial Offer'd to the Great Deservings of John Williams* (1692)

Hall, John, *Select Observations on English Bodies* (1679)

Harris, Robert, *The Works of Robert Harris* (1654)

Hall, Thomas, *Fuebria Florae, The Downfall of May-Games* (1661)

Head, Richard, *The Life and Death of Mother Shipton* (1667)

The Historie of the Damnable Life and Deserved Death of Doctor John Faustus, ed. H. Logeman (Amsterdam 1900)

Hoby, Margaret, *The Private Life of an Elizabethan Lady: The Diary of Lady Margaret Hoby, 1599-1605*, ed. Joanna Moody (Sutton: Stroud 1998)

Hopkins, Matthew, *The Discovery of Witches* (1647)

Ephraim Huitt, *The Anatomy of Conscience* (1626)

Huitt, Ephraim, *The Whole Prophecie of Daniel Explained* (1643)

Hutchinson, Lucy, *Memoirs of the Life of Colonel Hutchinson*, ed. N. H. Keeble (Everyman: London 1995)

James VI of Scotland, *Daemonologie* (1597)

Jessopp, Augustus, *Random Roaming and Other Papers* (London 1894)

Jocelin, Elizabeth, *The Mother's Legacie to her Unborne Childe* (1624)

Julian of Norwich, *Revelations of Divine Love*, ed Clifton Walters (Penguin: London 1966)

The Just Devil of Woodstock (1660)

Kempe, Margery, *The Book of Margery Kempe*, ed. Barry Windeatt (Penguin: London 1985)

Leigh, Edward, *A Treatise of Divinity* (1646)

The Life and Death of the Merry Devill of Edmonton (1631)

The Life of Mother Shipton, A New Comedy (1670)

Luther, Martin, *Commentary on St Paul's Epistle to the Galatians* (Philadelphia 1875)

The Merry Devil of Edmonton (1608), ed. William Amos Abrams (Durham, North Carolina 1942)

Merry Drollery Complete (1670)

Milton, John, *Paradise Lost*, eds., Stephen Orgel and Jonathan Goldberg (2008)

Milton, *Prose Writings*, ed. K. M. Burton (Dent: London 1958)

The Miracle of Miracles (1614)

Morton, Thomas, *Ezekiel's Wheels: A Treatise Concerning Divine Providence* (1653)

A Most Certain, Strange and True Discovery of a Witch (1643)

Most Fearfull and Strange Newes From the Bishoppricke of Durham (1641)

A Most Horrible & Detestable Murder Committed by a Bloudie-Minded Man Upon his Owne Wife (1595)

The Most Strange and Admirable Discoverie of the Three Witches of Warboys (1593)

A Most Straunge and True Discourse of the Wonderfull Judgement of God (1600)

The Most Wonderfull and True Storie of a Certaine Witch Named Alse Gooderige (1597)

Mother Shiptons Christmas Carrols with her Merry Neighbors (1668)

Nashe, Thomas, *The Terrors of the Night* (1590)

Newes From Hell, Rome and the Inns of Court (1642)

Norwood, Richard, *The Journal of Richard Norwood*, eds. W. F. Craven and Walter Hayward (New York 1945)

Perkins, William, *The Foundation of the Christian Religion Gathered Into Six Principles* (1641 edition)

Perkins, William, *The Art of Prophesying* (Banner of Truth Trust: Edinburgh 1996)

Perkins, William, *Lectures Upon the First Three Chapters of the Revelation* (1604)

Perkins, William, *A Discourse on the Damned Art of Witchcraft* (1608)

Potts, Thomas, *The Wonderfull Discoverie of Witches in the Countie of Lancaster* (1613)

Powell, Vasavor, ed., *Spirituall Experiences of Sundry Believers* (1652 edition)

Powell, Vavasor, *The Life and Death of Mr Vavasor Powell* (1671)

Powell, Walter, *A Summons for Swearers* (1645)

Preston, John, *The Saints Daily Exercise. A Treatise Unfolding the Whole Duty of Prayer* (1629)

The Prophesie of Mother Shipton in the Raigne of King Henry the Eighth (1641)

Raworth, Francis, *Jacobs Ladder, or the Protectorship of Sion* (1655)

A Rehearall Both Straung and True of Hainous and Horrible Actes (1579)

A Relation of a Strange Apparition (1641)

Reynolds, John, *The Triumphs of Gods Revenge Against the Crying and Execrable Sinne of . . . Murther* (1634)

Rogers, John, *Ohel, or Beth-Shemesh* (1653)

Rowley, William, Decker, Thomas, and Ford, John, *The Witch of Edmonton* (1658)

Sad and Dreadful News From Horsley Down (1684)

A Sad Caveat to all Quakers (1657)

Scot, Reginald, *The Discovery of Witches* (1581)

A Short, Compendious and True Description of the Round-heads and the Long-heads (1642)

Sibbes, Richard, *The Saints Safetie in Evill Times* (1634)

Six Strange Prophesies Predicting Wonderfull Events (1642)

Southerne, Lawrence, *Fearefull Newes From Coventry* (1642)

Sprint, John, *The Christian Sword and Buckler* (1623)

Stearne, John, *A Confirmation and Discovery of Witchcraft* (1648)

Stand up for Your Beliefe, or A Combat Betweene Satan Tempting and A Christian Triumphing (1640)

A Strange and True Relation of a Young Woman Possest With the Devil (1647)

The Strange and Wonderful History of Mother Shipton (1686)

Strange Newes From Antwerpe (1612)

Strange Newes From Warwicke (1642)

Stubbes, *A Christall Glasse for Christian Women* (1618 edition)

Tales and Quicke Answeres, Very Mery and Pleasant to Rede (c. 1530)

The Tryal and Examination of Mrs Joan Peterson (1652)

A True Relation of the Great Floods Which Happened in Coventry (1607)

Turner, Jane, *Choice Experiences of the Kind Dealings of God* (1653)

Whitford, Richard, *A Werke for Housholders* (1530)

Williams, Gryffith, *The True Church: Shewed to All Men That Desire to be Members of the Same* (1629)

Willis, R., *Mount Tabor, or Private Exercises of a Penitent Sinner* (1639)

The Witches of Northampton (1612)

Woolton, John, *The Christian Manuell, or Of the Life and Maners of True Christians* (1576)

The Wonder: or The Devil Outwitted (1736)

A Wonderfull and Strange Miracle, or Gods Just Vengeance Against the Cavaliers (1642)

The Wonderfull Discoverie of the Witchcrafts of Margaret and Phillip Flower (1619)

The Young Man's Conquest Over the Powers of Darkness (1683)
The Young Mans Second Warning-Peece (1643)

EDITED COLLECTIONS OF
CONTEMPORARY TEXTS

The Euing Collection of English Broadside Ballads (Glasgow 1971)

Gibson, Marion, ed., *Early Modern Witches: Witchcraft Cases in Contemporary Writing*
(Routledge: London and New York 2000)

Haining, Peter, ed., *The Witchcraft Papers* (Robert Hale: London 1974)

Happe, Peter, ed., *English Mystery Plays* (Penguin: London 1975)

Mother Shipton: A Collection of the Earliest English Editions of Her Prophecies
(Manchester 1882)

Porter, H. C., ed., *Puritanism in Tudor England* (1970)

Raymond, Joad, ed., *Making the News: An Anthology of the Newsbooks of Revolutionary
England,* 1641-1660 (Windrush Press: Gloucester 1993)

Rosen, Barbara, ed., *Witchcraft in England*, 1558-1618 (University of Massachusetts
Press: Amherst 1969)

The Roxburghe Ballads, ed. W. M. Chappell (1871-1880)

Seymour-Smith, Martin, ed., *The English Sermon*, 1550-1650 (Carcanet Press:
Cheadle 1976)

Sisson, C. H., ed., *The English Sermon*, 1650-1750 (Carcanet: Cheadle 1976)

Trinterund, E. P. ed., *Elizabethan Puritanism* (Oxford University Press 1971)

SECONDARY WORKS

Almond, Philip C., *The Witches of Warboys* (I. B. Tauris: London and New York 2008)

Ambler, R. W., *Ranters, Revivalists and Reformers: Primitive Methodism and Rural Society
in South Lincolnshire,* 1817-1875 (Hull University Press 1989)

Ankarloo, Bent and Henningsen, Gustav, eds., *Early Modern European Witchcraft:
Centres and Peripheries* (Clarendon, Oxford 1993)

Behringer, Wolfgang, *Witches and Witch Hunts* (Polity Press: Cambridge 2004)

Briggs, Robin, *Witches and Neighbours* (2nd ed. HarperCollins: London 1998)

De Bruyn, Lucy, *Woman and the Devil in Sixteenth-Century Literature* (Compton Press:
Wiltshire 1979)

Cheyne, J. A., et al., 'Hypnagogic and Hypnopompic Hallucinations during
Sleep Paralysis: Neurological and Cultural Construction of the Night-Mare',
Consciousness and Cognition, 8 (1999)

Clark, Stuart, *Thinking With Demons: The Idea of Witchcraft in Early Modern Europe*
(Oxford University Press 1997)

Clark, Stuart, ed., *Languages of Witchcraft: Narrative, Ideology and Meaning in Early
Modern Culture* (Macmillan: London 2001)

Crawford, Patricia, *Women and Religion in England,* 1500-1720 (Routledge:
London 1993)

Cust, Richard, and Hughes, Ann, eds., *Conflict in Early Stuart England* (Longman:
London 1989)

Davey, Peter and Hodges, Richard, eds., *Ceramics and Trade: The Production and
Distribution of Later Mediaeval Pottery in North-West Europe* (University of Sheffield
Press 1983)

Davies, Stevie, *Unbridled Spirits: Women of the English Revolution, 1640-1660* (Women's Press: London 1998)

Davies, Owen, *Witchcraft, Magic and Culture, 1736-1951* (Manchester University Press 1999)

Davies, Owen, 'The Nightmare Experience, Sleep Paralysis, and Witchcraft Accusations', *Folklore*, 114 (2003)

Dickens, A. G., *The English Reformation* (2nd ed. Pennsylvania State University Press: Philadelphia 1990)

Dixon-Smith, Denise, 'Concealed Shoes', *Archaeological Leather Group Newsletter*, 6 (1990)

Doran, Susan, and Jones, Norman, eds., *The Elizabethan World* (Routledge: London 2010)

Duffy, Eamon, *The Stripping of the Altars: Traditional Belief in England, 1400-1580* (Yale University Press: New Haven and London 1992)

Durston, Christopher, and Eales, Jacqueline, eds., *The Culture of English Puritanism, 1560-1700* (Macmillan: London 1996)

Eales, Jacqueline, 'Thomas Pierson and the Transmission of the Moderate Puritan Tradition', *Midland History*, 20 (1995)

Emmerson, Richard Kenneth, *Antichrist in the Middle Ages: A Study of Medieval Apocalypticism, Art and Literature* (Manchester University Press 1981)

Evans, E. J., *Seventeenth-Century Norwich* (Clarendon: Oxford 1979)

Ewen, C. L'Estrange, *Witch Hunting and Witch Trials* (Dial Press: New York 1929)

Ewen, C. L'Estrange, *Witchcraft and Demonianism* (Heath Cranton: London 1933)

Fielding, 'Opposition to the Personal Rule of Charles I: The Diary of Robert Woodford, 1637-1641', *Historical Journal* 31 (1988)

Finucane, Ronald C., *Miracles and Pilgrims: Popular Beliefs in Medieval England* (2nd ed. Macmillan: London 1995)

Fincham, Kenneth, ed, *The Early Stuart Church* (Macmillan: London 1993)

Fletcher, Anthony, *Gender, Sex and Subordination in England* (Yale University Press 1995)

Fletcher, Anthony, and Roberts, Peter, eds. *Religion, Culture and Society in Early Modern Britain* (Cambridge University Press 1994)

Forsyth, Neil, *The Old Enemy: Satan and the Combat Myth* (Princeton University Press: Princeton and Chichester 1987)

Friedman, Jerome, *Miracles and the Pulp Press During the English Revolution* (UCL: London 1993)

Garrett, Clarke, *Spirit Possession and Popular Religion* (Johns Hopkins University Press: Baltimore and London 1987)

Gaskill, Malcolm, *Crime and Mentalities in Early Modern England* (Cambridge University Press 2000)

Gaskill, Malcolm, *Witchfinders: An English Tragedy* (John Murray: London 2005)

Gaskill, Malcolm, 'Witchcraft and Evidence in Early Modern England', *Past and Present*, 198 (2008)

Gibson, Marion, *Reading Witchcraft: Stories of English Witchcraft* (Routledge: London 1999)

Greenblatt, Stephen, *Shakespearean Negotiations: The Circulation of Social Energy in Renaissance England* (University of California Press: Berkeley 1988)

Griffiths, Paul, Fox, Adam, and Hindle, Steve, eds., *The Experience of Authority in Early Modern England* (Macmillan, London 1996)

Haigh, Christopher, *English Reformations* (Clarendon: Oxford 1993)

244   *The Devil in Tudor and Stuart England*

Haigh, Christopher, 'Success and Failure in the English Reformation', *Past and Present*, 173:1 (2001)

Haigh, Christopher, *The Plain Man's Pathways to Heaven: Kinds of Christianity in Post-Reformation England* (Oxford University Press 2007)

Helm, Paul, *The Providence of God* (InterVarsity Press: Illinois 1993)

Holmes, Clive, 'Women: Witnesses and Witches', *Past and Present*, 140, (1993)

Holmes, M. R., 'The So-Called Bellarmine Mask in Imported Rhenish Stoneware', *Antiquaries Journal* XXXI (1950)

Hughes, Ann, 'Thomas Dugard and his Circle in the 1630s', *Historical Journal*, 29 (1986)

Hunter, Michael, 'New light on the 'Drummer of Tedworth': Conflicting Narratives of Witchcraft in Restoration England', *Historical Research* 78:201 (2005)

Johnstone, Nathan, *The Devil and Demonism in Early Modern England* (Cambridge University Press 2006)

Jones, Karen, and Zell, Michael, "The Divels Speciall Instruments': Women and Witchcraft Before the 'Great Witch Hunt'", *Social History*, 30 (2005)

Jupp, Peter C. and Gittings, Clare, eds., *Death in England* (Manchester University Press 1999)

Kelly, Henry Angstar, *Satan: A Biography* (Cambridge University Press 2006)

Kieckhefer's *European Witch Trials: Their Foundations in Popular and Learned Culture, 1300-1500* (Routledge and Kegan Paul: London 1976)

Richard Kieckhefer, *Unquiet Souls: Fourteenth-Century Saints and Their Religious Milieu* (University of Chicago Press 1984)

Kittredge, George Lyman, *Witchcraft in Old and New England* (Harvard University Press: Cambridge, Massachusetts 1929)

Lake, Peter, with Questier, Michael, *The Antichrist's Lewd Hat* (Yale University Press: New Haven and London 2002)

Lamont, William, *Puritanism and Historical Controversy* (UCL: London 1996)

Levack, Brian P., *Witch-Hunting in Scotland: Law, Politics and Religion* (Routledge: London and New York 2008)

Link, Luther, *The Devil: The Archfiend in Art from the Sixth to the Sixteenth Century* (Harry N. Abrams: New York 1996)

Lock, Julian, 'How Many Tercios has the Pope? The Spanish war and the Sublimation of Elizabethan Anti-Popery', *History*, 81 (1996)

Lohse, Bernhard, *Martin Luther's Theology: Its Historical and Systematic Development* (T & T Clark: Edinburgh 1999)

Lowe, B., 'Religious Wars and the Common Peace: Anglican Anti-war Sentiment in Elizabethan England', *Albion*, 28 (1996)

Luttmer, Frank, 'Persecutors, Tempters and Vassals of the Devil: The Unregenerate in Puritan Practical Divinity', *Journal of Ecclesiastical History*, 51:1 (2000)

Macfarlane, Alan, *Witchcraft in Tudor and Stuart England* (2nd ed. Routledge: London and New York 1999)

Marshall, Peter, *Beliefs and the Dead in Reformation England* (OUP 2004)

Maxwell-Stuart, P. G., *Satan: A Biography* (Amberley: Stroud 2008)

McCalman, Iain, *Radical Underworld: Prophets, Revolutionaries and Pornographers in London, 1795-1840* (Clarendon: Oxford 1993)

McGinnis, Timothy Scott, *George Gifford and the Reformation of the Common Sort* (Truman State University Press: Kirksville, Missouri 2004)

McShane, Angela, and Walker, Garthine, eds., *The Extraordinary and the Everyday in Early Modern England* (Macmillan: London 2010)

Merrifield, Ralph, *The Archaeology of Ritual and Magic* (B.T. Batsford: London 1987)

Niccoli, Ottavia, 'The End of Prophecy', in *Journal of Modern History*, 61 (1989)

Obelkivich, *Religion and Rural Society* (Clarendon: Oxford 1978)

Oberman, Heiko, *Luther: Man Between God and the Devil* (Yale University Press: New Haven and London 1989)

Oldridge, Darren, *Strange Histories* (Routledge: London and New York 2005)

Oldridge, Darren, ed., *The Witchcraft Reader* (2nd ed. Routledge: London and New York 2008)

Orme, William, *The Life and Times of Richard Baxter* (1830)

Pagels, Elaine, *The Origin of Satan* (Penguin: London 1995)

Parish, Helen, and Naphy, William, eds., *Religion and Superstition in Reformation Europe* (Manchester University Press 2002)

Parker, Geoffrey, 'Success and Failure During the First Century of the Reformation', *Past and Present* 136 (1992)

Plantinga, Alvin, *God, Freedom and Evil* (William B. Eerdmans: Michigan 1974)

Porter, Roy, *A Social History of Madness* (Weidenfeld and Nicolson: London 1987)

Power, Amanda, 'A Mirror for Every Age: The Reputation of Roger Bacon', *English Historical Review*, 492 (2006)

Pumfrey, Stephen, Rossi, Paolo, and Slawinski, Maurice, eds., *Science, Culture and Popular Belief in Renaissance Europe* (Manchester University Press 1991)

Rack, Henry, *Reasonable Enthusiast: John Wesley and the Rise of Methodism* (Epworth: London)

Reay, Barry, *Popular Cultures in England, 1550-1750* (Longman: London and New York 1998)

Roper, Lyndal, *The Holy Household: Women and Morals in Reformation Augsburg* (Clarendon: Oxford 1990)

Roper, Lyndal, *Oedipus and the Devil: Witchcraft, Sexuality and Religion in Early Modern Europe* (Routledge: London 1994)

Russell, Jeffrey Burton, *The Devil: Perceptions of Evil from Antiquity to Primitive Christianity* (Cornell University Press: Ithaca and London 1977)

Russell, Jeffrey Burton, *Lucifer: The Devil in the Middle Ages* (Cornell University Press: Ithaca and London 1984)

Russell, Jeffrey Burton, *Mephistopheles: The Devil in the Modern World* (Cornell University Press: Ithaca and London 1986)

Sands, Kathleen H., *Demon Possession in Elizabethan England* (Praeger 2004)

Scarisbrick, J. J., *The Reformation and the English People* (Clarendon: Oxford 1988)

Scribner, R. W., *For the Sake of Simple Folk: Popular Propaganda for the German Reformation* (Clarendon: Oxford 1981)

Scribner, R. W., *Popular Culture and Popular Movements in Reformation Germany* (Hambledon: London 1987)

Sharpe, James, *Instruments of Darkness: Witchcraft in England, 1550-1750* (Hamish Hamilton: London 1996)

Shephard, Amanda, *Gender and Authority in Early Modern England* (1993)

Six Strange Prohesies Predicting Wonderfull Events (1642)

Spufford, Margaret, *Small Books and Pleasant Histories* (Cambridge University Press 1981)

Strickland, Debra Higgs, *Saracens Demons and Jews: Making Monsters in Medieval Art* (Princeton University Press: Princeton and Oxford 2003)

Tankard, Danae, 'The Reformation of the Deathbed in Mid-Sixteenth-Century England', *Mortality*, 8:3 (2003)

Taylor, Charles, *A Secular Age* (Harvard University Press: Cambridge, Massachusetts, and London 2007)

Thomas, Keith, *Religion and the Decline of Magic* (Weidenfeld & Nicolson: London 1971)

Walker, D. P., *Unclean Spirits: Possession and Exorcism in France and England in the Late Sixteenth and Early Seventeenth Centuries* (Scolar Press: London 1981)

Walker, Garthine, and Kermode, Jenny, eds., *Women, Crime and the Courts in Early Modern England* (UCL: London 1994)

Walsham, Alexandra, *Providence in Early Modern England* (Oxford University Press 1999)

Watt, Tessa, *Cheap Print and Popular Piety, 1550-1640* (Cambridge University Press 1991)

Wedderburn, Robert, *The Horrors of Slavery and Other Writings*, ed. Iain MacCalman (Edinburgh University Press 1991)

De Welles, Theodore, 'Sex and Sexual Attitudes in Seventeenth-Century England: The Evidence from Puritan Diaries', in *Renaissance and Reformation* 12 (1988)

Wilby, Emma, 'The Witch's Familiar and the Fairy in Early Modern England and Scotland', *Folklore*, 111 (2000)

Wilby, Emma, *Cunning Folk and Familiar Spirits* (Sussex Academic Press: Brighton and Portland 2005)

Willen, Diane, 'Godly Women in Early Modern England: Puritanism and Gender', *Journal of Ecclesiastical History*, 43 (1992)

Wilson, Stephen, *The Magical Universe: Everyday Ritual and Magic in Pre-Modern Europe* (Hambledon: London and New York 2000)

Woolf, D. R., 'The Common Voice: History, Folklore and Oral Tradition in Early Modern England', in *Past and Present* 120 (1988)

Wright, Thomas, *Narratives of Sorcery and Magic* (Redfield: New York 1851)

INDEX

Abbot, Francis, 181
Acts and Monuments (Foxe) 21
Adam and Eve 116
Adams, Thomas, 44
adulterers 89
Ady, Thomas, 179
afterlife, medieval depictions, 60
Alexander VI, Pope, 109
Allen, Hannah, 60, 65, 67, 69, 128, 149, 150, 151
  satanic thoughts 64–65
Allen, Thomas, (mathematician) 79
alvas 167, 174, 175
Anatomie of Abuses (Stubbes) 191, 192
animal guises
  the devil 80–82, 98, 170, 185
  witches 171, 190–191
anti-popery 109–113
Antichrist 20, 21, 44, 45, 52, 54, 76, 106, 107, 108
apparitions 57, 60–62, 105, 106, 130, 132, 133, 140, 171, 185, 186, 195, 197, 212, 214
Armada, defeat, 109, 113
Askew, Ann, 45, 51
Aubrey, John, 79, 83, 197
Augustine, St, 181
autobiographies 25, 43, 45, 50, 56, 58, 59, 66, 70, 73, 80, 102, 105, 125, 193

Bacon, Friar, 92
Bacon, Roger, 90
Baillie, Robert, 194
Bale, John, 45
ballads 7, 12, 13, 26, 27, 41, 45, 47, 53, 73, 74, 80, 84, 85, 86, 87, 99, 102, 103, 104, 105, 106, 108, 109, 110, 111, 112, 120, 121, 123, 124, 164, 165, 185, 193, 194, 195, 202
  anti-popery 109–113

civil war 53, 194
comic 7, 87, 120, 123, 202
  depicting hell 89
  godly 41, 45, 47, 73, 74
  popular beliefs 53, 103, 104, 105, 106, 121–124, 164
Balsom, Robert, 146, 151, 152, 153, 160
baptism 26, 34, 150, 160
Baptists 135, 194
Bateman, Stephen, 40, 49, 94, 95, 96, 118, 119
Baxter, Richard, 144, 153, 156, 189, 195, 196
Beard, Thomas, 28
'beast', the,: in Book of Revelations 44–45, 107–108
Becon, Thomas, 38, 43, 51, 69, 151
beliefs
  popular 28, 78–79, 82, 84, 97, 103, 105, 112, 141, 160, 164, 166–167, 169–170, 176, 179, 184–188, 190, 194–195, 197–199, 201
  suppression 51
bellarmines 174, 175
Bernard, Richard, 17, 186, 187
bewitchment 140, 142, 143, 165, 166, 172, 173
Bicknoll, Edmond, 76
Bilson, Thomas, bishop of Winchester, 117
blasphemy 66, 96, 98, 99, 141, 194
Bodenham, Anne, 123
Bolton, Robert, (pastor) 25, 43, 64–66, 149
Book of Common Prayer 22, 150, 160
Book of Martyrs, The, (Foxe) 21, 43, 45, 52
Bourne, Henry, 198
Boyle, Robert, 196

Bradford, John, 40
Breton, Nicholas, 116
Brettergh, Katherine, 74–76, 126, 154, 159
Briggs, Agnes, 143, 146
Brinsley, John, 185
Bunyan, John, 42, 43, 46, 61, 64, 65, 68, 77, 124, 125, 150
  apparitions 61, 64
  satanic thoughts and encounters 46, 65, 150
Burrill, Mary, 64, 128
Burton, Robert, (physician) 60, 62, 149

Caldwell, Elizabeth, 17, 100, 101, 128, 130
Calling of the Ministry, The, (Perkins) 176
Calumy, Edmund, 189
Calvin, John, 16, 18, 19, 39
Calvinism 18, 28, 197
Carlisle cathedral 33
Carpenter, Richard, 44, 69, 116, 142
Carter, Beezaleel, 48
catechisms 18
Catholicism 14, 20, 22, 41, 44–45, 48, 95–96, 110–111, 113, 131, 177
  as the Antichrist 20, 21, 44, 45, 54, 106, 108
  association with witchcraft 88, 177
  demonisation by protestants 20, 44–45, 54, 55, 80, 95–96, 99, 109, 110, 111, 181, 197
Cavendish, Margaret, duchess of Newcastle, 125
Cennick, John, 199
Charles I, king of England, 117, 160
Chelmsford witch trials 123, 172, 191

Chester mystery cycle 36
children: and possession 132,
  134, 137, 140–143, 145–147,
  150, 153–154, 174, 185
*Christall Glasse of Christian
  Reformation* (Bateman) 40,
  49, 94
*Cristall Glasse for Christian
  Women* (Stubbes) 73, 118
Christianity 11, 13, 15, 23, 43,
  55, 68, 76, 82, 84, 85, 94, 95,
  157, 200, 201
Chub, William, 39, 67
Church of England 18, 28, 41,
  48, 52, 56, 131, 198
  Thirty-Nine Articles 18
Civil war 7, 22, 44, 108, 117,
  121, 133, 134, 147, 156, 188,
  192, 193, 205
Clarke, Elizabeth, 172, 187,
  190, 191
Clarke, Hugh, (pastor) 97
Clarke, Samuel, 72, 75, 207
clergy 28, 52, 53, 109, 131, 132,
  138, 145, 147, 157, 159, 178,
  181, 183, 185, 197, –200
Cloud of Unknowing, The,
  31, 49
cloven hooves 44, 82, 95, 96
Colfe, Isaac, 54–55
comedy 27, 35, 36, 111
  in ballads 7, 202
  depictions of the devil 12,
  14, 35–37, 47, 87–89
Concealed shoes 174, 175
Conquest of Temptations, The,
  (Gerard) 73, 151
Conrad, Joseph, 10
Counter Reformation 130
Coventry: and Satanic
  murder 102–103
Cradocke, Edward, 19, 78, 79
Cullen, Abraham, 174

Darling, Thomas, 89, 137,
  139, 140, 142, 143, 147, 151,
  154, 155, 171, 172, 174, 184,
  185, 187
Darrell, John, (exorcist) 47,
  140, 142, 147, 148, 149, 157,
  158, 159, 160, 169, 171, 182,
  184, 185, 186, 189, 214, 215
  Sommers case 148
  folk beliefs 185, 214
  witchcraft 182, 184–185,
  214
Davies, Owen, 63, 198
Deacon, John, 147
deathbed scenes and terrors
  50, 72–76, 102, 126,
  134–135, 142, 151, 154, 159

Decker, Thomas, 89
demonic obsession 170
demonic possession see
  possession
demonologists/demonology
  28, 79, 164, 165, 167, 185, 191,
  see also Perkins, William,
demons 8, 11, 16, 17, 34, 36,
  46, 47, 63, 80, 84, 86, 91, 106,
  107, 109, 128, 136, 137, 138,
  142, 146, 158, 159, 160, 169,
  170, 175, 178, 179, 184, 195,
  197, 198, 205, 212
Dent, Arthur, 17, 18, 19, 41,
  49, 85
*Dialogue Concerning Witches
  and Witchcraftes* (Gifford)
  169, 179
Dinham, Edward, 136, 140,
  141, 142, 150
Discoverie of Witchcraft, The,
  (Scot) 169
Discovery of Witches, The,
  (Hopkins) 190
dispossessions 147, 150, 154,
  158, 159
*Dispute Between the Woman
  and the Powers of Darkness,
  A,* (Southcott) 200
doctrine predestination 18–19
Dod, John, (pastor) 73, 75
dogs 80, 81, 98, 99, 128, 130,
  165, 168, 170, 172, 185, 189,
  190, 191, 194, 206, 213
  and the devil 80, 81, 98, 99,
  128, 130, 165, 168, 170, 172,
  189, 194
  and witchcraft 185, 190, 191
domestic strife: and Satan
  127–130
Dovey, Joyce, 133, 135, 139,
  140, 141
Downame, John, 19
Dugard, Thomas, 54
Dugdale, Gilbert, 100
Dunstan, St, 33
dying: art of 9–10, 50, 73, 74,
  75, 126, 134, 142

Eales, Jacqueline, 159
East Anglian witches and
  witch-hunts 168
Easterbrooke, Joseph, 199
Elizabeth I, queen of
  England, 21, 22, 46, 116, 157,
  188, 196
elves 83, 84
Enchiridion (Erasmus) 51
encounters with the devil 46,
  50, 57, 59, 70, 72, 76, 83, 90,
  105, 114, 120, 169

epilepsy: and possession
  144, 147
equality of the sexes 116,
  118, 120
evil 14–20
  protection from 43, 46, 47
evil spirits traps 175
exorcisms 136–161
  accounts 32, 137, 141,
  150–151, 158–160, 207, 214
  Methodist 198
  see also dispossessions
exorcists 33, 47, 140, 142, 145,
  146, 147, 148, 149, 150, 151,
  152, 154, 157, 158, 160, 169,
  170, 173, 175, 184, 198, 200,
  207, 215
  see also Darrell, John

Fabell, Peter, 90, 91, 92,
  102, 111
Fairclough, Samuel, 189
Fairfax family 142, 143, 185
  Helen 132, 133, 135, 139
Fairford church, Glos. 32
fairies 82, 83, 84, 197, 198
'familiars' 84, 166, 167, 168,
  169, 170, 171, 172, 184, 190
  and the devil 168, 169, 170
Faust legend 80, 86, 90, 109
Fearefull Newes from Coventry
  (Southerne) 102
Fletcher, Anthony, 153
Flower, Philippa, 168
folklore 31, 34, 77, 82, 90, 120,
  183, 185, 187, 189, 190, 201
  the devil 31, 34, 77, 82, 90,
  120, 183, 189
  witchcraft 185, 187, 189, 190
Fox, George, 68, 117
Fox, John, (possession case)
  169, 207, 208, 209, 210
Foxe, John, (preacher) 44, 52
Friedman, Jerome, 116
Fulke, William, 44

Garrett, Clarke, 144
Gaskill, Malcolm, 163,
  187–188
Gaule, John, (pastor) 175, 177,
  189, 191, 192
Generall Martyrologie, A,
  (Clarke) 46, 151
Gerard, John, 73. 151
Geree, Stephen, 118
Germany: religious warfare
  52
ghosts and hauntings 10, 25,
  51, 58, 59, 60, 61, 66, 76, 78,
  79, 82, 106, 130, 134
Gibson, Marion, 137, 182

Gifford, George, 14, 18, 43, 53, 55, 78, 79, 158, 164, 165, 167, 169, 178, 179, 183, 192
Gilpin, John, 156
Glanvill, Joseph, 83, 195, 211, 212
Gloucester cathedral 36
God: and the devil 7, 10, 11, 12, 13, 15, 16, 17, 18, 19, 23, 39, 41, 43, 46, 47, 48, 49, 50, 51, 53, 54, 55, 57, 58, 61, 62, 64, 65, 66, 67, 68, 69, 70, 71, 72, 73, 74, 75, 76, 78, 79, 83, 86, 87, 93, 94, 97, 98, 99, 100, 101, 108, 110, 114, 116, 117, 118, 119, 120, 121, 124, 126, 127, 128, 131, 132, 133, 134, 139, 146, 147, 149, 150, 151, 152, 155, 156, 157, 158, 164, 173, 177, 178, 179, 180, 184, 186, 187, 189, 196, 198, 199, 200, 201, 205, 206, 208, 209, 210, 211, 215, 217, 218
'godly the' 8, 21
Gouge, William, 20, 40, 46, 47, 59, 96, 116, 117, 118, 179
Gough, John, 51, 108
Gower, Stanley, 136, 158, 160, 169, 207, 208
Grace Abounding to the Chief of Sinners (Bunyan) 61
Greenblatt, Stephen, 157
Greene, Robert, 90s
Greenham, Richard, (pastor) 49, 50, 196
Grymeston, Elizabeth, 43, 50, 68
gunpowder plot 109

Hacket John 132
'hag the' (sleep disorder) 170, 212
Haigh, Christopher, 51, 113
Haitzmann, Christoph, 144
Hall, John, (physician) 139
Hall, Thomas, (pastor) 64, 181
Hallywell, Henry, 196
Hampton Court Conference (1604) 22
Harris, Robert, 53
Harrowing of Hell, The, 36
Harsnet, Samuel, bishop of Norwich, 147, 160, 161, 184, 189, 215
Hartley, Edmund, 137, 140, 171, 184
Harvey, Joan, 173
Hawkins, Jane, 131, 132
hell: scenes from 32, 33, 36, 42, 54, 60, 63, 65, 70, 74, 76, 77, 80, 85, 86, 87, 88, 89, 91,

95, 96, 97, 99, 101, 103, 108, 110, 124, 128, 142, 149, 181, 186, 195, 197, 198, 199, 203, 204, 211
Helm, Paul, 51
Henry VIII, king of England, 21, 51
heresy 20, 130, 131
Herring, Julius, (pastor) 73, 75
Hoby, Lady Margaret, 126
diary 126
Hoddesdon, Henry, 19
Holmes, Clive, 122
Hopkins, Matthew, 165, 168, 169, 187, 188, 189, 190, 191, 192
Houlbrooke, Ralph, 126
Howson, John, 151
Huitt, Ephraim, 53, 54
humour 31, 36, 47, 87
see also comedy
Hutchinson, Lucy, 43, 45

idolatry 44, 99, 117, 121
images/imagery 9, 10, 12, 26, 36, 45, 75, 89, 93, 94, 95, 96, 97, 98, 116, 193, 194, 199
'imps' 63, 82, 83, 163, 167, 168, 169, 171, 172, 173, 178, 179, 183, 186, 187, 189, 190, 197
introspection: and religion 48, 50
invocation of demons 34, 35, 194
Irish rebellion (1641) 110

James VI (of Scotland), I (of England), 22
Jessey, Henry, 135
Jocelyn, Elizabeth, 82, 126
John, the Divine, St, 44
Johnstone, Nathan, 7, 13, 23–26, 59, 188, 207
Jorden, Joan, 170, 171, 172, 175
Julian of Norwich 37, 124
Kempe, Margery, 124, 127

Lapthorne, Anthony, 160
Laud, William, archbishop of Canterbury, 160
Leigh, Edward, 17
Levack, Brian, 21
Life and Death of Mother Shipton, The, 170
Life of Master Richard Rothwel, The, (Gower) 208
literature: popular 79, 80, 86, 103, 109, 110, 116, 120, 164
Lord's Prayer, the, 37, 74, 132, 141, 153, 184, 185, 217
Love, Christopher, 178

Lucas, George, 198, 199
Lucifer 11, 15, 122
lumps (bodily) 171
in possession cases 140, 171, 172, 183, 216
see also swellings
Luther, Martin, 16, 18, 20, 38, 39, 95, 108, 116, 118
Luther Link 12
Luttmer, Frank, 54

McCalman, Iain, 200
Macfarlane, Alan, 122, 163, 166, 188
magic 35, 90, 122, 162, 163, 164, 165, 166, 176, 178, 180, 181, 184, 187, 191, 192, 201
counter-magic 166
invocation of demons 34, 35, 90, 122
'white' 178, 180, 181
witchcraft 109, 122, 162, 163, 164, 166, 176, 178, 179, 180, 181, 182, 184, 185, 187, 191, 192, 201
magicians 110, 178, 180
Malin, John, 179
Malpas, Katherine, 143, 144
Malvern priory 36
Margaret of Antioch 114
Marshall, Peter, 106
Marten, Andrew, (courtier) 52
martyrdom 51
Mary I, (Tudor) queen of England, 21, 26, 51
medieval beliefs 30–47
rejection by protestants 45–47, 115, 184
survival 22, 78–93
Meditationes in Apocalysin (Foxe) 44
Merry Devil of Edmonton, The, 90, 111
Methodist movement 200
Middle Ages: beliefs and religion 105, 107, 115, 130, 141
military metaphors in religious conflicts 19, 20, 21, 24, 52, 55, 69, 76
millenarianism 200
Miller, Arthur, 76
Milton, John, 17, 55, 150
Mompesson John: and family 175, 211, 212, 213, 214
'monstrous' births 120, 121
Most Strange and Admirable Discoverie of the Three Witches of Warboys, The, 141, 182, 183
Mother's Legacie, The (Jocelyn) 126
murder/murderers 17, 31, 41,

44, 70, 86, 99, 100, 101, 102, 104, 105, 121, 126, 128, 162, 180, 193, 209

Nalton, James, (pastor) 69
Napier, Richard, (physician) 83, 105, 129, 136, 140, 170, 171, 172
  patients 81, 83, 105, 136, 140, 170
New Testament 11, 15, 158, 210, 212
Newcombe, Henry, 68
Newdigate, Lady Anne, 52, 72
Newdigate, Richard, (lawyer) 52, 59, 68, 177
Niccoli, Ottavia, 130
'night terrors' 49, 60, 62, 64, 129, 170
nightmares 57–64
Norrington, Alice, 175–176
Northampton Central Museum 174
Norwich cathedral 36
Norwood, Richard, (puritan) 63
Nowell, Roger, 185
Nynde, Alexander, 146, 153, 158

Obelkivich, James, 198
obsession: demonic 170–174, 211–214
Old Testament 11, 15, 44, 158, 210
Olde, John, 40, 41, 45, 51, 107, 177

Packwood, Josiah, 177–178
Pagels, Elaine, 55
pamphlets 41, 44, 47, 102, 105, 110, 168, 182, 184, 194, 203, 207
  see also tracts
Parker, Matthew, archbishop of Canterbury, 143
Paul, St: letters 107
Pendle witches 168, 185
Penny, John, 198
Perkins, William, 18, 38, 43, 53, 59, 89, 93, 105, 174, 186, 197
  catechism 18
  views on Satan 38, 64
  witchcraft 176, 180, 186
  writings and sermons 18, 43, 53, 59, 89, 174, 176, 180
persecution 20, 21, 43, 44, 46, 51, 53, 54, 72, 162–163, 182–183, 188
Pierson, Thomas, 159–160
Pinder, Rachel, 143, 145–146

political factors: and protestantism 11, 51
popular beliefs/culture 78–90, 110
  literature 120–124
  protestantism 19–20, 29
  witchcraft 164–176
Porter, Roy, 144
possession 25, 28, 65, 130, 131–134
  causes and symptoms 60, 63, 115, 132–133, 138, 139–144, 147, 148, 150, 153–156, 171–173, 214–215
  in children 139–140, 147, 171
  fraudulent 35, 143–145, 147–148, 171, 215
  lumps/swellings (bodily) 140, 143, 148, 171, 172, 184, 214, 216
  mental illness 58, 147
  religious ecstasy 154–157
  social context 144–146
  spiritual phenomena 59, 154–155
  temptation 149–154
  witchcraft 147, 170–174, 214–219
  see also dispossessions; exorcisms
Potts , Thomas, 168, 203
Powell, Vavasor, 28, 52, 62, 66, 69–73, 128
  apparitions 57, 60–61, 63
  temptations of the flesh 69
Powell, Walter, 98
prayer 60–61, 72
predestination doctrine 18, 19, 103
Preston, John, 61
pride: as a sin 39, 59, 68, 118, 119, 125–126, 159, 217
Primitive Methodism 199
propaganda 94, 95, 99, 101, 104, 105, 108, 110, 159, 170, 194
prophecies
  end of 130–134
  Mother Shipton 112–113
  printed 108–109
prophetesses 92, 93, 129, 156, 200, 201
protective objects 45–47, 174–176
protestantism 14, 20, 37, 39, 52, 62, 76, 82, 110, 113, 116, 130
  concepts of evil and the devil 7, 10, 12, 13, 14, 18, 19, 20, 21, 22, 23, 24, 25, 26, 27,

28, 37, 38, 40, 41, 45, 46, 47, 50, 51, 54, 56, 57, 59, 60, 62, 64, 67, 69, 72, 75, 82, 84, 91, 92, 95, 96, 99, 102, 111, 138, 164, 191, 192, 193, 194, 197, 205
  fusion with popular beliefs 77, 79, 80, 93, 97, 104, 105, 106, 113, 200
  popular culture 79, 93, 201
  possession 146, 147, 149, 150, 151, 152, 153, 154, 158, 159, 160, 161, 169, 207
  witchcraft 120, 166, 176, 177, 178, 179, 180, 183, 185, 186, 188
  women 114, 116, 118
protestants persecution of 43, 51, 52, 53
Providence 14, 17–19, 48–50, 61, 78–79, 101, 164, 186, 193, 196, 205
psychology
  of satanic thoughts 14, 24, 72
  of visions and apparitions 58, 64, 129, 149, 154
punishment: and Satan 33, 86–88
'puritan' as word of abuse 52
puritanism 21, 53, 62, 68, 77, 110, 111, 138, 139, 160, 184, 188, 194
  witches/witch-hunts 146

Quaker movement 117, 156, 194

Raworth, Francis, 17
Reformation 7, 12, 16, 21, 22, 23, 26, 53, 93, 113, 115, 130, 150, 157, 176
  images and imagery 10, 40, 89, 94
  individual introspection 48
  medieval beliefs 89, 92, 105, 124, 127, 167, 202
  perceptions of Satan 7, 20, 30–56, 90, 103, 114, 127, 162
  post- 10, 77, 82, 115, 193, 201
  religion 7, 10, 17, 21, 22, 23, 29, 41, 43, 44, 53, 57–58, 60–61, 67–68, 71, 73, 85, 93, 94, 100, 102, 110, 115, 116, 130, 132, 134, 135, 138–139, 144, 145, 146, 149, 150, 151, 152, 153, 154, 196, 197, 198, 200, 201, 208
    charismatic 131
    conflicts and divisions 20–21, 51–52, 54–55, 117, 131, 133, 146

intolerance and propaganda 104, 119–120, 183

medieval 20, 32, 37, 107, 114, 142

possession 139, 154, 156, 157, 158, 159, 160, 161, 195

social factors 77, 82, 119, 124, 127, 130, 135

witchcraft 21, 177, 180, 181, 182, 185, 186, 188, 199, 214

see also catholicism; protestantism; puritanism

retribution 97–99, 102, 194, 205

Revelations, The Book of, 44, 45, 96, 107

Reynolds, John, 41, 101, 177

Robbins, John, 156

Rogers, John, (preacher) 60, 61, 63, 70, 71, 155

Roman Catholicism see catholicism

Roper, Lyndal, 138, 153, 169

Rothwel, Richard, (pastor/exorcist) 67, 152, 158, 160, 169, 207

Rous, Thomas, 174

Rovere, Christina della, 130, 133

Rowley, William, 169

Rupert, Prince, 194

Russell, Jeffrey Burton, 11, 18, 39, 48, 50

sacramentals 34

Saducismus Triumphatus (Glanvill) 192, 212

St Andrews' church Greystoke, Penrith 33

Salve for a Sicke Man, A, (Perkins) 73

Samuel, Alice, 136, 137, 140, 143, 172, 182–184, 187

Sands, Kathleen, 137

Satan

agents and servants 16, 43, 45, 46, 96, 97, 102, 169, 173, 176, 190

anti-popery 44, 96, 98, 108–111, 159

comic depictions 7, 14, 35–37, 87, 96, 97, 112, 123

disguises 12, 27–28, 31–32, 60–61, 80, 85, 106, 149, 165

domestic strife 127–130

in popular beliefs/culture 8, 9, 10, 17, 20, 22, 26, 31, 54, 58–59, 78–80, 95, 103, 114, 116, 124, 135, 137, 175, 193, 194

post-Reformation 193,

198–201

powers and limitations 12, 13, 18–19, 33–34, 38–39, 46, 49–51, 55, 64, 70, 82, 131, 136, 146, 174, 180

protestant conceptions 12, 56–57, 62, 64, 69, 72, 82, 84, 91–92, 102, 104, 125, 146, 150, 154, 157, 191, 194, 196–197

punishment and retribution 10, 11, 27, 205

as tempter and deceiver 13, 23, 25, 27, 40–42, 50, 64–71, 74–75, 99–101, 105–106, 117, 126, 127, 145, 150, 195

witchcraft 113, 115, 119–123, 163–165, 168, 169, 176, 178–181, 186, 190

see also familiars; possession

Satan His Methods and Malice Baffled (Allen) 151

schizophrenia: and possession 144

Schorn, John, 34, 175

Scot, Reginald, 12, 122, 167, 169, 179

Scribner, Bob, 94

Scudamore, John, 79

sermons 53, 177–178

see also Perkins William

sexual equality 116, 118, 120

sexual temptation 40, 68

Sharpe, Jim, 122, 154, 163–164, 166, 192, 196

Shipton Mother 79, 82, 87, 90, 91, 93

anti-popery 112–113

prophecies 92

shoes (concealed): as protective objects 34, 167, 174–176

Sibbes, Richard, 43, 53

Simmonds, Martha, 117, 119

sins

blasphemy 66, 96, 98, 99, 141, 194

of the flesh 39

pride 125–127

sleep disorders 63, 170, 212

Smith, Henry, 106

Somers, William, 140–148, 154, 159, 174, 184, 187, 214–210, 219

Southcott, Joanna, 200–201

Southerne, Lawrence, 102, 103

Southernes, Elizabeth, 185

spiritual instruction: and protestantism 153

spiritual phenomena in possession 154–157

Spirituall Experiences (Powell) 63, 70

Sprint, John, 23

Starkey family 154, 174, 184, 185

Stearne, John, 188–192

Stile, Elizabeth, 108

Stretton, Elizabeth, 74, 75

Stubbes, Katherine, 74, 134, 135

Stubbes, Philip, 73, 75, 118

Styles, Anne, 140

suicide: and the devil 70, 72

supernatural entities/phenomena 10, 24, 32–33, 58, 63, 79, 82–84, 86, 120, 195, 196, 201, 219

superstitions 13, 76, 93, 108, 117, 175, 177, 178, 191, 192

swellings (bodily) in possessions 139, 144

tales

of the devil 28, 31, 35–37, 79, 82, 85, 86, 87, 90, 92, 93, 97, 98, 105, 106, 110, 170, 185, 194–195, 202

judgment 120–124, 205–207

merry 11, 32–33, 36, 45, 89, 124

of murder 99–103

of witchcraft 84, 145, 164–166, 191

Taylor, Charles, 24, 58

Temple, Anna, 117

temptation 55, 73, 77, 104

and the devil 13, 17, 19, 23, 24, 25, 40, 41, 42, 46, 49, 57, 58, 59, 60, 64, 65, 67, 69, 70, 71, 72, 74, 75, 78, 93, 95, 96, 97, 100, 102, 103, 104, 105, 106, 114, 116, 117, 119, 124, 125, 126, 127, 128, 129, 138, 141, 193, 195, 207, 208, 209, 211, 217

possession 150, 151, 152, 155

sexual 17, 40, 57, 68, 116, 119, 120, 123, 145

Tewkesbury abbey 33

Thomas, Keith, 82, 122, 163

thoughts: impious and satanic 64–77, 105

Throckmorton family 134–135, 139, 141, 143, 145, 150, 154, 172, 174, 182–183, 187

Tillotson, John, archbishop of Canterbury, 197

Tovey, Joyce, 133

tracts 31, 45, 93–104, 108,

109, 112, 115, 121–122, 194, 195, 201
see also pamphlets
Tragical History of Dr Faustus, The, (Marlowe) 34
Trapnel, Anna, 133
True Relation of the Grievous Handling of William Sommers of Nottingham Being Possessed with the Devill, The, (Darrell) 148
Turner, Jane, 67, 70, 117, 119, 155, 195

'unclean spirits' 26, 137–138, 148, 160, 180, 211, 213

vanity 114, 118, 119, 123, 125, 126
visionaries 130–132
visions 37, 60–62, 64, 124, 128, 130, 132–134, 140, 142–143, 149, 156
Voltaire F.M.A., de, 14

Walker, John, 147
Walsh, John, 166
Walsingham shrine 44, 177
war with Spain 21, 52
warfare
    religious 10, 52
    spiritual 76
watch (pocket) and the devil 79
Watt, Tessa, 95, 113
Wedderburn, Robert, (preacher) 200, 201
Werke for Housholders, The, (Whytford) 37
Wesley, John, 198
Whitford Richard 37–40
Whitgift, John, archbishop of Canterbury, 147
Whole Armour of God, The, (Gouge) 96, 179
will and power of God: and evil 14–20

Williams, John, bishop of Lincoln, 131
Wilson, Thomas, 52
Witch of Edmonton, The, (Rowley Decker and Ford) 169
witch-bottles 167, 174, 175
witch-hunts 179, 187–192
witchcraft 20, 21, 103, 105, 121, 132, 147
    continental influences 162
    and the devil 20, 981, 123, 162, 163, 164, 168, 169, 186, 190, 192
    'familiars' 83, 84, 166–172, 184, 186, 190, 122, 164, 166, 167, 168, 169, 170, 171, 172, 173, 174, 178, 179, 184, 187, 189, 190, 211
    as a female vice 116, 119, 122, 126
    folklore 82, 113, 165, 177, 181, 186
    magic 109, 162, 165, 166, 180, 191, 192
    obsession/possession 28, 63, 136, 137, 140, 141, 142, 143, 145, 147, 170, 172, 173, 174, 182, 184, 185, 202, 214
    in popular beliefs/culture 120, 164–165, 166, 167, 175–176, 179, 180, 183, 185, 187, 188, 190, 195, 198, 200, 202
    religion 88, 119, 161, 176, 178, 181, 186, 191
    trials 20, 22, 80, 82, 84, 119–120, 122, 125, 162–164, 166, 172, 179, 184, 188, 190–192
witches 20, 21, 82, 88, 91, 103, 121, 122, 123, 126, 132, 141, 143, 162, 164, 165, 167, 168, 169, 171, 172, 174, 176, 177, 178, 179, 180, 181, 182, 184, 185, 186, 187, 188, 189, 190, 191, 192, 199, 203

animal guises 190–191
East Anglian 126, 163, 168–169, 187–188, 191
as females 122–123
folklore 183, 185, 187, 189
of Pendle 168, 185
satanic connection 20–21
women 9, 10, 13, 14, 18, 24, 25, 37, 38, 49, 50, 51, 54, 56, 64, 68, 70, 73, 77, 79, 87, 96, 97, 99, 104, 106, 113, 115, 149, 154, 156, 159, 176, 202, 205, 217
    domestic strife 125, 129
    female authority 119, 123, 134
    perceptions of Satan 41, 46, 59, 64, 65, 66, 114, 116
    portrayal in popular litera-ture 89, 95, 115, 116, 119, 120, 121, 122, 123, 124
    protestantism 8, 39, 46, 114, 116, 119, 146, 161, 170
    religious/spiritual experi-ences 26, 28, 40, 53, 74, 76, 114, 117, 119, 124, 125, 126, 127, 129, 130, 131, 132, 133, 134, 135, 137, 143, 146
    sexual equality 118, 119, 120
    social roles 117, 119, 127, 129, 130, 145, 197
    witchcraft 122, 123, 126, 132, 165, 167, 181, 185, 187
    writings 200, 201
woodcuts: and popular imagery 40, 44–45, 60, 89, 95–96, 99, 104, 119
Woodes, Nathanial, 108
Woodford, Robert, 54
Woolton, John, 68, 150
Worcester cathedral 32
Wright, Catherine, 140
Wright, Elizabeth, 171
Wright, Sara, (prophetess) 129, 133, 135, 156